TRY

You Already Failed If You Don't

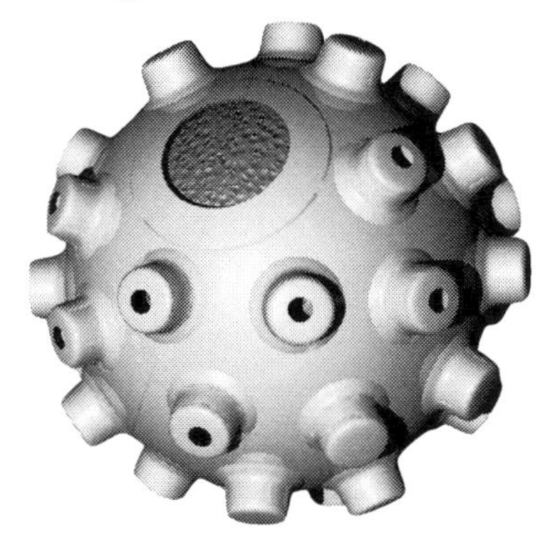

Mister Steamy the Dryer Ball

just one of the incredible stories of success that will motivate you to just "Try" when lightening strikes.

Williamson Howe

Creator of *multiple bars, well known products and clearly a guy who doesn't follow the rules. Stories of "How to" accomplish your dreams along with a bit of humor!*

SwagableStore.com is where I launch many of my current entrepreneurial dreams as I continue to be heavily involved in the bar & nightclub business. Who knows, maybe a few more inventions will come my way too.

Special thanks to my wife, Jilly, who patiently & enthusiastically sat with me each night going over my day's writing. Without her this book could have never been accomplished . She was also my editor-in-chief.

Arrogato buttercup-san!

Thank yous also go to...

Brad Bainbridge
Jeremy Buck
Kevin Carter
Chuck Crabb
Richard Deer
David DiVona
Dr. William "Billy" Graves
Jacqueline Howe
Chris Howe
Jim Irsay
Scott Marsella
Sue Nelson
Bill Niemann
Tony Parker
Kerry Payne
Ric Payne
Alicia Ruskin
Doug Sabotin
Brad Stout
Hiroto Uehara
Eisaku Yoshida
Helen Wells Agency
Dora Whitaker

ISNB 979-8-218-48263-3

Contents

∞∞

Contents Cont.

Prologue

•

"Effort only fully releases it's reward
after a person refuses to quit."
—Napoleon Hill

WHERE DOES one start out writing their life story, especially when they are still alive and kicking? I'm only 59 and honestly I feel like I'm still 22, although my liver may cry foul play. I've been encouraged by all the love around me to put my stories on paper, but especially by the love of my life, my wife Jill. She seems to think I have a good yarn to tell. I will say, I have managed to live a prosperous, I would say successful life without killing myself with the typical 9 to 5. I've invented some cool products you might know, owned some rentals, opened a small chain of wild bars, acted in Hollywood with decent success and lived in Japan for 4 years making money and creating adventures. So you're wondering, is this an advice book? Sort of, but not a "How To" book you'd be pressured into buying on a late night infomercial. See chapter 17, I've had infomercials. I wouldn't exactly call this book a memoir either. Damn, doesn't the word "memoir" sound pretentious? I, Lord Williamson Howe, have lived such an extraordinary life that your life cannot be complete unless you read more about mine, piss boy, piss boy, blah, blah, blah... This is a "grab the bull by the horns" advice book. The over used phrase carpe diem comes to mind. Seizing the day has been my lucky charm. I hope my crazy success stories spark something in you, inspire you to take chances. There will be some great "how to" moments as well.

I grew up in a divided home, but not broken. I didn't have a trust fund or a pot of gold to help me reach freedom. I did have a single mom who was a tough cookie. Obviously, I didn't know it at the time, but when she moved me and my two older sisters into International Village Apartments, not the nicest place, she had a plan. Mom took what little money she had and bought a duplex and we moved into the lower end of town. I'll get into that later, but yes I did see first hand, as a young boy, that sacrifices mean opportunity. And there you have it. This is a book about freedom. To me, freedom is the true meaning of happiness. I say "happiness" because success does not necessarily mean you are happy. All work and no play makes Will a very dull boy. I'm writing this book while sitting in a cabin in Nashville, Indiana. It's a Tuesday. It's raining outside, woodpeckers are pecking and I'm joyfully detached from obligations. Not having to answer to someone. Not having an alarm clock. Getting up each day and not having a boss is the way to make your one time chance at this life worth living. Can reading this book guarantee that you too can have this lifestyle? No of course not, but it could open your eyes to the possibility that it could be your life too.

This book is my autobiography - but it's also a larger story about creating your destiny, adventures and how to open up your mind, feed your soul and take on the challenges of life. You don't have to be the smartest or the best to succeed. I hope you find my story, my journey enlightening, humorous and it leaves you with the feeling that 99% of doing anything starts with trying. I have a lust for wonder. I listen to my inner voice, my "inner wonder" guiding me to my path. When I feel this wonder I make an extra effort. I become laser focused. If first you don't succeed TRY TRY again has always been my mantra. It's never too late to keep your wonder and lust for life alive.

“I say ‘try’; if we never try, we shall never succeed.”
—Abraham Lincoln

The people who are crazy enough to think they can change the world are the ones who do.

— Steve Jobs

The Impossible Mission
(with a Side of Gravy)

CHAPTER ONE

•

"Go confidently in the directions of your dreams!
Live the life you've imagined."
—Henry David Thoreau

ONE OF MY favorite expressions I say way too much is, "if you always do, what you've always done, you'll always get what you've always got." If you want something new to happen in your life you need to mix it up. Throw yourself into a challenge you see no possible way of succeeding, but you never really know until you TRY. I'm proof.

It's late spring 1985 in Bloomington, Indiana. I'm a 19 year old freshman. A girl I met the first day in my dormitory had broken up with me by running off with one of her high school crushes. We had taken a bus down to Daytona, Florida for Spring Break and I went to check-in our hotel and I saw her give a big hug to good-looking macho guy through the lobby window. The next thing I see is her loading her suitcase into his car and speeding off. I was devastated, broken. I spent the next 7 days alone. I didn't see her until I was back on campus at my dorm Teter Thompson 4. Long story short, she admitted she had always had a crush on this hunk of a guy and just abandoned me. Needless to say, we were through, but I was smarting. I only start this chapter with this bit of melancholy because I believe that kick in the balls motivated me to go for greatness. "I'll show her what she lost!" Revenge is powerful. Thinking back on my life often times when I leapt forward, took a risk, got super creative - it had come after some sort of crash landing. When the going get tough, well I got going to tryout for the impossible.

In late spring, being a freshman trying to get into the Indiana University School of Business, I was at Ballentine Hall for a review session for Economics 101. Ballentine Hall is a 10 story building. Built in 1959, it was recorded at the time as the largest academic building in the world. It's main lecture room has a theatrical setting with seating for 300+ students. The review session was at 3pm and it was packed. I mention the size of this behemoth space to emphasize the miracle of who sat next to me. This economics class was a real nail biter and the final accounted for 70% of your grade. I sat near the back, in the center, and to my smiling surprise one of the best known IU Cheerleaders, Kimmy Kelly*, squeezed in next to me. Just to put this into perspective, there was a guy on my dorm floor who had actually built a shrine to her. I knew exactly who she was. Kimmy was an upperclassman, not sure why she was taking E101, I think she might have told me in our small talk but I was in a daze.

Not one to be shy, I struck up a conversation, "Aren't you an IU cheerleader?" trying to act cool. She said she was - along with,

"Tryouts begin tonight at the HPER Center and go on for 2 weeks." I told her I played football & basketball in high school. She said that I should come and try out. "If you come I'll work with you for the next two weeks." I couldn't believe my ears. The thought of becoming an IU Cheerleader was not the driving force that was flowing through my body. There were other juices at work that were making my mind & body jolt with excitement. Two weeks working with Kimmy Kelly,

"Holy Moly, va-va-va-voom!" The review session was over at 4:45pm and tryouts were at 6pm. As we were leaving Ballentine Hall she said,

"Seriously, you should come to tryouts tonight!" I had a little more than an hour to run back to my dorm, change clothes and get over to the HPER Center. I'm huffing and puffing as I reach the 4th floor of Teter Thompson. I run into one of new best friends Lee Mann. It's

* Name has been changed

hard to describe Lee. He's from Richmond, Indiana which at the time was well known for RV sales and Hill's Roses. Lee is the 6th generation of the E.G. Hill Roses family business. He was 2nd in line, after the regimental commander, at Culver Military Academy. He's no nonsense but drops some of the best one-liners I've ever heard. I tell him the whole Kimmy Kelly story and that I'm thinking of going just to see her again, not to actually tryout. From that moment on he jumps to attention. He barks, "You've got to go. I'll grab my camera and snap some photos." I changed into my short-shorts (remember it's 1985) and he and I set off as fast as we could.

The HPER Center is a massive recreational building with 10 basketball courts, a full indoor track, swimming pool, racquet ball courts, weight room, gymnastics and countless volleyball courts. It's impressive design resembles a field house but made out of Indiana limestone. They have closed off 1/2 the basketball courts and there was a large group of men and women gathered at the east side. There were about 65 women and 25 men. They were vying for 6 spots on the Big Ten Men's Football & Basketball squad. There was also the 2nd team of 4 that would cheer for the Men's Soccer and Women's Basketball. I wasn't really thinking about any of that at this point, I just wanted to hangout with Kimmy again. Lee stays back about a good two basketball courts away with his Canon telephoto lens. I walk up to the sign-in table and grab an application. It's pretty standard with a release of liability. It states that you had to have experience either as a HS cheerleader or in gymnastics. I'm not one to fib... but I said I was a HS cheerleader. Speedway High School, my alma mater, had a few male cheerleaders cheering on the Sparkplugs and I know those guys couldn't do anything remotely as gymnastic as I could, so I felt I could hide behind that fact if I was called out. I'm looking over the crowd of beauties and I see Kimmy. I wave and she comes over with a smile and a hug. I don't think she had any kind of romantic feeling towards me at all. I wasn't getting that vibe. She was just a really good person. Full of energy for life and wanting to help someone. I, on the other hand, did think she was a total babe. "Total babe" was normal lingo back then. She looked different from the review session. This was her element. She had long, dark wavy hair. A bit puffy but perfect for that time. It was obvious she could tan really well too. If she had on a cocktail dress she'd be called gorgeous again & again. She had on little tight sports shorts and a tank top. She seemed older and more sophisticated than me. Totally out of my league, she's the cat's meow and I'm the fish out of water.

After a brief pep talk by Chuck Crab, not only the voice of the Hurryin' Hoosiers, but also in charge of all things cheerleader, we all separate into groups. Guys were pairing with girls to practice lifts. I had never done a lift in my life. A lift means throwing a girl up "lift" and catching her in a multitude of ways. The most common and the one we've all seen on TV is the chair lift. Kimmy asked me if I wanted to try one. We had spotters around us for obvious safety. "Put your hands around my waist, I'll put my hands around your wrists like this" she said. I look across the HPER and see Lee zooming in. I smile in his direction for a picturesque shot of me with my hands on her waist. Click. Click. Click. Kimmy gave me instructions, "It's all in the legs. We will go 1, hands around my waist. 2, we bend our knees and 3 we spring up, I will flick my wrists off of yours. You wanna try just the lift?" I nodded, glancing Lee's way, "Sure" and simultaneously we say,

"1 and 2 and 3!" With the strength of both our legs leaping us up, her flicking her hands down on my wrists and me thrusting my arms up, she was launched pretty darn high. Kimmy came down on two feet with a big smile on her face, "Wow, that was great! You're strong." I could see that other guys wanted to have a chance to toss her up but we were locked and loaded again and again. "Now, this time I'm going to sit with one knee bent and one leg straight," Kimmy demonstrated her position. "You need to put the palm of your hand on my hip." I looked confused. "On my butt," She laughed and patted her tush. 1-2-3, I launched her up and my hand landed perfectly on her perfect behind and we did a flawless chair the first time we tried. After that we did one right after the other. "You're a natural!' she blurted out. We were getting some attention because I was a complete unknown and everyone knew her. We then started having me throw her leg out while she is sitting on my hand. I'd bend my knees and pop her off my palm into a full layout sitting position. Kinda like carrying the bride over the threshold. I was really catching on. I was fairly strong back then and could bench press 300lbs several times with a spot. My weightlifting days from HS football were paying off. I was really starting to think I might be able to do this.

Lee was smiling from ear to ear snapping away photos. Kimmy said for tryouts you would need 3 lifts with a partner. We seem to have already mastered the chair in a matter of 25 minutes. "Let's try a split catch," she said. Now this is 1985 and unbeknownst to me several cheerleaders across the country had broken their arms doing this lift. I don't even think they are legal anymore in the NCAA if that tells you anything.

"What's a split catch?" This had my attention. I was totally confident.

"It's basically what we've been doing but instead of me sitting on your hand I do the splits," Kimmy said while mimicking the splits standing up.

I nodded, "That doesn't sound too hard. Where do I put my hands?"

Slapping both her thighs just above the knee, "Right here."

She pointed over to a couple of veterans that were doing a split catch and it looked easy. Later I was to learn that they were Bonnie Bright and Steve Clouse. Bonnie was just about the cutest thing you've ever seen. Steve was super cool. I think he's an optometrist now.

"Hey, we are going to need a spotter in front and behind me. We are going to try a split catch for the first time," Kimmy barked. A couple of guys got on either side of us. Once she's balanced midair the split catch can be wobbly. It's easy to have her plunge forward or backward without her feet under her, the cause of many broken arms. Kimmy looks me in the eyes enthusiastically, "You ready to try this?"
I put my hands around her waist. She put both her hands around my wrists.

"1-2" we both said simultaneously. We bend our knees together. I try and give an extra strong lunge upward. Kimmy really flicks her wrist to help get maximum height.

"THREE" we grunt. I think back now and I believe my extra enthusiasm caused me to push her up too fast. Kimmy's right wrist slightly slipped off my hand so we didn't get an even lift. Remember, I have NEVER done this before. I look up and she's flying above me, slowly going into the spread eagle position. She's off kilter. I try and snap my hands up as fast as possible to get under her. I get my left hand perfectly on her upper left thigh, but because we didn't get an even lift my right hand can't get under her fast enough. She's coming down and in a last ditch effort to try and place my hand on her upper thigh I accidentally hand plant my palm on her crotch. I wish I could say that was all that happened. Somehow in that split second my thumb slipped past her shorts, under her briefs and directly into.... her butt hole. I don't mean brushed near it. I mean that I fully dry docked her pooper. My thumb for a very brief moment was fully up her butt to the 2nd knuckle. No one "but" her and I at that moment knew what had happened. It was over so fast that the human eye could not have seen it. But she let out a sound that's hard to explain. It was sort of a groan, not a scream, but loud. It was the sound someone makes when they break their arm or hear nails on a chalkboard. Her wincing, painful sob followed by the fastest tears I've ever seen to this day. The whole incident took maybe 2 seconds. I felt terrible. We were both in shock. I apologized profusely.... after a few moments she seemed ok and to my relief said, "It was just an accident."

It caused an instant scene. Kimmy left, still wiping her tears and did not return. I don't mean did not return that night. She did not return to cheerleading. True or not, the rumors are that she went to a semester at sea. The most famous cheerleader on campus retired. Everyone was like, "WHAT THE HELL HAPPENED?"
I suddenly had a group of guys around me and I walked over to the water fountain to try and get away from the chaos and questioning. Lee walks over, "Why did she run away like that?"

"Dude, my thumb went up her butt. I feel so bad!" Lee, without missing a beat said, "You have Kimmy Kelly's butt gravy on your thumb!" The term "butt gravy" will forever be part of my college vernacular. Slowly word got out around the tryouts that some sort of embarrassing freak accident had happened.

Chuck Crab ended the night with an announcement and said the following things were mandatory for tryouts in two weeks, "We'll meet here again this Wednesday and Friday and again next Monday, Wednesday and Friday. 6pm. Then tryouts Sat April 26th."

1) 3 jumps
2) 3 lifts
3) Group Presentation Cheer (IU Fight Song)
4) Standing Back Tuck
5) Tumbling Run

I had lost Kimmy and now I had these athletic requirements that I didn't have the ability to do - yet. I would have only two weeks before the Saturday morning tryouts on the sacred floor of Assembly Hall. We would have 5 more group gatherings to go over the routines and whatnot. I felt empowered because I had done so well on the initial chair lift I even surprised myself. Plus, being active in athletics all my life I loved the idea of being involved, especially as a part of IU athletics! I also was enjoying the idea of the camaraderie and being part of a team. I had that in high school and I missed it. Let's also not forget the dish of revenge I wanted to serve my cheating ex-girlfriend. After that initial practice I met a guy that same night named Tom Swayzee who was a great gymnast. He told me we could go over to the trampolines, wear a harness and work on learning to do a standing back tuck. We exchanged numbers. I was feeling the team spirit already! I was not giving up just yet but was still thinking this is likely impossible.

And then, ANOTHER angel came to my rescue. Lori Coons was an IU cheer veteran. With so many guys trying out and me having zero experience it seemed likely I'd need to find a tryout partner from one of the newbie girls. Practice two, Lori came over and introduced herself to me. I didn't know she was a veteran, but she seemed like she knew what she was doing. I had a nip of stardom or should I say "infamy" over the butt gravy debacle.

Lori smiles at me and coyly says, "What happened the other night?"

Now, I don't want to look like a jerk, not knowing how Kimmy felt, I wanted to keep the whole thing close to my vest and not spread rumors. So I asked, "What do you mean?"

"I heard you...." she waved her head back & forth, "You know, you... may have put your hand where it doesn't belong," she said with a frowny smirk that let me know that she knew it wasn't fully my fault.

"I'm Lori Coons. Are you looking for a partner? Kimmy told me you have potential." she smiled.

I instantly put out my hand and said "I'm Bill Howe. I would love to team up for tryouts.... I need all the help I can get. I really don't have any experience doing this but Kimmy and I were doing pretty well with stunts until things went south."

"You mean north, don't you?" she laughs. "Seriously though, Kimmy said you're a good guy."

Hearing that made me feel better and just like that, I was back in the ballgame with one of the elite alumni showing me the ropes.

IT'S TIME, Saturday morning 2 weeks later. I'd worked with Lori and we've got our three lifts down pat. We will do the chair, a lift to the shoulder stand (super easy) and a side overhead into a sailor, meaning she'll roll down my body. It's not too difficult but looks cool. Great veteran suggestion because that lift is used in the games a lot. I have my three jumps. Pike, splits arm thrust and scissors. I knew the cheers really well (I had been been secretly practicing at night in the Teter dorm bathroom mirrors...think "Glee" but 1985) I over exaggerated my pops and knew how to play the "cheesy" game well. The standing back tuck was mandatory. Do you know what it is? From a standing position you jump in the air backwards and do a complete flip, hopefully landing on your feet. I had practiced these 4 days on the trampoline with a side harness lifting me up in case I was going to land on my head and crack my neck. I almost broke my neck even with the damn harness. I landed on my head day 2 and had that hot searing bolt of heat go down my neck. Awful. That put fear in me.

Chuck Crabb asks me, "Do you need a spot?" He almost seemed to know I was the guy who was involved in the Kimmy debacle. How did he know I could not do a standing back tuck? How did he know I might need a spot?

"I don't think I need any help, but I guess you could have someone stand next to me."

I knew the physics of this flip. I had an expert gymnast tell me you stand on your tip toes and jump as high as you can, fly your arms back, flip up your knees and wrap your arms around them and throw yourself backwards...then look for the ground. Mentally, in my mind I knew what to do. I had never had instructions so ingrained in my muscle memory. Although I had NEVER done a complete back tuck/flip while not on the trampoline, I went for it and NAILED IT. I raised my arms in a triumphant pose and as Chuck Crab would later describe, "he had a complete look of shock" as I landed firmly on my two surprised feet. I had done the perfect standing back tuck! These 6 judges had no idea that was my first (and LAST) back flip....that I would EVER do in my life. Looking back, I learned a lesson: *Doing the impossible is not something you make happen, it's something you allow to happen. We create success by not giving up before we start.* Nike's slogan "Just Do It" is pretty darn good. Don't just dream the impossible dream, get out of bed and see for yourself what is possible.

The tumbling run was the one thing I knew I could NOT do. I didn't even work on it. A standing back tuck is one thing.... but a complete tumbling run was out of the question. NO WAY!

> *My advice is to concentrate on the things that MAY be possible to do, but don't let the things that you CAN'T do stop you from trying to do the impossible.*

So back to the tumbling run, I thought I would go out and yell and scream. Show personality. I knew there had been other male cheerleaders who weren't gymnasts. I had worked out the math. If I did the absolute best I could, I still had a 30% chance of making the Men's Soccer and Girl's Basketball squad. If I could somehow overcome my "tumbling run blues" I still had a chance.

Chuck Crab calls my name, "Bill Howe" or my number or something, honestly I was so nervous that now I can't even recall. When the other guys went out, they would run directly to their starting spot. I went out and instead of running to my "spot", I ran up & down directly in front of these judges....and not just once, but TWO times. Yelling and screaming. I'm breaking down and waving my arms. I'm a super fan! I saw them smile. Suddenly, I had a genius (or terrible) idea. I wasn't sure yet. I stopped my screaming and stood in front of the judges like I was on The Tonight Show with Assembly Hall as my stage.

"Hello judges. I have something extra special planned for you today... but I will need TWO extra gym mats brought out to give me an extra long tumble run."
They already had 80 feet of mats (10) out, which made this request really intriguing. This meant that I needed 96 feet to do my "special extraordinary tumble run" one would assume.
Over the loud speaker there was a pause, "Barney, can you bring out two - no, three more mats?" Chuck said somewhat annoyed (or captivated), not sure.

Barney the janitor goes over to the closet, opens the double doors and lugs the extra mats onto a cart. In the silence of the room I can still hear my heart pounding, the wheels of the cart squeaking across this sacred wooden gym floor where the likes of Ken Benson soared.

Barney sets the three mats grudgingly down to extend my run. I am lined up facing the mats. The six judges are to my right. I look over at them and I raise my arms with purpose and absolute confidence. Now for some history: The 1984 Summer Olympics were just in LA. The Men's Gymnastics team won the GOLD medal! They were the first American squad ever to win the Olympic gold in team gymnastics. So, now it's less than a year later. I remember watching how Bart Conner would do a presentation before he did his vault. The confidence, the stride, the galloping of strength.

I BECOME Bart Conner for 8 seconds. I look over, raise my arms, imagining I'm preparing to do a Pike Suki Hara. My strides are exaggeratedly long, I'm trying to look "part Bart", "part gazelle". I get a little more than half way down the 104 foot run of mats and I do a half "guy" cartwheel with my legs mostly bent (A chimpanzee might come to mind). My momentum flows into a pseudo swat roll and I land flat on my back. I wait a beat (for drama) and do a couple of cardiac arrest convulsions, a virtual fish flop for visuals. I suddenly jump to my feet and give the old Broadway "Ta-Da" jazz hands gesture and a big cheesy smile. My best Mel Brooks.

"That's all I can do, but I can learn!" I shout.

There was a brief silence and then.... genuine laughter. I could tell that my ballsy move had worked. I had done the math. I now thought I might actually make it.... not onto the 1st squad of course, but possibly the 2nd squad - and I was thrilled!

They posted the results on the back of the locker room door. It felt like the cast of Chorus Line waiting to see the audition results. "God, I hope I get it!" I'd tried out for sports before but I've never felt the excitement of looking up onto a wall and trying to find my name. The lead for THIS theater would be to be cast in "Men's Football & Basketball"..... On the floor with Bobby Knight. IU Basketball was King. Appointment TV in every home, bar and nunnery. Before I could fight my way to take a look I saw there were some pissed off guys in front of me, disappointment was excusing itself past me with nasty glares. I stepped forward and scanned the list of the chosen few and BAM - shockingly, I saw my name:

William Howe - S1 Men's Football & Basketball

Holy shit! I had made the top squad. The LEAD ROLE! I was one of 6 guys and 6 girls who would be cheering on IU Football, Bill Mallory's team. Bobby Knight's Season on the Brink with Steve Alfred, Rick Calloway, Delray Brooks, Daryl Thomas, Todd Meier, Steve Eyl, Joe Hillman... to name a few. You see, I am an Indiana Hoosier. I love IU basketball. If I'm going to write a book, I'm going to mention a few of the guys who made my life fun. Oh yeah, also Brian Sloan, Jeff Oliphant and I loved Stew Robinson. You see, I might be a technically bad cheerleader....but I'm very big IU Basketball Fan. My basketball knowledge and expertise is a "triple back tuck" above, any and all, other cheerleaders.

I have several Bobby Knight stories but one that hit particularly close to me, literally, was 1985-86 season. We were playing Illinois and Coach Knight received a technical foul for shouting at the ref and then kicked one of our megaphone. It was Merritt Becker's he launched across the floor. Tom Dempsey would have been envious. He was pissed off because the crowd was mimicking Steve Alford's motions, his routine, before he shot his free-throw. They chanted "Socks, shorts, 1-2-3" as Steve bent down to wipe his hands off on his socks, again across his shorts and then he'd dribble the ball 3 times. Steve Alford was shooting something like 93% from the line. He left college the 4th best in NCAA History at 89.7% (535 out of 596) which is still the 9th best in history today. The man could shoot. Going a bit off-point, Steve Alford was also my lab partner in Geology 101. We licked, smelled and scraped rocks together. He didn't come to class as much as he should have but he was good guy. I got along with him well. Anyway, Steve missed a free-throw with a couple of seconds left going into halftime. IU was in a battle with the Fighting Illini and this miss made Coach Knight lose his mind. After the tech and the boot we headed to our locker for halftime and Chuck Crabb came back and said Knight is furious and if we don't stop the crowd from chanting he would end the cheerleader program. "Wow, I thought, how the hell are we going to get them to stop?" We devised a plan that we would scatter up into the stands anytime Steve was going to shoot and try and wave our arms downward into motion of "be quiet" but we had doubts this would work. Chuck Crabb made an announcement over the loud speaker every time Alford went to the line. I have to admit it would be a distraction for him to hear the crowd chant his routine. Home crowds are supposed to support their players, not annoy them.

The MORAL of the story.... NEVER, EVER think you can't do something. I had no experience at cheerleading at all. Zero gymnastic skills. Find a way to get it done. It's not who is the most talented. It's not who is the smartest. It comes down to drive. Who wants it more. There were some breaks and some luck involved in me making the top squad, but you have to put yourself in the position to get those breaks. Like my mom used to say that I mentioned earlier, "Can't never did anything!"

• *Progress over perfection* • *What's the worst that could happen?* • *Not trying is losing* • *Don't think something is out of reach* • *Be driven*

Later, a few chapters from now, you'll see how this story you just read is the gift that keeps on giving. It's the motivation that keeps on motivating. It's the story that shows others that I'm the guy they want in their company. Good energy, good karma, good deeds, good effort, good perseverance, good at going for something you really had no way of getting. Your life, my life, is a pile of experiences that somehow sense and know when you are naughty or nice. People make a split second evaluation of you from head to toe in seconds. A blink of their eye and they've put you in a box, a category. The best way to improve your snap judgment, your instaYOU is to make it genuine. Life's experiences, what you do or don't do, give you an energy that people can unconsciously sense.

Statistically, our instaYOU is accurate. It's an inner chi, your life force of energy, that creates what people feel when they first meet you. One of my favorite books I read fresh out of college was "The Tao of Pooh" written in 1982 by Benjamin Hoff. It taught Taoism as more of an introduction to Westerners. I read this a long long time ago but there are a couple take-aways that I still cling to today. Winnie the Pooh would be meandering, lumbering along a path. "Doopty, doopty, doo..." and he comes to a fork in the road. What does Pooh do? Nothing, he just keeps walking and does not stop and ponder which direction to go. This is a deep zen philosophy. Taoism says don't force your way through life, follow your natural order to have harmony. It is also, in my opinion, a metaphor for following the blueprint that is embedded in your soul. Oh wow, I didn't expect to get this intense in chapter 1, but here we are. So Pooh chose his path organically. He went with the flow, what he felt in his mind, his inner voice. What happens when we stop listening to our inner voice? What happens when we don't follow our genetic desire to do certain things in our lives? It creates conflict within our own selves. Messing up your yin & yang balance. We've all experienced someone who just seems bitter, unhappy. Maybe you're in a Walmart parking lot and an older person feels you cut them off and shakes their fist at you. "Thanks for taking my spot asshole!" they creak out from their Oldsmobile Cutlass. Key word here is Old. I'll add bitter because somewhere along their path they didn't listen to their natural gut, their inner voice. That secret storyteller in your mind that knows what you want to do in your life. What you are designed to be.

SIDE NOTE: on a completely different scale away from my life story. This is me being purely opinionated, or dare I say enlightened to how and why we are programmed to be the way we are. This is something I've always felt but rarely had a platform to voice it, "Enough about me, let's talk more about me!" I like to think about the adventures we create when we are dreaming. We have NO CONTROL over why our 6th grade gym teacher is in his underwear making omelettes in a room with chicken wallpaper. We throw completely different groups of people together in our dreams that don't line up chronologically in our lives when it comes to months and years. It's crazy.

Could this same craziness also be connected to an unconscious blueprint to how we would most like to live our lives? I've thought about this for years. Our unconscious dreams, that we have no control over, could also be similar to an unconscious path that we are supposed to follow. Outside influences like family or religion could hamper our true best destiny. By destiny I mean path. We can't all be doctors, we can't all be artists.... we need people who are happy and acceptable at all levels of society. We should all be given the opportunity, free of external pressures or restrictions to be the person our internal voice is yearning us to be. Nature vs nurture. I chose nature.

> *Listen to your inner voice. Go with your gut feeling. You know better than anyone who you are and what you are supposed to do in life. Listen to the pulls of your destiny.*

Trying out for cheerleading at 19 in 1985 was me following some inner voice telling me that I can be whoever I want to be. Listening and acting on it led me in the right direction.

The 1985 IU Cheerleaders

I'm dead center 6th over from the left. Lori Coons on my lap.

The Whole Fun Crew at Cheer Camp

Infamous "Split Catch" with Lori

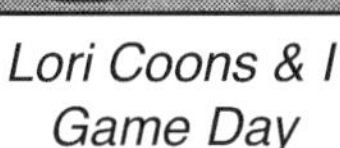

Lori Coons & I Game Day

My Signature Yell & Breakdown

Me Lifting Steve Clause

Life Lessons from a Bison

I read a story about bison and a life lesson stuck with me. Most creatures, including humans, often run away from an oncoming storm. It's natural to try and avoid mayhem, but when the angry clouds & thunder are rolling your way you can't outrun them. In fact, you end up moving along with the storm and prolong the dread.

Not bison, they wait. As the storm comes across the plains, bearing down on them, they begin charging towards the darkness. They hit it head-on and in doing so endure it's wrath for a far less amount of time. The storms of life will follow us all until we turn and face it. Debts, relationship issues, tough business decisions, health concerns and, any an all of the issues, that lay weight on your shoulders do not go away until you face that storm. Avoidance, procrastination, hiding… does not solve your problems. I had so much fear trying out for IU Cheerleader. I wanted to runaway and not try. I had a million excuses telling me "NO" but something in my determined soul, my wonder & lust for trying the impossible, put the heart of a bison in me. Many more times in my life I ran towards the challenge. Run toward your storms! ***TRY TRY TRY***

Billy Howe (left) draws admiring glances from Rene LoPilato, a "coed" in his kindergarten class, when he dons his fireman's hat. They and other Wheeler Elementary School pupils were kept busy as blazes trying on hats and seeing fire engines that pulled up yesterday at the school. It was part of the Speedway Fire Department's program for Fire Prevention Week. Billy is the son of Mrs. Beverly Howe, 2924 Consulate Lane, and Rene is the daughter of Mr. and Mrs. Joseph LoPilato, 2912 Consulate Lane, Speedway. (Star Photo by William A. Oates)

Kindergarten: Little 5yo me getting my first bit of press when the local firetruck came to visit my school. PR is in my blood!

How(e) **I Got Here**

CHAPTER TWO

•

"Nearly all men can stand adversity, but if you want to test a man's character, give him power"

—Abraham Lincoln

I HOPE it comes across that I really did feel badly about accidentally sticking my thumb in a place it did not belong. Lee called on his family, Hill's Roses, to try and send an olive branch of "I'm sorry" to Kimmy. We had a dozen, one of a kind, newly genetically formulated, bouquet of roses sent to her. You probably didn't know this but Richmond, Indiana was known as "Rose City" in the 1970s. I never saw them but Lee assured me they would be the most exotic colors of roses she had ever seen. I never heard from her. I guess I was the pain in her butt she wanted to forget.

I almost titled this book "Willfull" with an extra "L" to be clever. Willful (spelled correctly) usually has a negative connotation. Webster defines it as • *having or showing a stubborn and determined intention to do as one wants, regardless of the consequences or effect.* • *intentional; deliberate. Will,* the name I mostly go by, is also used in the English language as a verb. The word "will" suggests a stubborn persistence in doing what one wants. People sometimes say, "That willful child disregarded his parent's advice." I felt and still do feel willfull because I am going against a predestined future that was laid before me by circumstances. It goes back to The Tao of Pooh again. We all have an inner, innate fortune that can reveal itself if we follow it's calling. Fortune can be very fickle. I'm not really talking about it in regards to money. I'm talking about good fortune. Having life smile on you. To believe in fortune, you have to also believe it can go away. Lady luck will not always be by your side. You have to leap at the chance when you are fortuitous enough to taste that "fortune" and given the chance to succeed. Later I will discuss accepting the loss of fortune and how it should not be groaned upon. It's part of the glorious cycle of following your dreams. It's a loaded gun. Because no matter how far you go, you will have defeats. Mark Cuban loses. All great winners have defeats. In all diversity of fortune, the absolute worst is to have once been happy, content, but feeling you lost your mojo. Trust me, you DID NOT! It's a game of dodge-ball. Just don't let it hide for too long, your fortune is there if you let it breathe. Do NOT start believing you've lost your creative spark, the positive, unique energy that has made you who you are.

If you want a doctor's help you need to reveal the wound. The same goes for "Why are you stopping being the person you were or should be?" Find that wound. Pluck it out.

Before I get into my upbringing I want to share a success I had in my life that I directly feel was influenced by my mother and, as hard as this is to say now, Donald Trump. My mom was a go-getter in real estate. I saw at a young age her success and wanted to be a chip off the ol' block. It felt like child labor laws were being broken growing up. Mom & dad were divorced when I was 4 years old and being the only "man" in the house I got stuck helping with mom's rentals. I was the muscle, the trash remover, the painter, the roofer, toilets, carpets, windows... I was her handyman. I hated it.

My early feat (success) of entrepreneurism was in real estate. The first summer before heading off to college I was working at Steak-n-Shake. I also decided to take a course to get my real estate license. I was inspired by my mother as I mentioned earlier. I saw R.E. as my future even before college. I'll jump ahead 2 years. My freshman year I saw that some new condos were being built right across the street from Memorial Stadium in Bloomington, IN (Indiana University). They were selling for $65,000. They were two bedrooms with a shared bath & shower on the 2nd floor. A guest bathroom on the 1st floor and a basement with another full bath & shower. I thought I could build a wall in the basement and turn it into two rooms as well. This would make it a 4 bedroom townhouse. Game changer. In 1985 interest rates were 10% for a first time FHA homeowner. That's about 2% less than conventional and I only needed to put down 3%, but I convinced mom to loan me 5% and I put down $3,250. When I say "loan" anyone who knows my mom will tell you she treated these types of situations as strictly business. I explained to her she would be either paying IU, my fraternity or an apartment, a minimum of $300 a month. In less than a year she'd be ahead of the debt meaning by my senior year she'd be scot-free on paying my room and less board too. Yearly, the property tax would be $813 a year and home insurance $228. Monthly, I'd have a $40 PMI and a $75 homeowners association fee. My grand total expenses would be $744 a month. Mom agreed to co-sign on the loan and her name could be removed in 3 years. My land baron dreams were bouncing inside my head. If I could find 3 roommates to pay $300 I'd live for free and turn a profit. Amazing! My sophomore year I pledged Sigma Phi Epsilon and spent my 2nd year in college living in the Frat House. Varsity Villas were now selling and I had recruited 3 fraternity brothers and we were all excited to live off campus. Living in a Frat House is no picnic. My junior & senior year I thoroughly enjoyed my roommates, living off campus and reaping the benefits of owning it. I had a sense of pride being so young and being a landlord. I felt respect too. As my senior year was winding down I saw that many parents who bought condos at Varsity Villas wanted to sell them once their kids were graduating. Having only owned them for 1-2 years they hadn't built much equity and most of them feared becoming absentee landlords to college kids. A real estate agent would want 6% commission. If they tried to sell for $68K they'd owe $4,000 in commissions and closing costs. They'd be at a loss. I went down to the city county building and opened the plats (plots of land) that showed who owned each unit. I jotted down their addresses and sent out letters. I ended up buying 4 more condos pretty much overnight. Two (2) I bought for $2,000, one (1) for $550 and the fourth I got by just assuming their loan, so FREE! My worst deal was the one I bought for myself before my junior year. I was doing well. I mentioned Donald J Trump earlier. His book Art of the Deal came out in 1987. With my mom's RE background and his book I was motivated. This was long before I started seeing the chinks in Trump's armor. My first jump into being my own boss man was going well, but it was a lot of work too. Managing properties is a tough business, especially when college students are involved.

Anyway, back to chronological order. I graduated from Speedway High School in Indianapolis, Indiana in 1984. I was headed to Ball State University. That summer I had to earn my freshman year spending money so I got a job at Steak-n-Shake. They were launching a new location across the street from the Indianapolis Motor Speedway. I grew-up in Speedway, our mascot was the Speedway Sparkplugs. That mascot may have helped me land a national TV commercial many years later.....I'll get to that when I go into my Hollywood years. God, that sounds funny to say, "Hollywood Years" but it's part of the unplanned plan of my life. While working at Steak-n-Shake I was busting my butt. It was fast & furious. It was my first time being a waiter but not my last. One night a man came up to me, that I had not noticed before, and said he was impressed with my work ethic. He asked me about my future plans and I told him I was heading to Ball State in a few months. He was an associate professor of law at Indiana University. He told me that IU would be a better choice given that I wanted to study business. I'm not sure why I had chosen BSU. I would be rooming with one of my best HS friends, Tony Sarkine, and I was just mindlessly moving forward. But once the opportunity to go to IU was planted in my head, I started to get excited. I grew up loving IU basketball, Bobby Knight was royalty. When I mentioned IU to my mom she thought it was too much of a party school. I think somewhere around this time PLAYBOY Magazine ranked Indiana University as the #1 party school in the country. Long story short, I took a visit to IU with my Steak-n-Shake admirer, and it changed the entire course of my life. I followed my inner voice. I felt something draw me in this direction to be the person I should be. It's the trim-tabs of life *(Chapter 13 explains this theory)*

I landed down at IU in late August 1984. I was 19 years old and had a room in Teter-Thompson 4 with a roommate named Harry Westcott. He was an upperclassman from New Palestine, Indiana. He was in ROTC. His goal was to become an Aviation Officer, a pilot. I'm proud to say he did become a pilot and now works for Alaskan Airlines. Harry and I got along like two peas in a pod. We were quite different but that's what makes college so special. Harry was disciplined and had a set "quiet time" for us to study. He was the perfect rudder for me at that time.

Undoubtedly, when you are writing a story about your life, your experiences and possibly passing along some inspiration, you need to give some description of your upbringing. My dad worked for Citizen's Gas in Indianapolis, Indiana for 36 years. He was in ditches installing gas meters. My mother got into real estate when I was about 3 years old. Instantly she was a natural at selling homes. Both my parents grew up humble. Somewhere I read a quote by G. Michael Hopt:

My grandfather walked 10 miles to work. My dad walked 5 miles to work. I drive a Cadillac, my son drives a Mercedes. Likely my grandson can have a Ferrari, but my great grandson will have us walking again.

Tough times create strong men
Strong men create easy times
Easy times create weak men
Weak men create tough times

Does success (unearned) leads to entitled unhappiness and/or inherently false happiness? *(This question could be a whole book)*

"Tough times create strong men" sticks with me. My parents grew up in tough times. Dad, who I was named after, grew up with 3 brothers and 3 sisters. So including my grandparents, there were 9 people people living in a small two bedroom duplex. My grandmother was Mary Margaret Lenihan born in a place called Suckeen, Woodquay, Galway, Ireland in 1904. She left Galway, Ireland around 1921 at the age of 17. I'm sure that would have been a helluva journey in 1921: a single woman coming through Ellis Island alone, seeing the Statue of Liberty. She made her way to Indiana via some family connections I'm told and got a job at Central State Hospital in the laundry room. To us Naptowners (Indianapolis), Central State was the local mental hospital. Growing up it had a mystical scary reputation. Rumors have it that's where my grandfather Willie Howe met his future bride - in the laundry room. Yes, my dad's name is William and so was my grandfather's. My dad preferred to be called Billy or Bill. I, for some reason, remember my grandpa went by Willie. Growing up and going to their house was old school fun. You'd hear a clock ticking, hourly chimes. Grandpa would be on the couch watching sports while grandma was always cooking in the kitchen. If the Dallas Cowboys Cheerleaders came on TV, by God, grandpa better pretend not to be watching or grandma would have a conniption fit. Her jealousy was charming, and even at a young age I knew it was sweet.

Grandma & Grandpa Howe grew up seriously blue collar. They didn't have a pot to piss in, but they'd give you the last dime they had in their pockets. I don't think they ever owned a car but grandma would take us grandchildren on the best bus trips downtown that we all still remember today. We'd get our picture taken in the photo booth at William H. Block department store. They raised their 7 children

Catholic and taught them right from wrong. They were rich in ways people look past now.

My mom grew up in Brownsburg, Indiana. A farming community back then and still is to a certain degree. She was born in a home with no indoor plumbing, a wooden stove in the middle of the room to heat the whole house and very few modern luxuries. As a child her Christmas present would be a very small toy if she was lucky. Her main gift was a special dinner and oranges for dessert. I know a lot of us my age have this same story about their parent's childhood. The generations born in the 30s & 40s really saw their quality of life soar upward. Both my parents grew up in this humble era, but my mother had the type of wiring that would make sure they strived for more. They met in high school, dad joined the Navy and was shipped out on a navy destroyer at the end of the Korean War. He traveled all over the world. Mom moved to New Jersey where dad was stationed but most of her time there he was out to sea and she was alone.

Once his Navy career was over they moved back home again to Indiana. Dad got a job with Citizen's Gas and they started our family. I have two older sisters, Jacque Sue being the oldest (7 years older), Mary Lou (4 years older) and finally me, William Roy Howe, born on June 28, 1965. I was nearly 3 months premature which at that time was dangerous. When I finally came home from the hospital I expected the same 24/7 care I got with the around-the-clock nurses. I'm told that I was quite the handful, but also I was quite welcomed as a son. Mom told me that she felt pressure to have a boy because my dad was a great athlete and wanted a son. Obviously, I was spoiled rotten by my doting dad and two older sisters. I'm not a child psychologist, but it must add to your personality to be raised with such love. To feel special and wanted from the moment you took your first breath. Although I was a "blessing" as mom had said, I did not save their marriage as mom had hoped. I was 4 years old when they divorced. I don't really remember them being married, but I do know it must have been a profound moment for me the day dad left. He picked me up and put me on the bed of his blue truck. He told me he was leaving. That moment is emblazoned in my memory and nothing else from that young age stands out - so that must mean something.

Divorce sucks but it might have been for the best. As I grew older I realized that they weren't right for each other. I do want to say a few things about my parents that I feel influenced me before their divorce. Once they came home from the East Coast and dad got his workingman's job, it became apparent that they both had bigger dreams. With the knowledge of hindsight, it's obvious to me that it was my mom who was the driving force in striving to have more. I love my dad to pieces, but he was not nearly as motivated as mom, which shined through even more once they were splitsville. While dad was working at the gas company they had this wild idea to open their own trampoline center. It's funny when you hear about things your parents did before you have any real memory and it can just blow your mind. I can't see my parents trying this, but it makes me smile. Their first try at entrepreneurism. From what I gather they rented some space, had 12 trampolines and charged people to jump up & down. Mom said they had insurance through Lords of London, sounds so fancy. I'm still not sure how they pulled all this off because they did not have much money. Grandma Hamill (mom's side) may have mortgaged the farm? The business did well, but not great. The hours were long. After a couple of years they "jumped" out of this business and they both started taking night classes to get their real estate license. Mom says the guy teaching the class warned married couples that if they both got into real estate together they'd be divorced soon. I'm sure they scoffed at that.... but he turned out to be right.

The divorce must have had an affect on me, but I'm blind to it or have chosen to not be a victim. I heard people discussing *Equality vs Equity* and it's a hard subject to wrap my mind around. *Equality* has a straight forward definition. Individuals or even groups of people should be able to have the same resources or opportunities. That is fair. Someone should not be treated differently, lessor or greater based on their age, gender, sexuality, race or religion. There are lots of grey areas such as education & upbringing that can add confusion to the unfairness. *Equity* in some terms means a value you possess or a build up of value. Having been born with certain equities was a blessing. The barriers that would get in the way of my success were there but maybe also a driving force for me to try harder. I was given opportunities and resources. I also had challenges, but being a white male can be forgiving. That's impossible to ignore no matter your hardships. My parents were divorced when I was very young. My mother became a working mom. I would classify myself as a "Latch-key Kid" meaning when I came home my mom was not there. I didn't have much adult supervision. I learned to cook on my own. I did my own laundry. I became very self-sufficient. My equities (bonuses in my life) were that I was loved, grew up in a safe environment and had good friends. I didn't know what I didn't have. Maybe it is DNA or just a God-given personality, but I was a good kid. I had all the freedom in the world. Instead of getting in trouble I got into sports. I was in FCA (Fellowship of Christian Athletes). I was very active in school. I learned around 3rd grade that school was not going to be a cakewalk for me. Mom's hard work was paying off. We went from living in one side of a double in the old part of town to a two-story house in new Speedway known as Meadowood Park. I was devastated to leave my current school. Although I would meet back up with many of my old friends once we hit junior high, as a 3rd grader I didn't understand that. It was only an 8 minute drive but a 44 minute walk. It might as well have been the moon for the next 4 years. I was crushed. On top of this it was decided I should take 3rd grade over again at the new school. It made me feel stupid. Mom explained to me there were two reasons:

"You struggled with your reading and math" she bemoaned.

I knew it was not coming easy for me, but I didn't think it was so bad that I needed to take the whole year over again.

"Plus, you can either be the youngest in your class or the oldest. Your dad and I discussed it we and think that extra year will help you in sports" she smiled.

Now, looking back and maybe even then, this second reason was giving me face. I was addicted to sports. I was excelling but being younger meant I was smaller. I accepted this fate and when we moved to Wheeler Elementary I started 3rd grade... AGAIN!

I always did fairly well in school but I had to work 3 times harder than anyone else and do it without letting on that I was struggling. I soon realized that my life, my strengths could <u>not</u> be measured by tests in school. I needed to be smarter in ways you don't learn in school. That's damn near the THEME OF THIS BOOK!

"Comparison is the thief of joy"
— Theodore Roosevelt

I learned early on that I did not need to worry about what someone else could do better than me. I knew my strengths. Life is more than regurgitation. I could be creatively smart. I often attack challenges with these objectives in mind:

1) Overcoming an obstacle by thinking outside of the box. You have to believe in your own abilities. Your mindset in believing, being happy, and willing to take risks is a key to success. Break some rules, legally!
2) Don't wait until you're ready. You're never ready to jump in head first. No-one is ever ready. You have now, today. Stop stopping.
3) Failure is an affirmation that you are trying something big. Can't never did anything. Get to bat. Take a swing.

When I changed schools I was treated differently by the teachers. At my old school I was in Reading Group 3. That hurt my pride, it felt like a punch in the gut. It becomes obvious to you, but more importantly, to EVERYONE that you may not be the sharpest tool in the shed. You've been put into a category of lessor intelligence. True or not true, it becomes your label, your stigmatism. I think my reading got worse because I became nervous after being made to feel stupid. It still bothers me today. At the new school I had challenges too, but no one knew of my previous reading group. Taking 3rd grade over again, I had a step-up and graduated to Reading Group 2! In my entire life since then, I look at the "Reading Group 3" people of the world (meaning the "looked-down-on" or underprivileged for whatever reason), with different eyes. I was one of them. I was labeled. I befriended and related to everyone. Even though I was feeling better about myself, I was knocked down a notch yet again by my new teacher that Christmas. We were going to start cutting out ornaments from colorful card stock construction paper. I was so excited! I enthusiastically raised my hand because I could not WAIT to start cutting out these ornaments! The teacher looked at me and basically said that I wasn't very good at cutting along the lines of a pattern. I was shocked! It shook me. And still, EVERY freakin time I cut out anything TO THIS DAY, I am thrust back into Mrs.Lawrence's class and I fear that I might not cut paper very well. It's made me cut extra carefully. Is that crazy or what? I was learning that I had to work my magic in other ways. I also have been a voracious reader my whole life. *Instead of retreating from perceived weaknesses I attacked them.*

Groundless Fears

'There are more things likely to frighten us than there are to crush us; we suffer more often in imagination than in reality'

—Seneca (65AD) *2,000 years ago

I think in this day and age, with social media, the cruelty of people (young & old) is far beyond our mind's ability to filter it. We all need to look at "Groundless Fears" for what they are and take a breath. We humans don't stop and consider how the person we are holding authority over may feel. We need to put ourselves in their shoes and try to have compassion for how our actions may affect them. Equality, especially feeling equal, is essential for us to develop. The equities we came into this world with help shape our lives, but we are not limited by them, we can still improve. I learned early that many of my fears were completely unfounded and mostly in my mind. Looking back, I now know that if I was feeling these social pangs, then many of my fellow students must have had it worse. I was popular, athletic and overall lucky as hell in my fortune in life. I didn't grow-up 'rich' as in money but as many of my fellow Speedway alum will likely say, "We didn't know we didn't have something or someone was better off than us." It's likely a blessing growing up when I did. Kids these days want to keep up with the Kardasians or some TikTok star. Oi vey, I'm plotzing. Anyway, I got through grade school.

Four grade schools fed into Speedway Junior High. It was a new beginning with so many new people. I was self motivated. Mom was working a lot and I wanted to play football, basketball, track, baseball, choir, clubs, church groups... It set the ground work for High School too. I ended up having a good athletic career in high school. I was a starting forward in basketball and never left the field in football. My senior year we were 10-0 going into the playoffs and that season I had many touchdowns and a few interceptions. I even dated a cheerleader. Finishing out Speedway High School was a very good experience for me. I could tell stories and go into details but I want this book to be a motivator and I have more stories to tell.

Wonderlust is not in the dictionary, but the combination of these two words sum up the drive & attitude that has led to my success. Looking at life with curious desires has also led to many unknown adventures. What's behind that door? You'll never know until you knock, or better yet, kick it down.

WONDER: *Webster (n) provokes a feeling of surprise mingled with admiration, caused by something beautiful, unexpected, unfamiliar, or inexplicable. (v) desire or be curious to know something.*

LUST: *A strong, powerful desire, whether it's a noun or verb: you lust for things you deeply crave.*

I have *wanderlust* too, with an "a" that is is in the dictionary. A strong desire, an impulse, a longing to wander, to meander and explore. I love to travel, but to build success you need wonder. That childlike innocence to believe and hope in something. To be curious, to have that wonder of life in your soul is a magical driving source of energy & hope for entrepreneurs. Finding yours is often listening to the universe. You have a determined blueprint in your DNA. *Listen to it!*

Mom inspires with ZEAL

Doug's on the ticket! (see page 57)

OVERACHIEVER 101

CHAPTER THREE

•

"You gain strength, experience and confidence by every experience where you really stop to look fear in the face... You must do the thing you cannot do"
—Eleanor Roosevelt

"DO THE THINGS you cannot do" is music to my ears. The summer before my senior year at Indiana University I decided to stay on campus and take a particularly difficult statistics class in hopes that it might be easier. Plus, it was my last summer as a "footloose and fancy free" college student. I was only taking two classes, so I had plenty of time on my hands. I was starting to think about buying more condos at Varsity Villas, which I did, as mentioned in the previous chapter. The biggest thought consuming my mind was *"What am I going to do with my life?"* Entering your senior year you start to sweat a bit thinking the "real world" will soon be comin'-a-knockin' and it's scary. So my goal that summer, besides passing that ridiculous statistics class, was to figure out what I wanted to do after graduation. That is a deep question that feels so urgent when you're almost 22 years old. In hindsight, I know this is ridiculous. There is no need for most of us to know our life's path at such a young age. Hell, I'm <u>still</u> working on it. But that summer of 87' I was thinking not only of WHAT CAREER, but how I would get it.

On my quest for the answer for my future, I wandered into the BPO (Business Placement Office) at the School of Business. It's now called the Kelley School of Business due to a donation of $23M by someone who's last name is Kelley, duh! Anyway, like now, back then IU's business school was consistently ranked in the top 20 in the US. It's a great school, which also means even greater competition. I befriended a woman working in the BPO and asked her how it worked. She explained that some of the best Fortune 500 companies come to campus to conduct interviews starting in late fall. Students get a full list of companies coming to interview and they fill out a submission card with a #2 pencil (again, it was the 80's and nothing could get done without a #2 pencil!). There would be little circles to fill in much like an SAT test. You could rank your top 10 most interested companies in order of desire. The top feeders may get a lot of interviews, meaning it was a plug & play numbers game. Your numbers were put into a computer and mathematically I knew I'd be in trouble.

> *"Talent is cheaper than table salt. What separates the talented individual from the successful one is a lot of hard work."*
> *— Stephen King*

I throw this great Stephen King quote in here because I'm writing a book and he's one of our modern literary "Kings" (pun intended). It's probably apparent but I am not a *natural* student. I had to work so hard all through college to keep my grades above average. I still lack traditional book smarts, but it has made me more successful. I knew regurgitation would not be my ticket to success. No PHDs or doctorates would bring me financial freedom. I had confidence and had succeeded in thinking outside of the box. So, when the Business Placement lady laid out how it worked, it was a punch in the gut. I would only be guaranteed ONE interview and any additional ones would be based strictly on my GPA. Basically, if one of my choices was one of the more popular companies (like a pharmaceutical sales rep position with Pfizer) the chances of me acquiring that interview would be determined by my GPA. She looked me up on the computer and shook her head, "Darlin, you're gonna have a hard time with a 3.12 GPA" she apologetically whispered. If you dug deeper into my grades it got even worse. I had F-Xed a couple of classes too, meaning I was doing terrible in them and took a voluntary F by dropping out. It's sort of a free pass but stays on your record and does some sort of average into your ultimate GPA. It's a lifesaving Catch 22. The summer stats class that I was trying to get through is one of my previous F-X disasters. I already had one go around at this beast of a class. It's data science combining algebra & algorithms. "Give me association data or give me death" was ringing in my head. I hated it. "It's not rocket science," novices would say. "No, rocket science would be a joy compared to this." I told my advisor that my brain was not wired for stats. My summer school teacher resembled Einstein and was crossed-eyed. Seriously, I can't make this up. When he called on you, he'd literally be looking one row over from where you were sitting. It was comical except for the fact that this one class held my future in it's balance. I was looking straight ahead into disaster.

My brain is wired on how to get ahead. I looked at the BPO woman, flabbergasted. But then she then said something magical, a door had shut.... but a big freakin' window was about to be opened.

"If you have a '*letter of invite*' you are guaranteed to interview with whoever gives that to you."

"How can I get that?" I asked.

"There are files that can be accessed by students that list all the companies coming to campus, including their contacts and what positions they are interviewing for," she proudly exclaimed.

Holy crap! No one I knew, knew about this golden nugget loophole! The BPO in 1987 did not make it super easy to access the info. I went over to their office, right off of E. 10th Street for the next 3 days and started jotting down all the companies I wanted to interview with. It also made me think of jobs in life I might not have even considered or knew existed. I got the names of the actual interviewers. I knew I had stumbled upon a sort of secret. It wasn't encouraged by the BPO, it would put a kink in their elite system that held the almighty GPA as the Holy Grail of success. I began working on my resume and the all important cover letter. I knew presentation would be a big factor for me - frankly, it was my biggest asset! This was the beautiful time in our history when you could *'Wow'* someone with the right white 32lb linen paper with premium texture. You could actually see criss-cross strands of excellence in this paper. I then went to a professional resumé company. They sat down with me and laid out a masterful presentation with bold titles, different fonts in just the right places. It was a work of art. I used raised black ink...in fact, it was almost braille! Everything had a superior quality to it. Classy yet not dated. I must say, looking back now: I nailed it. My cover letter was professional but also intriguing. The company reps all told me later at my interviews they were surprised by my request for a *letter of invite.* I think it set the bar early on that I was a go-getter. I was interviewing for sales positions, so that sort of gumption was part of the DNA of a good peddler. I made sure to use the same paper & printing ink as the resume. They were a team. I also arranged to have the resume company print the 8.5x11 envelopes which I slightly customized for each letter. I signed them with an excellent pen. NOTE: You DO NOT want to sign a cover letter with the first pen you see. Test it out. Make sure it has strong ink. I mailed out about 25 requests in late July. Keep in mind, no one else was doing this, I was going rogue with this secret that had landed on my lap. I was not about to let my entire future ride on a computer scan-tron and a #2 pencil! I was stealth. I was as busy as a beaver and no one but me knew what I was up to.

Within a week I started getting responses. It was exciting! I did get some rejections saying they preferred to follow the "typical submission process" they had used in the past. As I mentioned, many of them also didn't know about the "letter of intent" and actually asked me what I needed from THEM to help guarantee ME an interview! After a few correspondences back & forth, I had 14 companies asking to see me!! I was on top of the world. The

Valedictorian, the Summa cum laude, Magna cum laude.... none of these "super smart people" would get anywhere NEAR the number of chances to sit in an interview room with potential employers like I would. Now, getting the interview was a crucial first step. There are other ways to help an *overachiever* achieve things he cannot do. I need to continue to be that "wunderkind" kid. I went to the Men's Warehouse and bought a dark navy blue suit, white dress shirt with a basic collar (no buttons, no bars) and I went with a maroon tie with some blue highlights. I wanted to make a serious statement - navy is not only a power color but it also depicts dependability and loyalty. I didn't want to be red, white & blue, I mean I wasn't running for office, but I did look slightly candidate-ish, which I was a bit worried about. However, it was 1987 when I was interviewing Ronald Reagan was president. I may or may not have been channeling "the Gipper" which was a good look back then. "There you go again!" is classic Reagan.

My girlfriend's father, Robert Milligan, was an executive at Continental Bank in Chicago. He showed interest in my plight and explained that he would be annoyed by potential employees if they didn't know anything about his company during an interview. He suggested that I research any company I was meeting with. He even used some of his bank contacts to get me history on several of them. Remember, there was no internet back then and researching anything took time and energy. I began making crib notes on flash cards for every company I would be meeting. The Indy 500 driver Bobby Unser said, "Success is where preparation and opportunity meet." I was prepared and ready for success.

It was only September into my senior year and I was interviewing for jobs that would likely start soon after I graduated in May 1988. The companies I remember meeting were in three different industries. The large industrial corporations were Dow Chemical, US Steel & Alcoa.

Financial houses JP Morgan, Caldwell Banker & Charles Schwab showed interest. I also met Kaiser Permanente and Pfizer Pharmaceutical. I felt like a rockstar. For me, wearing a suit always had a bit of pageantry to it - Halloween for adults. I still cannot understand why tying a knot around your neck so a piece of cloth can dangle down to your dingle-dangle is considered business appropriate. The ascot, bow-tie, bolo, zipper tie, craven and knit ties, the whole lot is extremely uncomfortable and dated, but at 22yo it was exciting. As stated earlier, I was in full bloom of business fashion. I was ready to play the part. They all seemed to show interest in me. I remember US Steel (USS) very well. I was sitting in one of the more modern buildings at Indiana University. It had glass & metal strewn about in a "we are progressive" type of manner. Indiana University was founded in 1820 and many of the buildings on campus are made of Indiana limestone and have a majestic quality about them. The campus is just beautiful. The BPO was striking out to be contemporary... dare I say stark? Not the warmth you feel in Memorial Union. There were several small rooms down a narrow hallway that must have been designed just for the purpose of interviewing. Thinking back, it resembled a Japanese hospital in Toyota-shi that I unfortunately had to visit many years later. You'll hear more about that later.

A well put-together man of about 40, dressed conservatively, called out, "Bill Howe!" I rose and marched over to him with confidence and shook his hand firmly, of course. Confidence 101. I followed him back to our little room. I was all smiles.

As what seemed to be the norm in my interviews, "I got your letter and resume in late summer and was impressed," he exclaimed.

I decided I would somewhat cop to how and why I went the "letter of intent" route, "I really wanted to meet with United States Steel and my counsellor told me that the opportunity to contact you directly might help me get an interview," I explained. In all honesty, I actually told *every* company I did the "letter of invite" just for them. I noticed the company reps seem to know each other. They were on the interview circuit. I then got worried the different reps might go out for drinks and compare notes and that I'd possibly be caught as a liar, but then I laughed at myself and said, "I'm interviewing for SALES, they may love me more!"

"The first thing that caught my eye on your resume was that you are an IU Cheerleader," USS pointed out.

"Well, I was a cheerleader my sophomore year, and I loved it," I smiled. "Why did you only do it one year?" he asked. This is another time I decided the truth was my strength. Plus, it was a helluv' a story.

I began with, "I was sitting in a review session for economics and Kimmy Kelly, the most famous cheerleader on campus sat next to me.... blah blah blah!" I, of course, skipped over the butt gravy part, but laid on thick the part where I pulled a Bart Connors gymnastics stunt / farce. I had this guy in stitches. He even started asking me questions, "How were you able to do the standing back tuck?" I went into serious details of how I pulled off the major coup. I even told him how the cheerleader coach at nationals was pissed off because I couldn't do 75% of what she had designed. Suddenly it became crystal clear why this guy was so interested in my cheerleading career,

"I was a IU Cheerleader," he blurted out, laughing.

"No way, really?" "Yes, when I saw your resume I was looking forward to meeting you," he confessed. "Cheerleading changed my life," he confessed again.

We continued on with some of the more traditional questions and I was completely prepared. It was less than a month later that I was being flown to Pittsburgh, PA to have my 2nd round of interviews. I was on top of the world. To be a kid of 22, have someone buy me a plane ticket, pick me up at the airport, book me into a beautiful hotel and give me $50 cash per diem, holy cow - that was a lot of money back then! I felt like I was a basketball player, 5 star recruit, a McDonald's All-American - doing a campus visit. It was amazing.

In Pittsburgh I was taken to a fancy white tablecloth gentleman's type club restaurant. I was definitely wet behind the ears. My girlfriend's dad, Mr. Milligan *big shot*, had advised me to not order anything messy or complicated to eat. Spaghetti was a no-no. I settled on fried chicken and used a knife & fork to eat it as he instructed, that was first. Put your napkin on your lap, don't order like it's your last meal, follow your guest's lead (meaning - do what they do) and no elbows on table or talking with my mouth full. I love all this advice because it's Mom 101. I had two Outside Sales Reps as my interviewers. The good thing about interviewing for a steel company is that it's a man's man type of world. Not hoity-toity at all, but a delicate balance of rich BS and locker room talk. They were drilling me. I think one of the guys naturally wanted to not like me. He was 30ish, blonde hair, ambitious and I learned later maybe a bit insecure. 2nd guy was mid-thirties, dark hair, kinda looked like Mr. Big from Sex in the City. He and I hit it off more.

"What is it you like about USS?" blondie probed. I started my history lesson on United States Steel. "Andrew Carnegie, JP Morgan, Charles Schwab founded this company in 1901.... blah blah blah." I went into details on how USS was the leader in the "Birth of America", how it helped "build America" and I named several big projects that US Steel had supplied the steel for across the US. I proudly barked, "US Steel at one point had a larger budget than the United States of America!" Later, after I accepted the job with United States Steel I hung out with both these guys and even went on sales calls with blondie to some major accounts. "You know more about US Steel than anyone I know who *works* at US Steel," they later joked with me. They said I had blow them away. I had a glowing review from the on-campus (cheerleader) recruit, but these two guys had decided before meeting with me they would give a hard time. They wanted to haze me with difficult or stupid questions. "You came out of the gate with that fucking US Steel history lesson, all patriotic and shit, and we knew you had out-played us before we even got to harass you," they teased me later. *Some thoughts I have about WHY I got the interviews and then got several job offers:*

Your BRAIN is your most IMPORTANT tool

Meaning, it's not all about intelligent regurgitation. Your brain has the creative function to go outside the box. Use the "Smarts" you've been given to your advantage. It can be a blessing to not be the smartest kid in the class. I fart in the direction of "reading group A"

You will NEVER be TRULY ready, Ever

Do you think a movie star is ready for instant fame? Was I ready to tryout for cheerleader? You have to make action. Don't let road blocks in your mind halt you. Nike again, "Just Do It!" Go for your dream (goal) now! Don't doubt yourself. Try, try, try…

Create your OWN SUCCESS

Make a plan. Prepare for what you want to happen. Take a step-by-step approach. I did that. I jotted down who was coming to interview and made a kick-ass letter & resume. How can you get around the conventional method of whatever you're doing? Be fearless!

Corporate America, Oh NO!

CHAPTER FOUR

•

"We all have big changes in our lives that
are more or less a second chance."
—Harrison Ford

THE US STEEL (USS) success was not my only exciting adventure during my interviewing time. I remember Dow Chemical flew me into Midland, Michigan. I thought I had landed on Mars. I still had that rockstar feeling that someone believed in me enough to want to put time, energy & money into me. At the end of all my interviews, I decided US Steel was the place for me. They had offered me a spot in their Detroit office off of Big Beaver Rd in Troy, MI in the Somerset Township. It was an amazing suburb with TGI Friday's, Bally's Gym and a huge mall. My first place, solo, was at the Somerset Apartments. The #1 spot for young urban professionals. It had a golf course right in the middle of it and a kick-ass swimming pool.. I was in heaven!

Now, up until this point in my life I had *mostly* followed the All-American Dream of what path a successful good boy takes. Of course, I wasn't all good, I mean I had experimented with a few drugs, I had pre-marital sex like it was going out of style (but with my girlfriend at the time). I was NOT perfect, but for the most part I was a parent's wet dream. I was ticking the boxes of how to live a good life. I think even my mom was surprised I got the job offer with US Steel. I could see the glint of proudness in her eyes. I had that job by November my senior year at Indiana University, meaning I could basically skate by last semester. Man, that was great! I still needed to graduate, but I felt an enormous relief knowing I had a good job waiting for me.

Hitting the real world was a total drag. I only got one week vacation my first year. What a complete wakeup call being an adult was! It sucked. I mean, the pay check was nice. I was being paid $29,500 in 1988 right out of college. My rent was $520, which was a lot back then, being the average income in the US was $24,450. I was doing well. A movie was $3.50 and a gallon of gas was .91 cents so I was feeling good about that aspect of my life. Every two weeks that check came like clockwork. It's stability. What I hated were the hours. I often joke, "What's the worst thing about a 9 to 5 job?" I answer with a smile, "the 9" because getting up M-F everyday at 7:30am is not pleasant. In Michigan you have to scrape the ice off of your car, defrost it for 15 minutes, and freeze your butt off in the process, all while you are wearing that god forsaken suit & tie. It was "glamour chic" to me for about a New York minute. I went all in when I started. I had the Bally shoes, the right tie, I looked smart. Smart in fashion. There is nothing smart about putting on a monkey suit every morning of your life and clocking in to Corporate America. That's the big lie. I loathed it more & more. I was so tired at work that I could barely keep my eyes open. I started thinking, "Is this the meaning of life?" If I stayed another 5 years I'd get 3 weeks vacation. Yay me! On top of all my personal internal bitterness for being a cog in a big machine, I was being bombarded by the old codgers that had been with US Steel for 20+ years, "You need to get the hell out of here!" "This company doesn't care about you!" "They will suck the life out of you!" The water cooler talk is real. I'd be approached by so many lifers asking me "why are you wasting your time" at this company? They say things like, "If I was young again I'd travel the world" or "Life is too short to be cooped up in this office for eternity." They seemed genuinely pissed off that I would throw my life away like they did. It was a constant theme. I was starting to drink their beautiful Kool-Aid. I wanted out. I was thinking of expanding my condo rentals in Bloomington, Indiana. I now owned 5 and was socking away the monthly profits to invest in more condos or a few doubles. I was miserable they were tightening the noose of understanding.

About a year later, just when I was about to pull the ripcord and escape, US Steel transferred me to Pittsburgh and set me up in a beautiful company apartment right downtown. It was amazing. Their headquarters is the USX building. It's facade is rusting steel, designed to erode, which made it a futuristic design concept for that day and age - it is still the tallest building in Pittsburgh at 64 floors. Pittsburgh had just been named "The Most Livable City" in the US. It was hopping. The nightlife was great (which totally flipped my switch), the food, Steelers football - I was really enjoying it. I didn't mention this earlier, but US Steel had a down period when Chinese Steel was kicking America's butt. USS was not doing well. That's why some of the long term employees in Detroit had a bad taste in their mouths for USS. It's understandable. They had lived through a bad time with the company. USS had not had a new college recruiting class in many, many years. I'm not sure how many but something like 15+ years. They recruited 16 of us from all across the US, which was a big deal for them which was not lost on the media. They hand-picked us to be the proud example of "US Steel is back!" We had our picture in the paper. We were the great hope of their future. So, when I was living in Pittsburgh I felt like a successful young executive. Many people in Pittsburgh had a connection with US Steel. It was the backbone of the founding of the city. It still is a major part of the city's identity. I was now 23 and then turned 24 living in Steeler Country - although those years 88-89' the Steelers were not good. But the fans were still awesome back then. The Three Rivers were beautiful, there was an art scene I had not experienced in Indiana or Michigan. Pittsburgh was hip. Who doesn't want to be drunk and wander into Primanti Brothers along the river at 2:30am? They give you everything you love all on the sandwich: grilled meat, melted cheese, french fries, coleslaw, tomatoes, oil & vinegar all smashed between two thick slices of Italian bread. So to clarify, this is all ON THE SANDWICH. French fries & coleslaw on the sandwich made it an original. The location I knew about was down in the Strip District that served the workers who unload produce to the area at the wee hours of the morning. Back then regional food was so unique. We are all sort of dumbed down now with everything we want everywhere. It kills the experience of going someplace new. That's why I still make a hard effort to find mom & pop places wherever I go.

So, Pittsburgh was great but corporate America still was a struggle for me. I just couldn't imagine working for a company the rest of my life. I'm thankful people do that and I get it. It's secure and comforting. It's what we have been conditioned to want to do. It was the "American Dream" they say. I was so torn, because US Steel had been good to me. I had a future with them. I could stick with them and definitely have an upper middle class life. Maybe even an upper UPPER middle class life if I dabbled in real estate on the side. But, but but, I'd have to put the hours in, the years in, my entire life in. At 24 I just could not sign that deal with the steely devil. I say "devil" because that's how it felt. I did NOT have exactly a vision of a bigger life or dreamt of the things I would eventually do, but I did know I wanted more freedom. I wanted more control of my destiny. I wanted to drive the bus. I knew I needed to plan my escape. It was really hard for me. Corporate America gets a hold of you and you feel connected. You feel a part of something and it's alluring. I knew to leave I would have to rip the band aid off in one swoop. The big cheese for me was Greg Spencer. He was the GM of all things Human Resources and his office was on the 61st floor. He was in charge of the 16 Elite Recruits that were to be the backbone of the USS comeback. His office was big and impressive, larger than most apartments. He was very high up on the food chain and I knew I had to tell him personally that I was leaving. I would be the 2nd person of the 16 Elite to leave and I was super nervous.

My First Encounter in Greg's Office

Actually, this was NOT the first time I'd been in Greg Spencer's office. When I was still living in Detroit they would often have all the recruits come in from all the other offices for training. I always felt special because Detroit was the biggest outputter in terms of sales volume. We had the Big 3 (Ford, Chrysler, GM) along with a bunch of stamping plants. One of my fellow recruits was Andy Anniken. He and I were the only two in Detroit. Andy was a badass and has gone on to a successful life in big steel thru & thru and is now CCO & EVP of Bull Moose Industries. So anyway, we were in Pittsburgh and all 16 of us went out on the town. We headed to the waterfront area called the Strip District (not a strip "club" area, it's a place on the water where the shore-men work) and went to a nightclub called Metropol. It happened to be close to the Primanti Bros sandwich shop I mentioned earlier. This was one of those industrial steel (no pun intended) clubs. 3 floors, girders, metal catwalks, flashing gobo lights, big dance floor. Dance clubs in the late 80s were the real deal. New Wave/Industrial dance music was the rave. Open floor plan so you could look down onto the dance floor from every floor. It was dark, loud and super artsy, crazy. The USS recruits were all probably too square for this place. It was an alternative crowd way before we even labeled anyone that way. We had gone to a Japanese restaurant for dinner and drank quite a bit of sake. None of us were that familiar with sake and I think it gave us an odd buzz. Once we got to the club we kept drinking. Everyone sort of split up and I was hanging with a couple guys I knew best. The place was hoppin. Over the next couple hours the group slowly started heading out. I wanted to go because I knew I had drank too much and we had an early training session at USX for a role-play Xerox Selling Skills course. My co-worker Mark did not want to leave just yet. Mark was from a line of steel executives and being part of the elite 16 was a really big deal for him.

"Come on man, let's get out of here. Everyone's gone but us," I insisted. "It's late! We've got a big day tomorrow."

"There's this girl I've been checking out all night I want to talk to," he replied.

I commiserated, knowing that I was stuck baby-sitting him. He was drunker than me and I knew he needed me to get him back to the hotel.

"Where is she?" I asked. He pointed up to the floor above us and sure enough there was a goth looking chick waving at him. "She's waving at you." Mark did the hand gesture for her to come down to our level. Maybe it was the lights, the new wave trans music, but I seemed to zone out for a while and when I looked up I saw Mark and this girl making out along the rail. It was dark, flashing lights, fog in the air, it all felt like a David Lynch movie. Suddenly, I see three guys approach Mark and start beating the hell out of him. I ran over, "What the hell's going on over here?" I yelled and started to try and pull one of the guys off of Mark. A bigger fight broke out and suddenly someone sucker punched me from the side. It's NOT like the movies. This punch cleaned my clock. Before I knew what literally hit me I was on all fours. I was dazed & confused. By the time I had my wits about me several of Pittsburgh's finest had come in and were separating everyone.

Pittsburgh cops are the real deal. They looked like they chewed nails for breakfast. I'm drunk and stupid at this point.

I demand, "Who punched me?" and someone pointed at a guy over in the direction near the cops. Stupid me staggers over and drills this guy right in the face in front of the cops. I haven't punched too many people in my life, but I hit this guy hard. He went down and I was jumped by the square-jawed men in blue. The next thing I know I'm being dragged towards the exit by the cops. I'm handcuffed. There was a loading dock attached to this club and I'm being moved down it's side ramp by two large men. Suddenly, I hear a girly scream and the guy I had punched upstairs leaped over a rail and was strangling me. I had no defense because I was cuffed. The cops started beating him off me with billy clubs. Before he let go of my neck he dragged his very long nails across my throat. It was as if a leopard had attacked me in my sleeping bag. My neck had four clearly visible scratches on each side of it. They were deep. I was bleeding all over my newly purchased Cosby type sweater. Anyone my age remembers those Cosby sweaters. They were expensive and our pride and joy. MINE was now blood soaked. Thinking back, I must not have fit in too well with that sweater and my clean-cut demeanor.

"Whats the hell are yous doin' down here?" the cop asked me dumbfoundedly with a profound Pittsburgh accent.

"We work for US Steel and are in town for a training session," I replied, "we had no idea this club was like this."

The cop marched Mark and I over to a Paddy Wagon. This was an authentic paddy wagon that looked like it had been picking up drunk Irishmen since the 1830s. I'm surprised it wasn't being pulled by horses. It was wooden and old. In we went. I looked over at Mark and he was a mess. He had a bubbling knot on his forehead, a black eye and just looked like crap. I'm sure I didn't look too good either. We were sitting opposite each other in the paddy when to our surprise a small window slid open and the same cop who put us in the back was now talking to us through this confessional. Once out of the limelight he lightened up a bit.

"Yous guys shouldn't be in this place, it's a bunch of freaks. Do yous know who you punched?" his eyes gestured towards me.

"No idea, but he sucker punched me," I explained. He shook his head in a way that I knew I had got myself in a pickle.

"Dat dare, the owner's gay-o-la lover that he's flew in for this shindig. He's pippin' fury. We's got his boyfriend in 'nother paddy and he wants yous arrested for assault," he explained morosely. This cop's James Cagney, long ago Pittsburgh accent, made him seem tough. It all seem surreal. I strangely felt like a real man. I had arrived.

We got taken to the city lockup, but it looked like prison. As normal protocol they took off our belts and removed our shoestrings. They put Mark and I in the same cell in the basement. It was dark and old. Our cell walls were covered with feces and blood. It was disgusting. We had a metal bed and a stainless steel toilet. If we looked straight up there were thick block windows about 2 stories above us but directly in front of us was a dark brick wall. It was like a dungeon. That's all I can say. Mark was not taking the confinement nearly as well as I was. The hours went on and on. It felt like we were in that dark gloomy cell for 2 days. We lost all track of time. No one came to check on us. We'd hear distant screams of agony. We could see that the sun had come up but that seemed like eternity ago. Mark was losing it. He jumped up on the bed and tried to stick his nose between the bars.

"HELLO, HELLO CAN ANYONE HEAR ME?" he yelled as loud as he could. Occasionally, we'd hear another inmate moan or shout something incoherent.

"We are going to lose our jobs, it's over. They're gonna fire us," was Mark's constant theme, "I just bought a new car, my parents are going to kill me!" (It was a 1989 Ford Probe, in my opinion it was the ugliest car in the world but it was his pride and joy)

I thought it must be about 9pm the next day. We had no water, no communication and of course no food. Then finally, we were taken in front of a judge. We found out it was 3pm. We had been in that hole for 17 hours. The judge basically charged us with nothing. We apologized profusely and were let go. We grabbed a taxi and headed back to the hotel. We looked rough. In 1988 when you had a message on your room's voicemail a little red light would flash in the upper right corner of your Bakelite rotary phone. Mark and I had separate rooms but we both had a red flashing light, it was blinking & blinking. It was 3:30pm and both our messages were from Greg Spencer himself. Terrifying.

"I need you to call my office the minute you get this message," was all he said plus leaving me his direct number.

I was startled by a loud knock at my door, "Did you get a message from Greg Spencer?" Mark exclaimed.

I sighed, "Yeah, let me call his office now."

I dialed 9 to get out of the hotel and then the number he left for us to call. His secretary answered and asked us to be at Mr. Spencer's office by 4:30. Oh crap, it was 3:45pm. We had no time for a shower. We both scrambled and tried to clean up the best we could. We put on our best suits and headed to the 61st floor of the USX building.

"We're fucked," Mark kept saying, "he's going to fire us."

I felt more confident and I wasn't married to this job and didn't feel my future relied on not getting fired. I had multiple scratches on both sides of my neck and I was trying to lift up my dress shirt collar to hide my bright red, bloody wounds. It was so painful. Mark looked worse than me. He had a golfball size knot right on his forehead, a black eye, reddish contusions, that just didn't look right, in several spots on his face. Plus, he looked sickly. Pale and out of sorts.

"We were about to leave the Metropol when a fight broke-out around us and we were "accidentally" corralled in by the police unfairly," was the story we concocted in the cab on the way to judgment day. I felt like Ralphie in A Christmas Story when he shot himself with a BB gun and then stepped on his glasses. He lied & cried to his mom that it was caused by a falling icicle. Our fake story was so ridiculous, but maybe Greg Spencer needed to accept it?

We tried to maintain our composure. Neither of us had been to the 61st floor. It was 4:26pm. We had at least made the deadline. Mr. Spencer's office was impressive, with floor to ceiling windows and executive-like decor. We were in the clouds. Mark and I sat across from Mr. Gregory R. Spencer. Mark had suggested he speak for us, but I could tell as soon as we walked into the interrogation that I should be the one to lead the defense. I was our best counsel.

Matter of factly, "What happened?" was his first words.

With our obvious outward wounds of war I knew we had a yarn to spin. Mark did not speak up right away so I did. I told him the story we had decided on. I went into some details but I also truthfully talked about the conditions of our lockup and that we had no way to communicate with the outside world. Mr. Spencer nodded.

"Does any of the media know about this?" he asked concerned.

This was a revelation. Sure, he wanted to know what happened but what he really wanted to know was if there was any need for damage control. This never crossed our minds. We both thought he would be upset that we missed the Xerox Selling Skills mock sales training.

"Did they know you were with United States Steel?" he wondered.

Well shit, we did tell the copper, who looked like he ate nails for breakfast, because we were trying to save our souls. But of course, we didn't tell Greg that. We explained, truthfully, that we weren't charged with anything, not arrested or set to go to trial.

This is my favorite part of the story because of what I said next to Greg. In fact, on the elevator back down, "I CAN'T BELIEVE YOU SAID THAT!" was all Mark could muster. He now knew I had balls.

(Five minutes earlier)

I could feel Greg was starting to ease up on us. He had put a lot of time & energy into his recruits. He didn't need the world to know he hired a couple of brawlers. He would need to stand by us. It was in his best interest. I could sense this and felt a bit cocky or maybe I wanted a moment of levity? Remember, we were selling steel not doilies. This was a man's industry and that machismo was everywhere.

"You know Greggie...." no I did NOT say that but that's the swagger I felt as I proclaimed, "Twenty years from now when we are both top salesman for UNITED STATES STEEL I'll tell the young recruits 'When I came to Pittsburgh for training I didn't even get a hotel room, I knew I'd be spending the night in jail' and they will look at us with awe."

I can't remember his exact reaction but we kept our jobs.

Now, Back to My 2nd Time on the 61st Floor

I had requested this meeting. I was more nervous now than I was the last time I was up here 9 months ago. I had written a great resignation letter. 100% cotton paper, raised letters, folded in a high quality envelope with "Gregory R. Spencer" typed out perfectly and centered (at this point, would you expect anything less from me?). It was hidden in my briefcase. I had a nice briefcase. There were certain things you have to ALWAYS remember - presentation. I'll get into that in more detail when I tell you about the products I've invented, but early on I knew that you had to look like you belong. I didn't like the saddle briefcases. It seemed too Indiana Jones. I had a Samsonite black leather briefcase that could be locked of course. It had two metal hinges on the left & right at the top on either side of the handle. They would spring out at one end. I can still remember the sound they would make when you opened them. It commanded attention. I knew at some point in my brief discussion with Mr. Spencer that I would pick-up my Samsonite. He'd recognize it was a Samsonite. I'd slap it down on my lap, click each metal hinge at the same time and I'd open it to pull out my letter of "Adios, mother fucker!" I have a whole life to live outside this corporate prison. I'm being funny and somewhat dramatic, but when I think of all the things I did with my life after leaving that structured world - it's not far off. Long story short, Greg seemed to envy me. I was even able to get a killer letter of recommendation from him on US Steel stationery.

I walked out of the USX building with a sense of freedom. It was so strange. My entire life changed just like that. I skipped back to my corporate apartment, packed up all my belongings and was literally on the road within an hour of being at the top of US Steel. I drove, not home, but to my best friend's college UNCG (University of North Carolina Greensburg). He was a 5th year senior and I had been out of college 2 years. I had some money saved. I had my condos making me some money too and I felt like I was FREE. Bill Niemann and I partied like it was 1999 but that wasn't for another 9 years. We met in 3rd grade and have been close ever since. He came to live with me in Japan and drove me out to Hollywood when I was going to try to be a movie star. You'll read about that if you keep flipping these pages.

After hanging with Bill for five days I headed back to Indianapolis - my hometown. A bit scary yet a much needed anxiety. The unknown is a healthy fear, keeps the soul alert. I had to ask myself what I value in my life, what do I want my personal journey to be? Sometimes you need to get off of a really good ride, because it's not your ride. Some people feel pressure from their parents, or society in general, to do the next "generic" step in life to be successful. You have to know when to pull the cord and get off on the next stop. That's what I did with USS. What do I value in life? We all know the normal idea of values. My values believe in *being good to others, being honest, not stealing, treat others with respect, integrity, humility, kindness...* these all have great worth and make the world a better place, but...

What about setting your CORE VALUES? I think I started to do this way back when I left US Steel. My mind shifted. I had an epiphany. I just walked away from a perfect future. Why? What was my motivation to do that? For whatever reason; youthful stupidity, laziness, unfulfillment or possibly an *inner voice*, I never wondered if I was doing the right thing. Even now, when I think about it, I want to give my younger self a high-five. Thank you 23 year old Will. This made me start to think about ways to live with fewer regrets. Which values do I want to make sure become part of my core?

Could my "best for humanity" values be more attainable if my <u>sub-core</u> values; *freedom, creativity, adventure and living happy* were a top priority? You need to decide what's important to you so it will shape who you are. It can bring fortune, meaning good fortune, but there is NOTHING wrong with money fortune being a byproduct either.

Just don't let the money desire trample all over your true desire to be a good human being. From my own life, when I'm following my inner desire and passion, money seems to follow. First things first, you need to think about what you want your *sub-core values* to be. They will help guide your life's path. These values may change as we get older as our responsibilities change. Questions to ask yourself:

> ***What Flips My Switch?***
> It could have been something you read, someplace you went or a feeling you felt during a certain situation. Really take the time and think about a *time you felt alive*.
>
> ***When Did You Want to Pat Yourself on the Back?***
> It could have been when you picked up a piece of trash on the ground. For me it was walking out of US Steel. Reach for the times you felt proud of what you were doing.
>
> ***Are You Living the Life You Planned to Live?***
> It's hard to answer this because it's not written down for us. I do strongly believe there is an inner voice that guides you in a certain direction. Don't fight that voice. DO NOT FIGHT IT!
>
> ***YOLO, How Would Live if You had a Do Over?***
> We only live for about 80 years. If we are lucky they are coherent years. Health is unpredictable. Seriously, write down five (5) things you'd do differently if you could. Then see how many of them you could still do. Probably most of them.

Back home again in Indiana I dabbled in commercial real estate and for the first time tried to create my own company called University Management. I went back down to Bloomington, IN where Indiana University is, and my five (5) condos are, and tried to entice owners to let me manage their properties for them. Once their kids graduated most parents didn't want the hassle of being an absentee landlord to college kids. Once again, I'm in the City County Office going through the plats trying to find who owns each parcel. It's pages and pages of maps with little numbers representing each plot. It's funny, it's plats with little plots. I'd jot down that number, take it to another area and flip through more pages to find out who owned that condo. It felt like "letter of invite" scheme again, but better. I had secret.

Once again, I had an amazing presentation. I had professional brochures made, cover letters, envelopes and mailed out about 50. I was asking for 10% of their gross rent. Most condos housed four (4) students and collected $1,200-1,600 a month. I hoped to manage at least fifteen (15) condos my first year and make about $2,250 a month on average. It didn't seem unreasonable to manage 50+ within a year or two possibly more. Well, things didn't go as planned. I had a failure on my hands. My response back wasn't good. I only had five (5) strong interests and I might only pick up a couple of those. It wouldn't be worth my while to do it if I didn't have a least 10 and even then it might be more hassle than it's worth. I was also second guessing myself about living in Bloomington, IN. My own five (5) condos were doing well but managing college kids can be a nightmare. I had my fair share of destructive behavior.

In 1991 the economy was shaky. The whole slow down put a damper in the commercial real estate business. There was overbuilding in the 1980s and it just killed the market. Unemployment was tittering around 8%. Unemployment now (2024) is consistently 3-4% if that gives you any indication how bad it was. Slick Willie became president in 1992, but Clinton actually took office in January 1993. He did a great job the next 8 years bringing our economy back to life, but here I was in 1991 thinking about my future. I had money saved and the condos were helping out, but I was antsy. I had met a girl named Christine. She was from Los Angeles, California. She was tall, exotic and just a real beauty. Her mom had been transferred to Indianapolis and Christiana tagged along between her international modeling gigs. Somehow I was lucky enough to catch her eye and we be began dating. Before me, she had dated the All-American Pro

Football Player Marcus Allen. He was one of the best NFL running backs of all time, playing for the Los Angeles Raiders for 10 years. I only mention him because this girl was intimidating. She had dated greatness before me. The reason she is being brought up in my book is I feel I need to give her credit for opening my eyes to exploring the world. She would jet into Indy, then off to Tokyo or Italy. She would come back with amazing stories. Ultimately, she met an American banker in Tokyo at the elite International Club & Gym and I was nato. Nato is stinky fermented beans the Japanese love. They say "fermented" but it's really just rotten beans. Ugh, I lost my international super model, but for whatever reason, I knew I would only be a speed bump on her fast track. She planted the seed in my mind to think global. You meet the right people at the right time if you allow yourself to be open to endless possibilities.

"I want to go to Europe for three months and I want you to go with me," I said eagerly to Doug Sabotin, "so many people do it and I want to do it too. I really want you to go with me!" Doug Sabotin was one of my best High School friends. He is a 6'4", blonde stud with a heart of gold. He was the best player on our Speedway Sparkplugs football team when we went undefeated my senior year. He went off to college on a full scholarship and had an amazing collegiate career. He was close to making it in the NFL. I remember going to see him play in college and his picture was on the ticket. Amazing. Anywho, when I came back into town after leaving US Steel I moved in with Doug in the trendy part of Indy called Broadripple. Doug had bought a house, which was impressive at 23. He did not come from money. He earned this house working his brains off in computers. He's a winner!

Doug looked surprised but not afraid, "How much do you think it would cost to go to Europe?" I had asked him to go get a sandwich at Subway and we were sitting on the patio. I remember this so well because him saying "Yes" literally set my life in a whole new direction. Of course, I didn't know that then but I can tell you now, it did.

"I'm thinking you will need $5,000," I calculated.

"That's not totally out of the question. What brought this on?" Doug asked.

I took a bite of my club with extra jalapeños, "When I was with US Steel I met so many people that had done it or knew someone who had. I know we never thought about it growing up in Speedway, but it's a thing. People graduate from college and they take off for Europe," I passionately explained. "We need to culture ourselves,"

"Have you done any research on it?" Doug was asking all the right questions. He could have easily blown me off. I needed a wingman. I know I would have NOT done that trip solo.

"It's amazing man, Europe is set up for it. We can stay at cheap youth hostels," and I pulled out Frommer's Europe on $15 a Day and started thumbing through it, "and we can buy a three month Eurorail Pass for $400 that includes trains, ferries and sometimes buses. It will be the greatest adventure of our lives," I promised.

Doug was diggin what I was throwing at him, "Have you looked how much a plane ticket would cost?"

"It's pretty expensive, but if we fly out of Chicago we can get a round trip ticket to London for about $450. That's by far the biggest expense. We can take the train up to Chicago." I could tell the wheels behind his blue eyes were turning. I saw a spark.

"Have you told your mom you are thinking about doing this?" he asked.

"No, but I'm pretty sure she'll be okay with it," I surmised.

Both my mom and dad knew Doug's mom & dad. His parents were solid down-to-earth people and Doug was a superstar and a super-son.

I won't go into many details about our trip to Europe, but obviously Doug said yes, "He said YES!" it's like I was proposing. Actually, I was proposing a life-changing experience but I don't think either of us knew it just then. Often when you're knee deep into something it doesn't register. I will tell a funny story at the very beginning of our adventure. We hopped a train in downtown Indianapolis to Chicago. The train ride was about 5 hours. It was all going well. We had given ourselves a huge cushion of time - something like 8 hours. As we were clacking along I got up to use the restroom. As I was standing in front of the commode trying to keep my balance as the train swayed back & forth along the tracks, I suddenly felt a jarring jolt. A mini-stop. The aggressive pause didn't faze me. I hadn't been on too many trains and thought maybe this was just part of the experience.

"I saw chickens fly across the windows," Doug said excitedly.

"What?" was all I could say, "are we slowing down?" I continued.

The train in fact was slowing down, down, down and then stopped. No one knew exactly what was going on. We sat motionless for over an hour and everyone was beginning to get restless. Murmurs began to leak among the passengers, "We hit a chicken truck that got stuck on the tracks? No freaking way!" I said as a guy with suspenders leaned across the aisle to give me his two cents worth. Another 45 min went by. I was starting to get worried. Yes, we had some time to kill, but now it was becoming critical. I was getting worried.

Suddenly a man and two police officers walked slowly past us. The train was still dead stopped. Then they walked through our train car again. On their 3rd pass they stopped and looked at Doug. He was sitting along the window looking out. He turned to look at them.

"Can you slowly show us your hands?" a police officer asked. Doug looked surprised but slowly raised his hands. I can't make this stuff up.

"Can you slowly show us some form of identification?" he asked.

Doug slowly pulled out his passport. Our first passport reveal.

"Are we living in the 1870s?" was all I was thinking. Apparently, we are on a train that hit a chicken truck crossing the tracks. The train needed to come to a complete stop to make sure there wasn't any

damage to the wheels before we can go onto Chicago. During the initial one hour stop a man had robbed a bank in *whatever* small town we were near. The police thought that the bank robber might have jumped onboard our train as a getaway. Doug somewhat fit the description of the bank robber. You can't make this stuff up. How hilarious is this that in modern day America; you are on a train, you hit a chicken truck, there's a bank robbery, the robber possibly stowed away on our train, the police are searching for Butch Cassidy & the Sundance Kid, by the way, one of the best movies ever written by the master of William Goldman, and now we might be late for our European Super Jet to London. What an adventure we started.

Doug and I got to Chicago late. Our backpacks were slung onto our shoulders and we ran as fast as we could to make our flight. Oh, to be young again. We landed in London and the "New World" was now my Europe. Traveling abroad at that time, or should I say age, changed me profoundly. I have always been a lover of history. I think Human Sexuality and History H103 (Europe: Renaissance to Napoleon) were the only two classes I got an A+ in while at Indiana University. That might tell you something about me. We traveled on a backpackers budget and stayed in hostels, often called pensions, which is a fancy word for a boarding house. Traveling within foreign countries nowadays is a breeze with our smartphones. Back then, you had to have everything pre-mapped out. It was challenging and made it a true adventure.

We started in London, then on to Paris via a rough ferry ride over the English Channel. We fell in love with Paris and I even managed to catch the eye of a beautiful young Parisian girl. I remember Doug and I sat under the Eiffel Tower, we pitched a blanket down and ate strong cheese, broke off pieces of a tough baguette of bread and a had a bottle of wine. Not that either of us were wine drinkers back then, but as they say "when in Rome" so tried to culture ourselves. Five days later we headed down to Nice and hopped over to Monte Carlo, which is in a district of Monaco, to try our luck in the Grand Casino de Monte-Carlo. The entrance was intimidating. Luxury was on full display. The exotic cars; Lamborghinis, Ferraris, Porsches, Rolls Royces and Bugattis were all parked out front. Even the taxis were Mercedes Benzes. The wall of opulent cars felt like protection to stop the riff-raff from wandering in. We'd read about this place in one of our guide books and had packed dinner jackets just so that we could get into this palace. I felt sure someone was going to stop us as we walked in. Two hicks from the sticks were going to be high rollers in the land of Grace Kelly and Prince Rainier. The only casino I had been to was in the Bahamas with my college girlfriend. I was soaking wet behind the ears literally and figuratively. I was nervously sweating but trying hard to look cool. Doug was sticking close to me. He knew that between the two of us, I was the better bullshitter if anything went south.

I was gung-ho to play blackjack but was shocked to see the minimum bet was €25. I think that was about $27 a chip in 1991. We were paying $15 a night for hostels and eating cheese & bread everyday to save money. To say we were on a budget is to put it lightly. We had travelers checks and no ATM card. We watched our money like hawks, but I had been dreaming of this James Bond moment (*Never Say Never Again)* and saw myself sitting at the tables as a waitress walks up, "Martini, shaken, not stirred" and then I hit blackjack and a beautiful girl takes my arm - to be so young, in the south of France, it's good to have fantasies. I was determined to say, "Hit me!" before we took our night train back to Nice. We couldn't afford to stay in Monte Carlo of course. I found a lonely row of slots that were €5 a spin. Still salty, but I had a bit more money than Doug. We had agreed to bring the same amount of money to keep us both on the same page, but on our train ride to Chicago I found my mom had slipped

$500 extra inside my book. That was like a million dollars to me. I got €75 worth of coins, so about $50-60 dollars worth. The Wheel of Fortune, "Big money, big money" was spinning in my head. About €30 in I saw 3 gold cherries line up straight across in front of me. Have you ever seen gold cherries? Me neither. Bells sounded and coins began dumping into the metal tray below my knees. That is a glorious sound to hear! Although the cherries were gold, my payout was roughly only about $150. I cashed out and now had €200 to play with guilt free. At the blackjack table that would give me only 8 chips. As Austin Powers says, "I too, like to live dangerously!" I bet big with 4 chips, 1/2 my money. My first card was an 8. The dealer had a 7 showing. I then got another 8. I had 16. The dealer asked me if I wanted to split, double down. I was a bit confused, but didn't want to look like I didn't know what I was doing. I knew 16 is never good. Plus, she had a 7 showing. When I said yes, she separated my cards and took my remaining chips. Holy Bond, I was betting €200 ($215) on one hand, my 1st hand. Lady luck was shining on me, I got two face cards so I had 18 which is the best I could hope for. The dealer flipped a Queen and she had to hold on 17 and yours truly just doubled his money! I played it safe for the next 30 minutes, got a free drink, and walked away. It was francs back then but for easy math I've been saying euro. I started with €75 and left with €530. I won somewhere around $490 dollars! I could tell Doug was a bit jealous, but probably just didn't like that we were no longer equal on the splurge scale. I remember I paid for a lot more drinks after that. I considered it our €.

From Monte Carlo we headed to Italy and hit all the hot spots; Florence, Rome, Venice and then down to the Brindisi's port on the southeast coast and sailed down to Corfu, Greece by ferry for 5 days. We stayed in the famous Pink Palace, saw more boobs in one day than I ever imagined I would. As an American, topless beaches alway seem so wild and free. Doug and I sliced through Italy onto Interlaken/

Switzerland, Salzberg/Austria, Munich/Germany. We took lovely trains from city to city often sitting in a dining car eating potato soup and drinking a stout beer. We had the time of our lives. Our last stop was a doozy, Amsterdam/Netherlands, before we trekked back to London and back home to Indiana changed men.

Amsterdam had the famous Bulldog Cafes that sold a plethora of marijuana and hashish. Neither of us had smoked much pot and we decided we didn't want to risk the Space Cake experiment, but did want to try a joint. We went in and instead of a condiment caddy holding mustard, ketchup along with salt & pepper, the Bulldog's caddie confused us. There was loose tobacco, rolling paper, grinders and few other items which I'm still not sure what their usefulness is. We tried to fit in and follow my favorite rule *Monkey See, Monkey Do*. We looked around and were trying to figure out how this all works. I went down into a basement area and the menu was like a TGIF happy hour. So many choices: Indica, Sativa, Hash with names like Super Glue, Skunk 3, Candy Kush, Amnesia Haze... I was overwhelmed and undereducated. A hipster stoner saw my hesitation and ordered Super Polm for us from Morocco. It looked like a piece of poop, yet sticky. I brought it back to the table. Doug just stared at it. The group next to us saw we were confused and they showed us how to crumble up the hash, mix it with the tobacco and I made my best effort to roll a spliff. This story does not end well. We got so messed up that we lost each other and separately wandered the canals blown out of our minds. I found a receipt in my pocket for 52 guilders from Burger King. That was about $29. Our pension was only 40 guilders ($22) a night, of which I paid half, which included breakfast. Stoned, and on a munchy madness feast, I ate nearly 3 nights worth of room & board in burgers & fries, of which I have no memory of. I truly ate like a burger KING! Somehow we both got back to the room. Doug faired better than I did. I didn't make it back until sunrise. That morning we stood over the toilet and flushed the remaining hash poo down the toilet.

When I got back from Europe, and that amazing trip could be a book on it's own, I was a changed man AGAIN! I was soul searching. Traveling to Europe put the bug in my ear to do something bold, something different. I didn't have a scintilla of what that was - I knew now this is a much bigger world and I wanted to be a part of it. I grew up in small town America, which I LOVE, but now tasting the sweet allure of differentness I was a addicted. The traditional life of 9-5 was fading fast as any part of my future. Europe was the seed that was planted into my soul of wanting growth. Traveling from city to city, experiencing people from such different cultures, opened my eyes to change.

"It's not the strongest of the species that survive, nor the most intelligent, but the one most responsive to change."
—Charles Darwin

I was flipping through the Sunday morning IndyStar looking for my change in the classified section. Man, classified used to be so popular. Now it's mostly CraigsList. I was back from Europe and needed a sign. I was sitting in the livingroom, cup of coffee in hand with the behemoth newspaper in front of me, the NFL was on and I was ready to dig in. I always cleaned it up before diving in, meaning I separated all the colorful ads and inserts. Then I'd stacked my favorite sections; first the front page, I mean it was the front page for a reason. Then it would be the Sports Section, possibly next the Metro if something caught my eye, the funnies (comics) was also a priority and then recently the UNEMPLOYMENT section. It was like it's own separate paper. Commercial real estate hadn't cut the mustard. Once again, the economy was down. I was doing okay because of my rentals but I was actively looking for a spark. I was working with the Helen Wells Agency in Indianapolis doing some modeling and commercial work. My best friend Bill Niemann's brother Dave was doing well with them and they were the best, most legit agency in town at that time. I had been working with Dave at The Charles E. Larmen Company before I threw in the towel and headed to Europe. He was my mentor in modeling & commercial real estate. I'd known Dave 15+ years. I had booked some jobs and met a great photographer named Pamela Mougin. I mention Pamela because about 4 years later she took the headshots that got me started in LA.

*"**Live and Work in Japan**"* was the headlines for an ad in the IndyStar. To me it stuck out like a sore thumb. I had just come from Europe. I had international travel on the brain. Christine (model girl) ranted & raved about how great Tokyo was. It said it was for a position in Toyota, Japan working in Toyota-shi (city) teaching business English but likely to Toyota executives who already had a certain level of TOEFL (Test of English Fluency Level). Coming from US Steel I felt a connection to Toyota Motor Company. The interviews would be in Cincinnati, OH which from Indianapolis is a little less than 2 hours away. I did my usual great cover letter & resume duo. In less than a week I got a phone call to come interview in Cincinnati with AEON School. I had no idea what I was getting myself into. I told no one I was skipping over to Ohio to interview for a job in Japan.

Change Change Change: is a song by Charles Bradley. Not to be confused with the song "Changes" by the same guy, Charles Bradley. He must like change. I recommend you look up "Change Change Change by Charles Bradley" right now. I felt a change coming over me and this funky song got my juices flowing.

"I feel a change coming over me. Change in my walk, change in my talk, change when I walk, change when I groove..."

Casino de Monte-Carlo
I Won Big Money!

Doug & I in London

Backpack & Fanny Pack

JAPAN

CHAPTER FIVE

•

"Trust is the coin of realm"
—George Shultz

WHAT DOES THIS MEAN, "Trust is the coin of realm"? When trust is in the room or in your soul, good things can happen. Trust yourself. Make that leap of faith. I was doing it again! "Coin of realm" is an old school way of explaining something of value or used as if it was money in a particular sphere. I like this phrase because I love saying, "You can take that to the bank" meaning it is secure. You need this level of trust to take on a new challenge. I always figured in anything I did I could always quit and run back to safety in a matter of days. Once you're in the middle of doing something it doesn't seem nearly as big of a deal as it did when you were planning it or just contemplating it. It's the same for business ventures or going to talk to a cute girl. *Breaking the ice melts away all your fears.*

I was 25 years old, but closing in on 26 in a few months. I was aboard JAL (Japan Airlines) going through Chicago. No train this time. O'Hare to Narita (Tokyo) is about 13 hours. Having just traveled to Europe less than 6 months ago I felt I had a good grip on international air-travel. Going from New York to London is about 7 hours, so this was by far the longest flight of my life up to that point. The minute I got onboard JAL I felt a presence of being in Japan. The flight attendants were mostly Japanese. They had dark blue military type suits on with tiny little matching hats. Many of my fellow passengers were Japanese and I got my first sense that I'm going to feel taller, much taller, than I do in the United States. The Japanese are extremely polite and bow a lot. My first impression of the Japanese people was very good. In 1991 foreigners (gaijin) were still a novelty.

The JAL economy class menu had traditional Japanese bento box type food along with a "Western" dinner choice. I remember very well that I had never used chopsticks before. When dinner was served I decided to try them out. Soon a smiling flight attendant came over to me and took the time to show me how to hold "hashi" chopsticks properly. Holding them correctly is a definite must to master them.

She grinned, "You need to practice," as she showed me exactly how to put my fingers around the sticks. "Here, use these peanuts!" she said dumped them onto my dinner tray.

"This is a lot harder than I thought," I shook my head, "I can still find forks everywhere in Japan, can't I?" I asked hopefully.

"You really need to learn to use chopsticks. Most places only have them," she unfortunately declared.

I began picking up peanut after peanut. I spent hours practicing. I got cramps in my hands. I was using tiny muscles I never had used before.

"Oh, very good," she proudly said to her pupil. "You may not starve now!" as she walked by during breakfast service. Giving me the thumbs up.

I had a few more people around me (Japanese) smile at me in approval too. This is a lesson we can all learn - *people generally are very appreciative, all over the world, when you make an effort to adjust and learn their customs and ways.* It shows character. I try and follow the general etiquette rules of whatever country I'm in. It could keep you out of jail or just help you receive general random acts of kindness.

It was a long flight to Tokyo but with my excitement it went by fast. Getting off the plane in Tokyo was a complete shock to my brain, even after all my foreign adventures in Europe, this felt like pandemonium on crack. People were whipping around everywhere. Black haired human beings galore. It was crowded. Narita Airport was not my final destination. I needed to change planes and get to Nagoya.

Nagoya is not a well known city to most people outside of Japan. It's the 4rd largest city in Nippon and serves as a port and manufacturing hub. I've read it is the 37th largest city in the world right behind London at 36. I had finally found the gate to Nagoya, on the whole other wing of the airport. When I landed in Nagoya I felt thankful. It had been a very very long day of travel and a smiling face with a sign greeted me past customs, "Bill Howe-san?" was all I heard.

He had a sign with my name on it so I figured it was a safe bet he was my Nagoyian Sherpa. It was about a 40 minute ride from the airport to my hotel near Nagoya Station. I was put up in a "business hotel" which was a term I had no idea about before this experience. Japanese say "bizunesu hoteru". We all have seen Bill Murray in Lost in Translation staying at the Park Hyatt in Shinjuku. Well, my hotel was not this. This was a no frills high-rise and my first real experience at true cultural differences. These hotels are designed for Japanese "Salarymen" who are traveling on business, hence the name. The room was on the 17th floor. The elevator and hallways were very narrow. I kept thinking of the movie Inferno, meaning I felt I was in a deathtrap. Once in the room it was shocking. If I stretched out my left arm and my right leg, I could touch both walls. Meaning, my room was freaking narrow (94"). No closet, just three hooks on the wall and a bathroom that you'd expect to see in a mobile home. It was a compressed plastic unit with the shower, sink & toilet all molded into it's compact design. My bed was 70" long meaning being 6' tall, I'd be 2" short of comfortable. My window was long and narrow. It did not open. When I say narrow I mean the glass was 8" wide. You usually ONLY see these type of windows in prisons unless you're in Japan. If I pressed my face against the glass and twisted my nose to the far right, I could see a crossing street with hundreds of Japanese people milling about, criss-crossing the cross walk. I had a robe and slippers in front of my bed. Why on earth would I need either of these? The TV had some of the strangest programs I had ever seen. When I say strange, the first show I clicked on was a women in a bathtub nude (blurred out) with a live squid trying to swim between her legs. This was on general access TV. My hotel was my home for the next 3 solitary days and then for two (2) weeks of training at the AEON hombu (headquarters). I wanted an adenture and "if damned, didn't I find it!" was ringing through my mind. I was wondering about my decision. Being in Japan, and it STILL is, is like being on a strange planet. It is so completely different than anything we ever experience in our normal day to day lives. I think that is why, after you ride this wild bronco, tame it, come to understand it, that it consumes your soul. Once you have Japan running through your veins it's an addiction that is truly hard to escape.

Living in a new country or any new city you will always have a moment of loneliness. You literally don't know anyone. It's a crazy feeling. Going to a restaurant solo, seeing a movie alone, venturing to a bar - it's all the things that I feel make you a stronger person. Man is designed to chase adventure. Saying that, it is still a very strange out of body experience. Honestly, in Japan, I was not even thinking of making friends yet. I was in survival mode.

"I got a job offer in Japan and I'm going to take it," I declared at one of my usual family Sunday dinners. These dinners included my mom, of course, often my grandmother (grandma) and my two older sisters. Sometimes both my sisters wouldn't make it, but this particular Sunday they were both there. My grandpa had passed away when I was in 9th grade. We were super close. He always defended me from my grandma. She was the type of grandma that would tell me to go get a switch from the backyard because she knew I had done bad things since the last week I had seen her that my mom had not punished me for. Her name was Dorthy Hamill, not the famous skater. Her husband, Roy, was where I got my middle name. Grandpa (Roy) was my protector but he was not alive the day I proclaimed I was moving to Japan.

"Japs? You're moving to Japan to live with the Japs?" grandma said as she slammed down her spoon on mom's version of grandpa's soup and beans. "You've got to be kidding?!"

"I got a job offer from Toyota Motor Company and I think it's a great opportunity to explore life." I think I said. I had studied Japanese two semesters at IU to meet my language requirement. Japan interested me. I had just returned from traveling all over Europe. The real estate market was in the dumps and my 5 year college girlfriend had told me to take a hike. My state of mind was defiant and deliberate. I'm MAKING CHANGES. Changes, changes, changes!

Grandma stormed away from the table. I know I was her favorite grandchild. No doubt about it. She always gave me a hard time. It was in her nature. She grew up on a farm with no running water or heat. She pooped in an outhouse until she was 25 years old. Dropping out of high school at 9 years old, the same year she took up smoking, she was a tough cookie. I had many warm fuzzy moments with her too. My senior year of college I skipped going on a fun Spring Break. I hadn't had the best experience in Florida with my ex if you remember - Grandma (Dorthy Hamill) was a snow bird and she invited me to spend ten days with her in Tucson, Arizona. That was a helluv an experience that I would never take back. I learned that my family had a history of mental illness. Grandpa (Roy) had gone a bit nuts a few times in his life. My great defender had climbed a tree naked and threw poop at anybody who tried to talk him down. He was a foreman at a metal shop and had all the workers leave their machines and sweep the streets. He gambled away his paychecks. He once peed on an old Ford engine to put the fire out while on a double date. Grandma revealed a whole side to our family history I had no idea about. It was great. I loved it. I knew I had a side to me that wanted to pee on an old truck to put out a fire. I too was a bit crazy.

Mom was surprised, but not. "You're really going to live in Japan?" she asked curiously.

"I think so. I accepted the job." I admitted.

Mom, being the practical one, "Who's going to take care of your rentals? I'm not going to do it, if that's what you're thinking?"

When all the dust settled it was clear to my family that I was going on this adventure. Now, here I was a few months later actually LIVING the adenture. This was real. It felt like an out of body experience even as it was happening to me. It's strange to do something this monumental all alone. No one but me will know all the crazy stuff I'm experiencing. Japan touches so many senses. Everything is foreign. The sounds, smells, the infrastructures, menus, lighting, just getting from point A to B was a million different stimuli that I wasn't used to. My brain was on overload. This is where years later I understood why Japan drawls people in. All the different challenges are like crack. Nothing is easy. You are constantly on learning alert. I can criss-cross America like a zombie. I can read and understand everything. I mean, I might have a slight challenge in Tennessee when I accidentally order sweet tea from a gal with a very heavy southern accent, but Japan is an experience like "Everything Everywhere All at Once" but with a drop of mind fuck. Seriously, it's that great, yet seriously that bizarro.

Once training in Nagoya was over, I felt somewhat prepared for the start of my new career in Toyota-shi. The two weeks in Nagoya were stressful and full of occurrences. One good "occurrence" was running into three out of place Americans, who were with a band called Red Van Go. They played up on the Van Gogh pun and had a following in Japan. Their set was eclectic acoustic with some vocals. They had a song "Eyes that Burn" that reminded me of Chick Corea, but I'm not sure they'd dig that reference, then again, maybe they'd love it. Being a Southern California band, they somehow had a connection to playing in Japan. Later I learned that a lot of bands could have a level of fame in Japan and still be nearly unknown in their native country. Red Van Go took me with them to a restaurant in Nagoya that their Japanese handler had recommended. I only mention this because the place served live shrimp in a large wicker basket. They were jumping 8-10" up & down and you were supposed to snare one and bite into it while still alive. It was completely outlandish - yet so Japan. Four years later I had never seen those jumping shrimp again, but what a great way to start my first week in Nippon. Later I dined on raw horse, whale, blowfish, eel, but never those jumping shrimp again.

Toyota-shi was 35 minutes outside of Nagoya on the Meitetsu Line. A representative with AEON took me to the train station and told me to get off at Toyota station. As the train is clacking along it stops every 5-10 minutes. The first 4 stops the name of the stations were written in Romaji which is basically a romanized spelling of Japanese words. So if a station is called Kanayama I can read k-a-n-a-y-a-m-a, but if it was written in Japanese 金山駅 名古屋 I would NOT be able to read it, obviously. Well, soon after we were outside of the city all the train stops were in Japanese. The romaji stopped and my panic set in. Now I'm listening to the pre-recorded Japanese announcements for each stop. I can't read the station signs and I sure as hell don't want to miss my stop. I was loaded up with a backpack and a very large suitcase. I had all my worldly possessions for the next year with me. Suits, ties, shoes, underwear, toiletries, books... everything. I felt like the kid in A Christmas Story who's mom bundled him up with 5 layers of clothing. I was not easily mobile.

"Okay, desuka, daijoubu?" a middle-aged woman asked politely and a bit worried.

My Japanese was not good but I did understand that she was asking if I needed help. The train was clearing out with every stop and there weren't many of us left.

"Boku wa Toyota-shi hoshi," I was able to squeak out without exploding my brain cells. I said, "I want to go to Toyota City."

"Daijoubu, mo sugu," she smiled and pointed to a map on the curved part of the ceiling above the two sliding exit doors. I could tell that she knew I was a bit confused and did not understand her last sentence completely. I smiled and she gave me that beautiful international language of "I've got you" and at each station as the train slowed down she would wave it off as not Toyota-shi. Finally, she indicated that the next stop was indeed mine. I was so grateful. I bowed and bowed and thanked her profusely. The funny thing I learned later was that Toyota-shi is the LAST STOP on the train. It doesn't go any further. I was finally at my destination.

Toyota-shi is an industrial town. The population is 420,000 (300,000 in 1991 when I was there) so that seems fairly large but it really feels like a smaller town. It's in the countryside. Founded on the backbone of the Toyoda Family. They founded Toyota, the difference in the name is the "d" was changed to a "t" which they felt rolled off the foreigner's tongue easier. I also heard that the word "Toyoda" uses ten strokes to write (kanji) while "Toyota" uses eight strokes. Eight is a lucky number in Japan. Either way, the new name made it feel like a bigger company and no longer a mom & pop enterprise.

When I exited the station I had a smiling face greeting me named Kiyomi. She was my manager, although I did not know that at the time. I loaded my stuff into her car and she drove me just outside of town to a four story apartment (apārto). It was in the middle of nowhere. Nothing was around it except rice paddies. The building was grey with molded concrete stripes like grooves pressed into it. It looked modern compared to some of the buildings we passed on the way out of town. My unit was on the 3rd floor on the end. Each floor had 4 units. There was no elevator which I was surprised by. The stairs were molded concrete that hung to the middle of the building. As I entered my new apaarto I was surprised how narrow it was. I guess after leaving my salaryman hotel I should have gotten the hint that space is a different measurable quantity in Japan. What they see as small or normal I was seeing as tiny and abstractly restricted. The width of this apartment was 8' wide. I could touch (again) my hand and stretched out foot and touch both walls. In yoga there is a pose called Parshvakonasana. This is the way I could touch both walls. When I walked in there was a small landing where you are expected to take your shoes off. You take your shoes off a lot in Japan. Many restaurants have you remove your shoes, most temples and *always* when entering someone's living space.

"You should remove shoes here," Kiyomi said pointing.

Just to the immediate right, after stepping up about 6", was a door that led to a one unit, pressed plastic, bathroom with the toilet and shower combined in the same room. Meaning, when I showered I would be standing next to my closed toilet. There was a small sink and mirror. It had the RV bathroom vibe. The narrow hallway past the bathroom had laminate that resembled wood. To my left was a tiny sink and sitting on the countertop was a single burner. It was removable. I had cupboard space above that contained two plates, two cups and two tall glasses. Below I found a sauce and frying pan.

"Here is rice cooker," Kiyomi pointed out. All the instructions were in Japanese, so we spent a little time on how it worked. I liked rice at that time but it was not a primary course in all my meals. Also below, next to the cabinet that had the 2 pans, was a small "college dorm type" refrigerator. As I moved deeper into the place past the kitchen I needed to step back down 6" to enter my everything room. This room was about 8'Wx10'L. The floor was covered with a thin layer of hard grey carpet. There was a single, round, low coffee table and a TV sitting on top of a simple stand. This was the whole room. No chairs.

"Where do I sleep?" I asked Kiyomi baffled.

"Oh, you have futon for that," she said straightly. She walked over to a double door closet and opened it up.

"Here is your bedding," she explained.

"So I set it up here?" I asked, pointing to the room.

"Yes, you move the table back to corner and set up your bed here."

"This is my eating table?" I asked, but knowing the answer.

"Yes, it's also a kotatsu. Do you know what that is?" she smiled.

I shook my head "no" and Kiyomi took the thick blanket out of the closet and slung it over the dining/coffee table so it draped over the sides. She then reached under the table and pulled out a power cord.

"This is heater too." she proudly explained.

I looked underneath the coffee table and there was a small metal cage mounted under it that had heating coils. I didn't know it then because it was still warm in Japan, but it gets cold in the winter and their homes and apartments are not well insulated. This little kotatsu would become my best friend. I had many a warm night snuggled under that thing. Kiyomi then showed me how to use the AC which was mounted above the sliding glass door that led to my patio/laundry room. Using the AC was always a shot in the dark because I never did really figure out how to read all the buttons that thing had. The brain never gets a rest. On the patio was a very small washing machine and strings (clothes-line) that ran from end to end of the patio. They killed the vibe out there because you had to always be ducking them. Japanese rarely have dryers. They hang their laundry outside. After doing this for 4 years I got used to it but your clothes always felt stiff. It's also weird to have your belongings on display for the public to see, but when in Rome. On a side note, there are sexual deviants who steal under-garments from women's balconies. I even knew a few gaijin girls (foreigners) who complained of their panties & bras being stolen. They call this hentai. A type of sexual perversion. Outside of Japan the word "Hentai" usually refers to anime or manga that is pornographic, but inside Nippon or Nihon (their way of saying Japan) it is a word to describe a pervert. They call their sexual manga & anime "ero anime" meaning erotic cartoons. It's very common. You'll see people reading ero anime on trains, coffee shops, it's everywhere.

It was a Friday when Kiyomi gave me the grand tour of my mansion (what they call them!). She left me her phone number. The apaarto did have a telephone and she wrote down my new landline # too. Cell phones were still far in the future, there were only landlines. It just around 4pm when she bids me "bye-bye" and I decided to walk to town to see what Toyota was all about and maybe grab some groceries. Get a lay of the land, so to speak. Walking to town took about 15 minutes. I was careful to trace my steps. If I got lost I knew I'd be royally screwed. I realized quickly that a bicycle would need to be my main transportation in the future. I just needed to find out how to buy one. I marched all over town my first evening. People were friendly. I saw no non-Japanese. I felt special. I was different and I liked that feeling. Gaijin means foreigner, but it also means outsider. An alien. I did feel like I was on a different planet. Everything was so foreign to this alien, so different. I was getting a lot of attention for just being a gaijin. The attention factor affects every gaijin. It's nice to feel special, to be the odd man out. The new kid in school gets all the looks. I mentioned earlier that Japan always gives your brain food. It's a constant challenge that keeps you engaged and causes a slight addiction to that rush of permanent learning. The gaijin attention adds to that craving. The women seemed to be taking an extra long look at me and I wasn't hating that. I heard the word "kakkoii" several times since I'd been in Japan along with giggling. I quickly learned it was a great thing, I was being called handsome, good-looking or cool. Going to Japan I never even considered the dating scene. Growing up in Indiana I hadn't been exposed to that many Asians and I had never even thought about Asian girls in that way. I just wasn't exposed to them. Now immersed deep in the middle of Japan I started looking at the people, I mean really looking at them. Although Asians seem to all have dark hair & eyes, they actually are more descriptive and different than when you are describing a "Hakujin" - meaning white person. I was surprised when I learned in America police use about 20 markers to describe a suspect or a person in general. Sex, race, age, height, weight, build, hair & eye color, nose, mouth, complexion..., but the Japanese uses over 40 markers to describe someone. Often hair & eye color are a throw away. They really get into details of a person's body type, facial shape, eyebrows, ears - they get to a level of details that are fascinating. They can describe someone in Japan to a T. They say there are 14 types of eye/eyelids. They break down their looks minutely. Being a "homogeneous" race has lead them to know exactly how someone stands out. All this being said, I started to look at the Japanese people with a different eye. They all are so unique. I also was developing a "type" of Japanese girl I found attractive. I had only been in the country 15 days, but I was a walking and breathing social experiment. I loved the autonomy of living in a place where absolutely no one knew me. It was freeing. I felt invigorated. I was living a remarkable journey.

After exploring the downtown area of Toyota that first night, I found a small grocery store. Going to a grocery store in a foreign country is always a fun experience. I highly recommend it. It's a challenge to try and figure out what things are. There are always items you can guess with 100% certainty. Sure, the name is not readable, but you just know. Ketchup is ketchup, hotdogs are hotdogs. But there are a lot of assumptions going on too which can be a real hoot. Snacks are curious tidbits behind the curtain of what makes a country tick. Japanese snacks are often animated and playful. Colorful. The art on the bags are usually manga characters jumping out at you with a drawing of fruit or vegetables that doesn't look familiar. Manga like Pokemon, not ero (erotica). Visiting a foreign country and going into a food store to look around is one of the MOST entertaining things you can do, but when you live in that foreign country and are picking out food to make dinner in your kitchen - it becomes a whole new level of adventure and necessity. I love it. Once you are cooking your own meals you feel super cool. Nowadays, you can get that experience all over the world via Airbnb.

I grabbed some snacks that accidentally included dried squid. I didn't even know what it was until weeks later when I asked a Japanese coworker. It really wasn't bad. It was dried, chewy and salty. Octo-jerky is the best way to describe it. I still occasionally buy some for old times sake. Japanese have a word called "natsukashi" for something that evokes a fond memory of the past, what we Americans refer to as nostalgia. They use this word a lot! It means a gratitude for the past rather than a desire to return to it. We are fortunate to have natsukashi moments in our lives. It's a positive term. I have a NOT SO NATSUKASHI memory when returning to my new tiny home that very first night. It's about 6pm on that Friday and I get to my third floor apaarto and in a sheer panic I realize - I don't have my key. I had locked myself out! I don't have my manager's number, it's also locked inside. No one will expect me until Monday morning for my first day of work. What in the world have I done to myself? I go back down to street level and circle my building. There's no office or any indication that an onsite manager is around. I'm desperate. I go around the backside where the balconies are and pondered the possibility of scaling the building. I could see that it looked like I left the sliding door open on my balcony. I couldn't be 100% certain but it sure looked open. I quickly came to the conclusion it would be impossible for me to climb up this building 3 floors. It was built like a prison. No decor, no accoutrements, no fancy railings, just a sheer concrete wall with small groves running horizontal. Looking up, I could see each balcony had a concrete wall up to about your waist and then a plastic wall that went all the way up to the balcony ceiling. That's what separated them. I studied it harder and thought it wouldn't be hard to swing a leg around the plastic wall and carefully shimmy around from one balcony to another. At one point I'd have one leg on each side of the dividing wall while sitting on top of the railing. You'd be dangling a bit over the two rails but it didn't look like it would be all that dangerous. Young and dumb comes to mind as I write this now, plus desperation plays tricks on the mind. I NEEDED to get in my apartment, period. Whatever it took!

Obviously, I didn't know my neighbor. My Japanese was crappy at this point, but I knew I had to take an unusual action. My natural inclination is to be overly polite. I only had one neighbor since my apaarto was on the end. I knocked on the door. There was no peep hole so whoever opened the door was doing so blindly. I heard some rustling and knew someone was home. A gentleman of about 40 answered the door. He was wearing cloth pants and a wife beater type tank-top. He had a separation cloth hanging at his entrance where you step up into the kitchen area. Later I added this smart feature to all the places I lived in Japan.

"Sumimasen," I politely spoke. I bowed several times to show a subservient behavior and appear less threatening. He looked very surprised to see a gaijin (foreigner) standing at his door.

"Sumimasen, boku-wa anta no neighbor," I sputtered, as I pointed to my place next-door. I didn't know the word neighbor. "Boku no apaarto, koko," again gesturing next-door. Boku is the male version of "I" and I knew apaarto was apartment and koko means "here" so I was pointing and saying "I apartment here" which I felt he probably understood. He nodded and began speaking rapid fire Japanese at me. I had no idea what he was saying. I didn't know the work for "locked out" or even "key" in Japanese yet. I pointed to my chest and gestured, "Boku" and then pointed past his face into his apartment. I was basically miming that I wanted to come into his house. He was not understanding me. I felt embarrassed for what I did next. At this point of the story, looking back with a fuller understanding of their culture, *shameful* would better explain how I feel about what I did.

"Sumimasen, gomen-nasai," I said politely. Gomen-nasai means "I'm sorry" and with that I bowed, put my head down and charged into his apartment. When I tell Japanese people this story they ALWAYS ask me if I took my shoes off. I DID NOT TAKE MY SHOES OFF! It didn't even cross my mind. Now I realize that trampling through this man's place with my shoes on was a vile piggy thing to do. I was uncouth and had no manners. Plus, being a foreigner, I likely reeked of elitism, stupidity or just being born in a barn. Japanese have a lot of clean customs, many strict rules. Hygiene is a top priority. Most Japanese bathe at least twice a day. Showering does NOT count as a bath. You need to be in a hot bathtub to count as bathing.

I'm pushing my way into his apartment and he's lightly touching me asking me to stop. I was still being very polite and trying to show no aggression. I march through his kitchen and he had another hanging curtain that divided the step down area into his livingroom. He had already laid out his futon and his TV was on. One reason they say Japanese started taking their shoes off is because of the limited space in their homes. Your livingroom is also your dining room, it's your study and eventually your bedroom. You don't want people walking all over your bedding who have their shoes on. He's now behind me saying what I can only guess is, "STOP" or "Take your shoes off!" I'm like the Easter Bunny in Toyota City. Gaijin are a rare sighting. This poor man has the unlucky fortune of encountering an urban legend. I tiptoed and zigzagged around his bedding and made it out to the balcony. He was still right behind me.

"Gomen-nasai, honto-ne, gomen," I said again. I pointed to my apaarto and curve my hand in a gesture saying "I'm going over the balcony" and I can see this has him very worried. He begins waving his hand in front of his face. Japanese fan their hand in front of their nose to say "No" and he was doing this profusely. Of course he was speaking a lot of Japanese that I could not understand, but he said one word over & over. I later learned it was "Abunai" he kept saying it, "Abunai, abunai..." In English this means dangerous. I had no problem swinging over onto my balcony. Just like that, crisis averted. I apologized to him again and again. My balcony was unlocked and I was home free.

About an hour later my phone rang. It was Kiyomi. My neighbor understandably called the landlord to let them know a gaijin forced his way through his apartment, with his shoes on, and that he was not happy about it. I risked my life going over the balcony they said, but honestly it wasn't that difficult. The worst part was how rude I was to my neighbor. I felt I had no choice at the time and I still feel badly about it. My office bought him a delicious bouquet of fruit that I'm sure was well over $100. Kiyomi and I went to see him Monday night to apologize. He actually laughed about it. He told Kiyomi he thought he was in a movie. Several times after that he and I had beers together. He loved to act out how I rushed into his place. If he did that in America - he'd likely be shot. I was becoming legendary fast!

I don't think that incident made a good first impression at my office, but soon I had won over the staff and all my students. I was sort of a local celebrity in town and I was beginning to make friends. I have so many fond memories of living in Toyota City. Geographically, it sits along the Yohagi River. I used to go sit along the banks and feel total freedom. At night I fell asleep to the sounds of all the frogs "ribbiting" in the rice fields. It bothered me at first and then it became zen. I remember telling a few of my Japanese co-workers about the frogs going "ribbit" and they said that in Japanese frogs actually go "gero-gero"... which opened a whole list of how they hear animal sounds. It's funny, because as humans we all hear the sounds that dogs, cats, cows, pigs, roosters make and so on, but we don't always translate them the same phonically. In English we say a pig goes "oink-oink" but in Japanese it goes "bu-bu" which is completely different in every way! This is always a fun party conversation when you're in a mixed language group. Many times in life we can see or hear the same things but interpret them differently.

"Everyone is going to see things differently and that's the way it should be."
—Bob Ross (Joy of Painting)

One of the things about living in a foreign country that I treasure are the other foreigners you meet. One guy who became one of my closest friends in Toyota was Michael Garcia, an artist from Fresno, California. To me he's a national treasure. He told me he knew he wanted to be an artist from a kid. He went to the California Institute of the Arts. His art has amazing beauty in it's decay. He uses panels of wood, adding metal, oil, rust - layers and layers of paint, scraping, burning, his art looks old & damaged in the best way. He lived near me in a 250 year old authentic Japanese shanty. It had old sliding doors, tatami mat floors, it was going back in time for sure. He called it Club Jinnaka-cho. I hung out with Mike for hours and hours every week. After he graduated from college he hitchhiked up to Alaska to work in the canneries to help pay off his tuition debt, and by the way, CA Institute of Arts is not an easy or cheap school to get into. Mike was truly talented and still is. Up in Alaska he did his thing and painted a lot of fish. In Club Jinnaka I think he hit his stride. Meeting people "like

Mike" opens your mind to new doorways, you see things differently. His work has been displayed in the US Embassy in Nagoya. He's a living legend in my mind. I was thankful to get to know him as a friend and absorb his richness as sherpa in this world. I remember one night it was raining and Mike suggested we ride our bikes through town in our underwear (for that time, I'm talkin tighty-whitie Fruit-of-the-Looms). I was clinging onto the artistic vibe in Japan and feeling a bit invincible. My mind began to expand and dream to be unique.

I had gotten off the pre-destined train track of the All-American wet dream, meaning if two parents orgasmed over having the "perfect son" I might have been that scoop of goo you cleaned up with your socks. In reality, I was not genetically wired to follow the "American Pycho" toxic path of success in the typical way. Not that I was not capitalistic back then or now, because I am, but I just could not see myself clocking into a 9-5. I had tasted freedom and adventure. I was making friends with people who were living greed-free but creatively swallowing up the opportunities that could then lead to, quote on quote, commercial / societal success. I guess you could say, do what you love and you'll create your destiny the way you want to live.

I was breaking away from having the right white crisp paper for my resume, the perfect Brooks Brother suit, the Bally shoes, a Rolex watch and all the dangling carrot things that were artificially impregnated into my unconscious. My brain was rewiring itself and I didn't even know it. I was chugging along at AEON. I was teaching English to all types of Japanese, many of who were executives at Toyota Motor Company and were training to go to the US to live. I had a lot of freedom in my lesson plans and I loved teaching them cultural differences. I remember that I had my mom record (VHS) TV commercials. I'd have 50 commercials lined up in a row, one after another. We'd analyze the meaning, the brainwashing, purpose, angle, demographics and have debates on how effective they were. Commercials are an interesting breed, a cross-section of society. The unusual ways countries sell their wares to the public is completely different from society to society. This teaches us a lot about how people think. My students loved it. No one else was doing anything this interesting. We'd watch an episode of the Simpsons or Married with Children. They were learning American culture and how people really spoke "cowabunga dude"! I could tell that students were eager to join my class. I was popular. I learned so much myself by breaking down our TV shows and ads. We mindlessly watch the boob-tube (my grandpa's name for TV) everyday. When you stop and really study it, it's fascinating. It's a reflection of our society.

Fate knocked on my door. Luck is an opportunity you put yourself in. Once that knock comes, you better jump at the chance. This is one of the cruel fates in life. You can be the best singer, actor, musician, designer, race car driver - you name it, but often times to hit that true level of success you need a boost. You need fate. The hand of God needs to pluck you from obscurity. This is frustrating. If you study to become a doctor you can become a doctor. But many fields and dreams need a bit of luck. The one thing we can all do is to have ourselves prepared for that chance and once it comes around, believe in yourself and go for it. My mom used to say, "Can't never did anything!" and I don't let nerves or lack of anything stop me from trying.

As I stated, I was the pied piper of Toyota-shi and about 8 months into my time there I was asked by Toyota Motor Company if I wanted to model for their catalogs for Australia and Europe. This was the fate I was talking about. I said "Yes" as fast as I could or should I say, "Hai!" meaning "yes" in Japanese. It was just a one day job and I would be sitting in a couple different cars. I was to wear a dark suit. When I arrived at the photoshoot I realized I was inside an area of

Toyota Motors I had never seen. They had a studio set up and the cars would be slightly suspended off the ground. I would sit completely still inside the car and they would use time lapse photography. Someone would pull a sting and the two tires facing the camera would rotate creating a blurred image of the tires. It would look like we were moving. Funny now, but at the time I thought this was so clever, high tech! Of course, photoshop could do all this with a click of a button now, but that's what made the "good ol' days" fun.

Ingenuity was always on display. Part of the lighting crew, cameras and the overall setup was with an outside company called Central Fashion. My Japanese was greatly improving and one of the art directors asked me if I had ever done modeling. I said I had some experience and she gave me her business card (meishi in Japanese). Business cards were a big deal in Japan in 1991. I'm not sure about now, but back then it was a whole presentation. If you really wanted to show respect to someone, you'd hold your little business card out with both hands, bow down and offer it to someone. Then you'd bow a few more times thanking them. I didn't get that kind of respect, rightfully so, from the Central Fashion art director, but I graciously accepted it anyway. When you got someone's card you didn't put it away. You looked at it with both hands. Flipped it over. Gave it a thorough look over. Pretended you were thrilled. It would be as if Steven Spielberg gave you his phone number at a film festival your short had just premiered at.

"Arrogato gozaimasu," I said politely. "Tadaima meishi wo kirashite orimashite, moshiwake gozaimasen" basically saying "Sorry I currently am out of business cards" but in truth I wasn't out, I just didn't bring mine. I had them though. You ain't worth spit if you didn't have a meishi in Japan. Later, while we were breaking for lunch, this woman told me that if I came to Nagoya she thought Central Fashion could get me lots of work as a model. I didn't know the term for it then but it would be editorial print work. Catalogs, brochures some magazine print stuff but not really fashion. Later on, I actually did do some fashion and TV commercials, but in the beginning I was the token white guy who could make a Japanese company look more international if they used a gaijin to hock their wares. I'm getting a bit ahead of myself. I contacted her and about two weeks later. I took a day off from work which was very unusual. I felt like I was on a spy mission. I snuck out of Toyota and headed to the big city of Nagoya. Central Fashion didn't have a gaijin men's division. I would be their first male foreign model. They did regularly bring in American and European girls 18-23 years old for three (3) months at a time. That's how long working visas lasted. It was a constant rotation of foreign beauties. They wanted me to come onboard, but I would only be able to stay for 3 months if I wasn't on Toyota's (AEON) working visa. My plan was to tell AEON that I wanted to sign-up for an additional year. Then I would get my visa stamped, quit AEON and I could stay in Japan for the rest of that year. I'm not good at screwing people over and Toyota had been good to me, but I decided that sometimes you have to do the wrong thing to do right. What I haven't said yet is that they paid me ¥650,000 which back in 1992 was almost $8,000 for that ONE catalogue job for Toyota Motor Company. I was blown away that they would pay me that much money. I wasn't really expecting to get paid at all. That sealed the deal. I was going to be an "International Male Model!" To renew a visa you have to leave the country you're in and go to the closest US Embassy outside the country you are currently in. From Japan that was Seoul, Korea. Kimchi was in my future.

Seoul, Korea was only the 2nd Asian country I had visited. I was expecting it to be like Japan and it was completely different. Japan, although poles apart from the US, had some common bond that made it feel safe and comfortable. Japanese people feel like kindred spirits to me. Like "brothers from another mother" type connection. Getting to Seoul, all that warm fuzzy feeling was gone. The Korean people seemed more cold, standoffish. I can somewhat blame the American GI's. We keep a military base there for their protection and to let the US have a foothold in that part of the world. Obviously, North Korea and China are always a thorn in our sides and we look at each other with skepticism. We've got business going with China and that keeps us cordial, but North Korea is a wild card. If you ask South Koreans if they like the US base Camp Humphreys located south of Seoul, most will say they don't. If you ask them if they'd like us to leave? Most will say no. With about 28,000 soldiers, sailors, airmen, and marines based there we have a big presence. Typical love/hate relationship.

Just before I got there a US Second Infantry private, 20yo, murdered a young Korean girl on base. She was bloodied, bruised and found with a Coca-Cola bottle in her vagina and an umbrella about 10" in her rectum. This put a lot of tension in the air. While walking around Japan I felt prized, sought after, one of the good guys, but in Seoul it was a much darker mood when I felt the Koreans gaze upon me. I also think the Korean people aren't outwardly as ready to show their emotions. In that way, I feel the Japanese are more Westernized. I just did not feel welcome in Seoul and I understood why. I was there for a purpose and it would take three days for me to get my visa renewed.

I have two incidents that happened in my three days that I feel are worth noting, other than not feeling welcome in 1992. Maybe they have a harder candy coated outside and sweeter inside, but I wasn't there long enough to break that shell. The hotel I was staying in was a 25 floor high-rise with a bar/lounge on the top floor. Not feeling that welcome on the streets, I was having a drink in the upper lounge at about 2pm and mentioned to the bartender that I'd like to get a haircut. He nodded and called the front desk and arranged for me to have a cut in the barber shop of the hotel at 4:30pm. Perfect I thought. My Korean language skills were limited to "hello, good-bye & thank you" so any relevant communication relied completely on whoever I was interacting with's English. Few people spoke English that well so it was challenging. Even arranging my haircut involved miming my fingers as scissors. All part of the adventure of life in a foreign land.

At 4:25pm I headed to the 22nd floor to get to the barber shop. I hadn't been on this floor and when the doors opened it didn't seem like I was in the right place. It felt abandoned. No one was around and there were no signs or storefront decor at all. Instead of being on the 22nd floor, it felt like I was in a basement somewhere I shouldn't be. All the walls were white with absolutely nothing on them. If I could compare it to anything I would say a doctor's office except there were no chairs, it didn't have a "waiting room" vibe at all. There was a small window and a door to the right of the elevator. I peeked my head through the window "Annyeonghaseyo," spoken with very little confidence. I was saying "Hello" in Korean. I spoke louder "ANNYEONGHASEYO!" Looking through the window, a man dressed in a long white lab coat opened a door in the back of the small room that the window looked into. He looked surprised to see me.

"I have appointment at 4:30, haircut," I say slowly and using my hands as much as I could, not knowing if he spoke English. From the look on his face he didn't seem to understand anything I said. "Haircut." Using my fingers as scissors again, I put them up to my head. Surely, this was the international charades' gesture for haircut?

"Wait" or what sounded more like "Wāt" and then he put up his hands in the stop gesture as he said, "Gidalida." I learned later, as you often do, that was in fact "Wait" in Korean, but he did say English first and I nodded and smiled, "Okay." BTW, the word "OK or Okay" is international. This is understood all over the world. White lab coat man looked like he could be a barber, a doctor or a butcher. I was hoping it was not the latter. I'm not going to lie, it was strange up there alone on the 22nd floor. There was no music. I felt like I was in an office after hours that had gone out of business years ago. It did not make sense this floor existed in this hotel. Scary!

The hotel was not grand. It was rundown a bit but gave me the impression that it used to be very nice. It might be on the Lonely Planet list now for bargain hotels with a great location, but it was not a halfway house, except this floor had that vibe. He picked up a phone and I presumed called the front desk. He hung up and gestured for me to go the door to his left. Once again, it had the doctor's office vibe. He opened the door and said, "Haircut," in an asking tone, in broken English, but I was thankful. I always try to remember I'm in THEIR country and they are speaking MY language. He walked me down a hallway with rooms with no doors. The room he guided me into had a window cut out next to the open door. What the hell was this designed for? My mind was racing. None of it made sense. In the middle of the room was a barber chair, sort of, or maybe a gynecological examination table? It didn't quite fit into any particular category as far as what it was designed for. He was gestured for me to sit on this thing. I had to slightly hop up on it. He left the room briefly and came back in with a robe that was just a tick better than a hospital gown and slippers. He gestured for me to put them on. Obviously, I'm fully contemplating leaving. I'm nervous. WHAT THE HELL IS GOING ON HERE? screeches in my brain and this would not be the last time I say this to myself. Just as he was turning to walk out he gestured and said, "Bir?" I was confused.

"Bir?" I said mimicking his words, shaking my head letting him know I don't understand. He said again, "Beer?" he shook his hand to his mouth. "Oh, beer!" I said now understanding what he was asking. In my nervousness and confusion I said, "Ok" which is ridiculous. I'm being asked to undress and offered alcohol. On one hand I thought, "Does he think I'm here for a medical exam?" The room and his getup, the robe all point to that possibility, but now he's thrown in beer. WTF! He walks out of the room that had no door and comes back with a Hite Extra Cold beer. He hands it to me and points to the robe/gown and gestures for me to put it on. He leaves again and I decide I will take my shirt off, but leave my jeans and shoes on. I get back on the the chair table and it forces you to lean back uncomfortably. I'm sipping my beer awkwardly. I saw him open it just before handing it to me so I felt safe there. I was looking around wondering how this is going to play out? The room is carpeted, there is no washing sink, no barber tools that I can see and I'm just waiting. The whole floor smells stale. There's no air circulation. I hear the elevator ding in the distance. A door opens and then a young attractive Korean girl walks into the room. I can't remember what she was wearing (which in hindsight bothers me), but I'm pretty sure I had entered the Twilight Zone of my mind at this point. We greeted each other but she spoke no English, zero. I was still sipping my beer and then she offered me a cigarette. For whatever reason, I accepted it. When I went to reach for it, she bypassed my hand and put it directly in my mouth and pulled out a lighter. Wow, this was getting stranger by the minute. I'm sitting in this strange chair with a beer in one hand and a cig in the other. It was one of those moments in life we all have, that while it is happening you are already rehearsing in your mind how you are going to tell this story to all your friends. Allen Funt, or nowadays Johnny Knoxville, could have burst through the doors and been the ONLY thing that would have made any of what was happening make sense.

"Mesiji," this young cigarette girl was asking me something that I wasn't quite sure what she wanted. She said again, "Mesiji?" as I smiled she walked around the back of me and began massaging my scalp. Meiji meant massage. I'm thinking "What is going on here?" for the hundredth time. I had several haircuts in Japan in my last 11 months and they often do message the scalp vigorously and even shave your forehead and earlobes. You get the full treatment in Asia, but this "full treatment" seemed like something out of the ordinary. I'm still drinking and puffin away and her hands move past my hairline and she begins rubbing my temples. Honestly, with the beer, the nicotine high, her rubbing my temples, I was feeling pretty good - but somewhere in the back of my mind I knew something was off. My cigarette was nearing the butt and my beer was all backwash. She came around the side of the chair, took both of them from my hands and discarded them. She turned around and smiled. She climbed on top of me and then proceeded to straddle me. I smelled cinnamon & vanilla. I'm looking at her chest and she started to massage my scalp again from the cowgirl position. Not to get off point, but back in Detroit when I worked off of Big Beaver Road for US Steel, I had a late night haircut appointment and when she wanted to get my bangs just right she straddled me to get the perfect angle on that cut. We ended up going on a few dates after that! How many guys can say they've been straddled during a haircut? And its happened to me twice!

This Korean girl stopped massaging my head and made a gesture for money and asked in very broken English, "How much you pay?" Suddenly a lightbulb went off in my head. This girl is a prostitute. I know it sounds naive but I really had no clue up until that time.

"No, no, no I want haircut," I said with my finger gestures again. "No sex!" She jumped down off me and seemed apologetic, not mad. She seemed to be saying I'm sorry in Korean but I didn't understand. She quickly left the room. I needed to get out of there. I was also wondering what this was going to cost me? I know there are a lot of rip-offs out there, but this was inside my hotel. I wasn't down in a seedy part of town. Then the original man in the long white lab coat came in. He asked me, "You want haircut?" It felt like he had just looked that phrase up. I shook my head "Yes" and he left again and quickly came back with authentic looking haircutting shears. Believe or not, this man preceded to actually give me a mild haircut. I say "mild" because he took very little off but I was just happy to get out of there. I paid $80 which was a lot of money. My room was only $78 a night. I'd be watching my money closely the next two days. I later learned from one of my foreign friends that asking for a "Haircut" can mean asking for a comfort girl. I still do not know if that's completely true in 1992 but I'm very careful now.

My last night in Seoul was very eventful. At about 1am I hear yelling and screaming in the hallway. It sounded like a Japanese man and a woman were arguing. I looked out my peephole but couldn't see anything. The racket continued. I opened my door and stuck my head out, turning towards the uproar. I see a middle aged Japanese man standing in his doorway with an open robe on. A beautiful young Asian girl is standing a few feet away from him in the hallway. He sees me and tries to grab her arm and pull her back into the room. I only know he's Japanese because I heard him yelling. The girl squeaks some jumbled words at him that I can't understand. He gets aggressive with her and I step slightly into my doorway and he sees me.

"Jiubun no koto was kinishinai!" he barks at me in that familiar Japanese tone that is almost growling with the attitude of fighting wrapped up in it's delivery. He has no idea I could mostly understand that he just said, "Mind your own fucking business," as he motioned for the girl to again go back into his room. She was now crying and looked frightened.

"Daijōbu, deska?" I asked her, and she came running at me.

He yells, "Dame!" or "Yamero" or something like that means stop or stop it. He took two steps towards me aggressively as she rushed towards me. Now, whenever you spend time in a foreign country and you make friends with the locals you always get to know some of the colorful language only natives speak. I had just such a phrase up my sleeve, or should I say off my tongue, and the reaction was priceless.

"Ketsu no ana ga chiisai, YAROU!" I growled with my best yakuza (mafia) impersonation. The look on his face was complete shock. I threw at him one of the most vulgar Japanese expressions that is actually used in real life. It literally means "You have a small butthole" but it's slang for you are narrow-minded. It's a harsh way of speaking. This guy was NOT expecting me to speak Japanese and it froze him in his tracks. The beautiful young nymph pushed past me and ran into my room. The Japanese guy made one more gesture towards me but I could tell he had lost his power.

I spoke very calmly and matter-of-factly, "Bukkoro shite yaru," which was basically saying I'm going to "kick your ass." I made an aggressive move forward with one strong step in his direction. He turned, and I'd describe it as ran, back into his room while calling me a fool, "Bakka" and slamming his door loudly.

I quickly discovered this young girl was Korean, which meant I could not speak with her in Japanese and she seemed to know no English. I closed my door, wondering if the angry Japanese guy might cause me problems. I had never used my clever cussing words in an actual conversation and truthfully I wasn't sure how strong my words were. I was like a mockingbird mimicking a phrase. I realized this girl must be a prostitute. She was young, very beautiful and scared. I could think of no other reason she would be in that middle aged "salary man's" room. Obviously, they had some sort of dispute. She sat on my bed and the game of charades started. She pointed to the bed and then claps her hands in the praying style and placed them against the side of her face and closed her eyes. She was telling me she wanted to sleep in my room. I shook my hand in front of my face signaling "No" and shook my head again. She went over to my little table, opened the drawer, pulled out the note pad that has the hotel's logo on it, grabbed the pen and wrote down ₩150,000 (won) which was close to $100. Yeah, she was a working girl. I can't say "woman" because she looked very young, possibly as young as 16. Asian girls can look young for their age but she was not a day over 20, that's for sure.

I let her know that she was not sleeping in my room. I went over to the room phone and started to pick it up to have the front desk help me get out of this situation. This put the fear in her. She panicked. With much gesturing I got the message that she wanted me to accompany her downstairs, through the lobby and out the front door. I did just this. Once outside she ran towards a Korean man. At first he looked like he was going to be angry with me, but whatever she said got me off the hook. For a brief moment I thought my good deed might get me into a heap of hurtin'. I found out later that the hotel frowns upon this type of business going on and if a girl comes and goes unescorted it could lead to them being arrested. Her insisting I go with her outside the hotel made sense after the fact.

I finally got my visa and I headed back to Japan. It felt so good to be back where I felt welcome. The Vapors had a song *Turning Japanese* in 1980 with the main lyrics being "I think I'm turning Japanese, I really think so" and I felt like I was. When you are a foreigner you try to be more like the people of that country than they do. It takes over your soul. I remember I was back home again in Speedway, Indiana during a break from Japan. I picked up my dinner plate and moved it closer to my face and was almost shoveling the food into my mouth. In Japan you often pick up your plate. It makes using chopsticks easier. I can remember my mom & sisters looking gobsmacked and asking, "What the hell are you doing?" I didn't even realize it. Traveling had started to influence my life in ways I could have never predicted.

Nihon II

CHAPTER SIX

•

"There comes that mysterious meeting in life when someone acknowledges who we are and what we can be, igniting the circuits of our highest potential."

—Rusty Berkus

THIS STARTS MY second adventure in Japan and really a whole new path in life that I didn't know would happen. I'm being "Pooh-ed" again and didn't even realize it. Nihon or Nippon is what the Japanese call their country, hence Nihon II. I was back in Japan and I needed a new apartment in Nagoya. This is where I realize just how free we are in America. A foreigner in most countries, including Japan, cannot just rent an apaarto, you need a sponsor. You cannot buy land in many countries in the world unless you are a citizen. You could not buy land in China, period. Not allowed. We allow China to buy all the land they want in America. We even allow foreigners in the US to get mortgages. I often see on the news or hear someone complaining about America for one reason or another. Until you live in another country I don't think you truly understand just how free America is.

Luckily, *Central Fashion* agreed to be my guarantor or co-signer for my mansion. There was some discussion that my working visa was not with them but somehow I flew under the radar and got a place in Kanayama which in Japanese means "gold mountain" and it can be a surname too. It's a major hub in Nagoya served by the JR and Meitetsu Line, meaning I can get around really easily. It's a lively happening area and I finally felt like I was really living in Japan when I started this new chapter. In Toyota I was coddled and helped along the way, which I needed in the beginning, but now I was my own man. I had learned the art of gomi hunting. Gomi is the Japanese word for trash. It's an odd custom in Japan, but they rarely give someone something that they don't want or are throwing out. It would be an insult. The solution to this is placing things you don't want out on the street. You may drive around and see a TV sitting along the street near someone's home. It's likely that the people living there had bought a new one. Sometimes they may tell a friend they are buying something new, like a TV or rice cooker or even a whole new livingroom set. This is their "hint hint" I'm going to have some good gomi soon. Gomi hunting is a big deal in Japan. The better neighborhoods have better gomi. One of my Japanese friends had a truck and after several nights hunting I had a new TV, stereo, couch, kotatsu, rice cooker, a lamp and even some artwork. It was amazing.

Good story - My TV was 36", which was big in 1992-93, but I could not get NHK. That's the Japanese version of PBS. One day there was a knock at my door and a man was there from NHK. He asked me if I had a TV. I said I did and he told me I needed to pay for the public station NHK. I was fumbling with my Japanese trying to tell him I did not get NHK. He kept saying, "Minna-san" - blah, blah, blah and I knew "Minna" meant everyone. I had to practically drag him into my apartment. HE TOOK HIS SHOES OFF. Once in front of my TV he took my remote control and tried again & again to find NHK. It was funny. I actually wanted to have NHK, but this gomi TV somehow could not get it. He shook his head and apologized and left. NHK collectors never came back to my apaarto again. Another lesson I learned in Japan is to never compliment something in someone's house. There is a chance they will take it off the wall and insist you take it home with you. This can be very awkward.

In Kanayama I found a local bar called *Canal Street* that had a Western vibe that I liked. An Australian named Pete ran it with his blonde lassie wife. Pete was about 30yo and his wife was mid-twenties and a real looker. They came to Nagoya from Australia to export cars. He managed Canal Street while saving money and finding deals on cars. Japan has strict rules on emission fees and inspection costs. These fees happen every 2 years and cars just keep getting more & more expensive with age. Sometimes the inspections exceed the value the car. Pete was a smart cookie. He would fill 2-3 shipping containers with each holding 4 used Japanese cars. Australia, like Japan, had the steering wheel on the right hand side. Pete had a goal of saving whatever the equivalent of $1M dollars was down-under, and then head home a much richer guy. He would not have to work for the rest of his life. I connected with Pete because we were like-minded. I too, was always looking for unique ways to make the almighty dollar in untraditional ways. Being rich in my mind was having freedom. Japanese cars were sought after in Australia and he could more than double his money per car. God bless him! I hope his modern day merchant trading on the high seas made him comfortable. Canal Street had awesome food and a bar I danced on many a night. It was a port in the storm and brought me a comfort of being around other foreigners who were in Japan chasing new escapades, happenings in their lives. It was a great time to be in Japan. In 1992-93, Japan was coming off of a period of excessive living. They were fat cats in the '80s and the effects were still lingering during my time there. The tides were preparing for an economic downturn but NOT quite yet. The "Lost Decade" as you often hear in Japan, didn't effect my lifestyle there. It actually made the money I was making in Japan more valuable when I exchanged it for the dollar. In the 1980s, Japan had a beautiful bubble economy which was making it into an extravagant, mind-blowing party. In 1985 Japan's goods were taking over the world. Money was flowing into the country like never before. Decadence was the norm. Everyone had money. It was a country that resembled Studio 54, PARTY PARTY PARTY! When I hit the bar scene in Nagoya & Tokyo in 1992 the mega discos were still alive. They had rows & rows of ikke ikke girls (go-go) that were NOT employed by the discos, they were just regular girls that wanted to party 1/2 naked to techno music. They would dance along the side of the dance floor on raised platforms waving fans and gyrating their bodies. It was a crazy scene. These clubs were massive. The volume of these places was like looking into the Grand Canyon. Your depth to feel was off. The size, the spinning lights, the LED screens (new at that time) were all far and beyond anything I had ever seen. I was witnessing the end of an era. I'm proud I saw that level of outrageous lavish squandering. It was like being there when Rome was burning.

I got off track, of course I did - because that time in my life was something I never get tired of talking about. Central Fashion was lining up jobs for me left and right. If a Japanese company wanted to look international I was their token gaijin (white guy). I never had to audition for anything or go to any type of casting. They would call me with a gig at least once a week and sometimes 4 times. I don't even remember how they quoted my fee but I was on the payroll and making good money. It was hard to make a schedule because one week I might only be working one day. I had time to take Japanese cooking classes, I even did flower arranging and went to the gym regularly. Other weeks I was busy nearly everyday. I loved being busy with "International Modeling" gigs. I say this facetiously because the type of jobs I was landing were incredibly hilarious. I was doing things like - modeling nuclear hazmat suits that you'd wear if you worked at Three Mile Island or unfortunately Fukushima. In the opening of The Simpson's, Homer is wearing a white hazmat suit with a square opening to see through. Every-time I see that opening I point to the TV "That's the suit I wore!" and I'm not exaggerating. The closest thing I did in regards to fashion was wedding garb. I wore suits, tuxes, leather jackets.... I did major ads for Toyota (again), Panasonic, Yamaha, Sony, banks, restaurants and I even started to get paid to be a customer at one of those wild Japanese nightclubs. Before I get into that crazy story, I want you to know that I completely understood then and now that I was not a sleek fashion model. I had a commercial face. I was just generic enough to look the part of the everyday man. I wasn't too good-looking to distract from the product, but I was good-looking enough to make someone feel "I don't know what it is, but I want to buy that what-cha-ma-call-it" because I want to be that everyday good guy. This overall theme that is me, transferred countries. Later I'll tell you how this appeal landed me success in Hollywood too.

I was making great money, not working that hard & when I did work it was fun. I would be given instructions to get on the Shinkansen (Bullet Train) to Kyoto or wherever and then be treated like a king. It was amazing. I rarely had a bad experience. Nagoya is like Cleveland or Detroit - meaning it has a blue-collar heartbeat and services large industry and manufacturing companies. During WWII it was one of the most heavily bombed cities in Japan. 40-50% of Japanese combat aircraft and engines, like the Mitsubishi A6M Zero fighter, were made in Nagoya. When I landed in Nagoya in 1992 it was a major hub for the automobile industry, aviation, ceramics, technology, electronics and textiles. This boom gave me a lot of industrial print work. I booked some TV commercials too. Japanese call commercials "CM" for short, spoken just like we would pronounce it in English. Along with a few CMs I did hosting gigs too. The most memorable was for YAMAHA organ / electric pianos. It was possibly the most nervous I had ever been and given some of the crazy things I jumped head first into this is saying something. It was a live show inside of a large theater. If I had to guess I'd say there were at least 1,500 people there. It was packed. I was hired as the MC along with a Japanese co-host named Tomoko. They sent me the script in Japanese and I had a lot of dialogue. I was in way over my head. Thank God for Tomoko. We met a few days before to rehearse and she clearly understood my Japanese was not up to par. She wrote down my lines phonically. For example; "今日は元気ですか was written in my script. Meaning "How are you today?" then she would write it out as "Kyō wa genki desu ka" so I could read it properly. I was so confused. It was like hosting the Oscars. We'd come onstage, banter something funny and then introduce a band, which would all be using Yamaha pianos or organs in their performances. Now keep in mind, that I had never done theater or performed in front of a live audience except when I was a cheerleader at IU, but that didn't seem like this. Cheerleading seemed like a sport, but this was "to entertain". I wanted to back out so badly! It was thrilling and exciting, but also terrifying. My Japanese wasn't perfect and I was afraid of embarrassing myself, or worse yet, of letting them down with my language skills. Being afraid is not a sign that you are not supposed to do something. Fear is real and part of living. All creatures on this planet have it. If you ask any successful person about their journey they will have a story of fear.

Fear of Humiliation

This feeling is one of my biggest weaknesses. Is this a phobia? Is it egotistical? Something deeply rooted in a bad childhood experience? I believe it is human. That's my answer, my theory. It can be very destructive but also can protect us. It can destroy your creativity if it stops you from reaching beyond your comfort zone. Don't let the fear become the negative "go to" in your conscious choice. Failure means you are trying something.

Fear of Not Being Good

It can be hard to please yourself. You can be your own worst critic. Self doubt is achievement cancer. The doubt can take a success and make it a negative, "I didn't deserve this" attitude. Do not compare yourself to others. Listen to the people around you and believe them when they compliment or encourage you. Put the face of confidence on and force yourself to move forward.

Fear of Rejection • Fear of the Unknown • Fear of Failure
Fear of Being Judged • Fear of Inadequacy
Fear of Something Awful Happening • Fear of Fear

That is a long list of FEARS. Fear should not be disproportionate to the reality of the danger. Excessive worrying is not healthy. Fear should not put limitations on how you live your life. We can easily say YOLO, but are we living like we believe "You Only Live Once?" ***Stop the fear!***

I am rocked with even more fear when I showed up on the afternoon of the big show and the director said he wanted me to start out in the crowd. His plan was to have Tomoko come out on stage and tell everyone she has lost her really cool gaijin co-host and then she would pan the room looking for me. I was to be hiding in the back. A spot light would hit me, a curtain would rise on stage and eight Yamaha organs would play some funky dance music. I had a mic in my hand and I would call out, "Boku wa koko, desu!" saying "Here I am" and I would come dancing down the aisles as the audience clapped. Now, I'm not a bad dancer, but obviously I'm not Michael Jackson either. How this director had any idea that I could dance at all is still a mystery to me. We weren't even going to rehearse this part. It was all matter-of-fact, as if it was no big deal. My heart was pounding out of my freakin' chest! I was already worried sick doing this whole show in Japanese, but also because I had never done a live show in my life. After the run-through I had almost TWO HOURS before the show. I have never had a panic attack before, but I was trippin balls at this point. I went to speak to the director to tell him I didn't think I could do it. I'm not a quitter, but something about this show had me frozen with FEAR. I wanted to back out.

The director could see I was about to exit stage left and he asked me to join him for a "pep talk". I didn't realize it at the time but there was a coffee shop/bar on the top floor of the theater building. He ordered me a beer and was being very positive that he had full confidence in me. I think he did not want to let me out of his sight. I was a "jump bail risk" and he knew it. Kudos to him! He got me a bit liquored up and was keeping me company (imprisoned) and before I knew it, it was show time!

I remember I was wearing a purple vest, a black dress shirt along with dark pants. As planned, the spotlight hit me. BAM! I instinctually raised the mic and yelled my first line as if on autopilot, and then I literally had an out of body experience. The music cued and I "did things", meaning dance moves, that I had NEVER done before. I hip-hopped, popped, locked and bound down several aisles and the crowd began clapping. No, not clapping - Cheering! I get goosebumps to this day writing this because I still can't believe I actually did it, their enthusiasm was like pouring gasoline on a scared little spark and my engine ignited. It's still all a little blurry to me because something took over and I was ON and it was GO time! I know this is a book but I wish you could see it. It was terribly wonderful. Depending on if you use a comma, "terribly, wonderful" or "terribly wonderful" is true because it was both. I have a poor quality VHS copy of that show so maybe I can put it on YouTube for those who need a laugh. Overcoming that challenge, facing that fear, became an advantage in my life. Anytime I have had to do something that scared me, something I fear, the "I can't do this" monster has reared it's ugly head, I always think about that Yamaha concert. I overcame adversity. I did it when I made Big Ten Cheerleader at Indiana University although I could not do half the requirements. As you read on in this book, you'll see a common theme: that talent or skill is not always the true measure of acquiring success. Resilience and willing to TRY are a very strong part of making it happen for you. "Can't never did anything," as I said before. You cannot hit a home run unless you get up to bat. I didn't know it then, but I was slowly adding layers and layers of experiences to my life that would help me get to the next plateau. This would give me the confidence to try anything new that was thrown my way. In fact, if someone asks me now to "dance down an aisle," I am more than up for the challenge. I'll knock them down with my moves before the words are even completely out of their mouth.

I spent a total of four years in Japan. Going into my 3rd year I needed my visa renewed again and I was approached by a company called Exiv that was creating a business oriented cultural exchange division that would teach English but also set up an international vocational exchange program. It was perfect for me. It would eat into some of my modeling, but I needed a sponsor and Exiv was flexible. This time I came back to Indiana and got my visa renewed in Chicago. The great thing about Exiv was that they wanted me to travel to Universities, Colleges and Vocational Schools (trade) and develop a partnership with them to send Japanese citizens to the US to learn a variety of vocational skills ranging from language, culinary arts, fashion design, art, cosmetology, hotel & restaurant, massage, nails, hair salon - these programs would be anywhere from 6 weeks to 2 years long. It was a great way for an adventuresome Japanese person to go to America and explore while at the same time, learning a skill. I felt it was similar to MY experience in Japan, but reversed. I spent a lot of time contacting these schools in different parts of the United States. There was no internet so everything was much harder. It also gave Exiv an advantage because their clients could not easily find the information I was gathering. About 6 months later they sent me to the US to meet with the schools and set up an agreement. The Japanese would need housing assistance too. Most of the schools I contacted were eager to be on the list to send students their way. Especially, the smaller trade schools. It could be an out of the blue, new revenue stream they had not tapped into.

This was the perfect job for me. I could meld the new culture I adored, Japan, and America, the country I loved. I could use my business degree, travel free across the USA and get paid a good salary. I still had my apartment in Nagoya and was truly feeling like an international man of mystery. You've heard of the trifecta in horse racing where you predict the 1st, 2nd & 3rd places perfectly. I'm going to create the new word "bifecta" because I had two (2) countries in my corner and it was a winner-winner-chicken-dinner for my pocketbook and my life experiences. The layer of my onion was peeling towards sweeter things. I landed in Los Angeles to start this adventure. I had never been there before and the allure of Hollywood was real. I felt a pretty big matzo ball hanging over my head. I told LA I loved her but didn't get love in return. It's a tough city that only shows her goodies to a fortunate few. It would be more than a year before I returned and got that "swipe right" vibe that maybe LA is interested me, tell me more. I rented a car, bought maps and proceeded to explore the cantankerous Orange County before moving onto Oregon, Washington, Vegas, Arizona, Colorado, New Orleans, Chicago and New York City. I was gone for two months, completely on my own. Freedom was my friend again. It was like being on an amusement ride where I got to make my own tracks. I would check-in with Exiv once a week with updates, but I was unshackled, unchained, unfettered, a lot of wonderful "un" in my life. I had a swagger when meeting with the schools & universities. I believed in what I was doing. I was living what I was selling but in the opposite direction. Plus, schools knew our program would bring them revenue.

I was like the Mickey Mouse of Exiv. I was the lone foreigner in charge of one of their biggest expanding divisions. By this time in Japan, I knew what people expected of me professionally and socially. I needed to play the role of the fun, happy "American Gaijin" and the lesson I learned was *know what people expect of you and be sure to give them some of that*. Living up to expectations can ease tension. It can help your career. I'm NOT saying if you are a woman that getting coffee for a sexist staff is right, heck no. But I will say to be open to expanding your comfort zone. This leads me leads up to another infamous story of "performing" at our company's trip to the IZU Peninsula which is about 3 hours away from Nagoya. This was my first time to go to one of these old school year-end parties. In the 1990's they were legendary. That year it was held at a popular hot springs (onsen) area and all 127 employees were going, all expenses paid. I was the sole foreigner. These Japanese corporate events were often whispered about. They had a *Mad Men* type booze and babes reputation. All bets were off, meaning inhibitions, clothes, common sense - the only thing I can compare it to now is the Playboy Mansion, but those stories come later. It was known folklore that everyone would be drunk and you may as well leave your wedding ring at the front desk. The undertone that it was going to get wild had been building for months.

Our traditional ryokan hotel had tatami mat floors and paper walls. We bathed nude (men & women separately) in the thermal volcanic pools. Everyone walked around the hotel in a yukata or happi type kimono-lite, wrap-around robe. It felt like we were all in our pajammies.

What a way to bond! The second night we had a lavish dinner in a large Japanese style room with long, low tables with us all sitting on the floor. As stated several times, the alcohol was flowing like truth serum. We were all bonding and I was seeing sides to people I knew that I had never seen before. I heard there would be a talent show between the 5 divisions of the company. Wow! This all had a summer camp in the Adirondack's feel. I don't think any of the groups were too prepared. I had, for some ungodly reason, brought with me an elephant g-string. I had told one of my co-workers I had it and he told me I definitely should bring it. It was red with two giant ears and a trunk you could put your penis into. It had boggle eyes and if you squeezed the end of the trunk it played Yankee Doodle Dandy. It was ridiculously funny and when I showed my team I had it, they went nuts - no pun intended. All my naughty bits would be covered but it was still a tiny thong. I'm not overly shy and I guess this is an example of me missing that little tiny voice that puts "the fear" into our heads.

My group and I had it all planned. We were all wearing our yukata kimonos and as we started doing our skit& song my robe would occasionally (accidentally) flop open revealing something red & odd hiding away. I could see that the crowd was really focusing on me. I would spin or kick a leg out and I'd get roars. It slowly built up and I knew we were on the right track. Again, the gasoline had been tossed and I was the spark that flamed it. The grand finale was when one of my co-workers stumbled into me and pulled my yukata (my robe) completely off. Just naked Bill-san and the Elephant. Everyone went wild. Our Shacho, meaning president/CEO, was rolling on the floor with laughter. Many of my co-workers didn't know me that well, but after Izu I was legendary and had the run of the company.

As much as I loved Japan, I felt it was time to head home. I always tell people "I did NOT leave Japan, I escaped Japan" because it becomes an addiction. You truly feel special when you are living in a different country. You get a lot of attention. I don't need to go into details, but I had never had the kind of attention from women in the US like I did in Japan. It's not natural for a man to have women throw themselves at you like that. This was the early 1990s and I'm sure it's changed now, but being a gaijin back then was like being a rockstar. I saw many a gaijin (foreign) men become crazed. They lost their moral compass. I felt myself going down that dark road and I didn't like it. Getting back to America would help restore my soul. I had kept my moral compass mostly on track but I was seeing sides to me I didn't like. I missed my homeland - the size and infrastructure. I missed the ease of being able to read everything - television, the culture and not standing out every minute of the day. I love Japanese food but I definitely missed America's comfort food. Four years was a long time and "I think I'm turning Japanese, I really think so" was becoming too true. Darker temptations were knocking at my door and I knew it was time to go.

That "dark road" included such perks as being paid to be a customer in one of Nagoya's newest night clubs called *Heaven*. It was located in the middle of Sakae, Nagoya's main party district. They agreed to pay me ¥200,000 yen ($1,700) a month to be a customer 3 nights a week. They wanted to have a gaijin presence there because it could make the club seem trendy, more international. I had written a few articles for a local magazine called The Alien which was founded by an English teacher named Carter Witt and later joined by Neil Gorscadden. A satirical look at living in Japan from a gaijin's point of view. It started in Nagoya around the time I arrived and I think it eventually expanded across all of Japan. It was a go-to magazine for foreigners to get a laugh, but also to see what was going on. I had so many out-of-the-box experiences in Japan.

It was hard to leave Japan, but it was time. I was nearing 30 years old. I loved and still do love Japan. It gave me experiences that have led me to the life I'm living now. I still try to go back to Japan every year. I asked my wife Jill to marry me in Kyoto. I will always have strong roots there. "What would I do next?' was the big question on my mind. It was time to say "Sayonara" to Japan but I knew it was really "Ja-ne!" meaning "I'll see you later!"

Hurrah for Hollywood

CHAPTER SEVEN

•

"Not knowing when the dawn will come, I open every door."
—Emily Dickinson

"There is nowhere to go but everywhere."
—Jack Kerouac

FORTUNE WAS still shining on me, but I know this can be fickle. I couldn't get cocky or complacent. We are only as good as our willingness to keep reaching for the stars. I can't say I was headed to Hollywood to be a star, but I was looking to keep the adventure rolling. I was leaving Japan, so why not try my luck in Hollywood? I already had done some outlandish things that I had no business succeeding at so I was going West. *Maybe you are a big fish in your small pond, but unless you dive into the biggest seas you'll never know how big or far you can go.* People like Madonna or Brad Pitt tested their limits on the biggest stage. I believe in that concept all too well. Go big or go home.

I had only been to California one time a year ago when I was exploring trade schools for Exiv in Japan. Honestly, like most people, my first impression was not great. The terrible traffic is a real thing and the beaches aren't the attraction. Growing up, going down to St. Petersburg, Florida or Fort Lauderdale for spring break was what I thought of when I'm headed to an ocean. Sure you'll see beautiful palm trees and you're gonna assume LA has decent weather. Well truthfully, the weather can be suspect depending on where you live. It's very hit or miss. My favorite meteorologist is Dallas Raines, the local celebrity weatherman, who will tell you what to expect all over Southern California. In most cities you get one weather report, but not in Los Angeles. In one forecast you see San Fernando Valley, Santa Monica, Long Beach, Burbank, Hollywood.... and the differences are crazy. In Marina del Rey it might be the high of 71° while The

Valley may hit 96°. Each area is like it's own state. But weather and traffic aside, I learned to really love LA and I know complaining about the weather is nuts when you don't need to own gloves or a snow shovel. It never snows. I think I just expected LA to be warmer than it really is. But when SoCal gets into your system it grabs you by the balls and doesn't let go. There is always "the chance" when you leave your house that something magical will happen. That you'll get discovered or you'll sit next to Michael Keaton having coffee or Fabio sipping a margarita. Both of these happened to me. I have tons of stories, man I have tons of stories, and that is what living in LA brings to you, life stories.

My road to LA took a long time to get there. I'm speaking figuratively, but literally it's a far drive from Indiana. If you drive straight through it's about 33 hours. My grandmother had gotten too old to drive her 1982 Oldsmobile Omega Brougham 2 Door Coupe. It was in spectacular condition. I think Brougham meant the roof was two toned with the back *1/3* being padded with vinyl that resembled brown leather. Brougham came from an old term where the driver of a four wheeled carriage sat in front separated from the back passengers. I guess the thought on the Olds Omega was the vinyl top gave a crude nod to that concept? The car was a light brownish yellow and the vinyl top was dark brown. It had spoked wheels and the interior would please a Victorian prostitute with it's plush cloth (almost Terry Clothy). I know, "Clothy" is not a word but this car was more than a car. It was the least cool thing a young man could ever drive. I say young, but on my way to Hollywood I stopped in Las Vegas and turned 30 years old. Damn, my 20s were gone just like that. I felt so young. I spent the 2nd half of my 20's in Japan so to me it felt like time had stopped. I didn't feel aged. I was very appreciative to have this car for free. To drive out to California to chase a dream. It was reliable, well maintained, but it was just so square. It was the least glamorous car in the world but I knew I had to take advantage of this gift. It was embarrassing, that's for sure. The "glass 1/2 full" optimist in me did like the plush clothy seats. They were so soft and naturally collected sweat. The AC was strong and I never worried about anyone thinking I had any money. One look at this Omega and you'd think social security check. It almost had a pimp quality to it with the spoked wheels, *1/3* vinyl top and plush seats, but the stubby body and overall ugliness didn't make that a possibility. Pimp cars need to be long and lumbering. This car just didn't make sense. One of my new LA friends always teased me, "Park in the handicapped man, they'd never tow this grandma car," as we circled around the Ralph's grocery store parking lot. He was probably right.

What I didn't mention earlier was that I had convinced my best friend, Bill Niemann, to come live in Nagoya Japan with me. I was having the time of my life. Bill had graduated from North Carolina Greensboro (UNCG) with a degree in hospitality. He was kicking around ideas and I was selling him hard on Japan. I had asked around and found him a job teaching English in Nagoya not too far away from me and he'd get his own house to live in. The money was decent and he could do some side gigs like me to pad his wallet. I learned a lesson having Bill come over. One man's experience might not be another one's. He didn't have the support I did when I landed in Japan with AEON. He couldn't speak a lick of Japanese and I think he felt like a fish out of water. I could tell he wasn't enjoying the experience like I was. Another lesson I kind of knew, but now fully endorse is "Don't give up too soon" in a new environment. I've traveled a lot and have put down roots in new cities several times. My advice is to GIVE IT THREE MONTHS before you throw the towel in. It takes time to adjust. You miss the normalcy of routines and friends. It takes time for your equilibrium to balance. Opposing forces are battling each other. Your old ways are stronger at first. They are comparing, unfairly, the way it used to be. The new things you are experiencing start to balance out. You reach a serenity, a stability and a calm feeling like you belong. Three months after breaking up, three months on a new job, three months working out - it becomes your new norm. I took Bill everywhere. We went to all my favorite clubs, danced on the bar at Canal Street while Pete laughed, we ate amazing ramen, went sight-seeing and he had girls falling all over him too. The problem was, Bill decided after only 6 weeks that he wanted out, he was homesick. He put in his notice at his company and booked a flight back home again to Indiana. He would leave in about 6 weeks. As his THIRD MONTH approached, with only a week or two away from leaving, he started to really enjoy Japan. I think he pulled the trigger a little too early. Bill is an amazing talent and has a deep voice like Don LaFontaine. He should be a VO star. He did hit a level of fame several years later, after leaving Japan, as the head radio personality on the morning show Y101.9 FM in Lufkin, Texas. I know his first month or so in Japan Bill felt constricted, his big personality could not shine fully because of the language barrier. I understand that. He's the kind of guy who makes friends with everyone he meets and that's tough in a foreign country. He and I talk about the "good ol' days" in Japan now and I think he knows he left a bit too early but that was his path.

I had Nemo (nickname) again back with me *ON MY NEWEST PATH* to Los Angeles. Bill and I were going to drive my grandma's car across country. While in Japan I reached out to my 2nd cousin, on my mom's side, Sue Nelson. I always grew up calling her Susie, but I think along the way now she prefers Sue. Our mom's were good friends at one point in their lives. I knew her parents Grace & Clyde pretty well. Sue grew up racing go-karts along with her brothers. She doesn't look like a tomboy, which may be one of her superpowers, you wouldn't expect by looking at her that she's done some ballsy things. When I called her I knew she was chasing the acting dream in LA. She has legit talent. I was coming in as a hack, but Sue had an agent, she was going on auditions and had booked a guest spot on ER during it's height. We knew each other from family get-togethers, but with her living in Tucson, AZ and me in Indiana, we were not super close. I told her what I had been up to in Japan and that I was contemplating moving out to Los Angeles. Sue was absolutely the best. She more than welcomed me. She knew the ropes and told me I could stay with her when I first got there, and if things went well, maybe we would get an apartment together later on down the road.

Bill and I took the southern route west. We stopped many places along the way but especially enjoyed the Grand Canyon, Sedona and celebrating my 30th b-day in Las Vegas. We rolled in to West Hollywood and quickly learned why they call it "Boy's Town". It was the very end of June and the annual Gay Pride Parade was in full bloom just a few blocks from Sue's apartment. It was a bit of a culture shock but I loved it. Changes in latitude, changes in attitude.

To add to the excitement, that very first night there was a large earthquake. I had experienced a few big ones in Nagoya over my 4 years, but this one caught me by surprise. The blinds were swaying. It was an attention getter. I was ready to make the earth move myself!

Sue's place was a perfect landing spot, but we both quickly agreed we needed to find a two bedroom apartment. We found The Summit Apartments at LaBrea & Franklin about a block from Mann's Chinese Theatre a couple days later. It was an awesome apartment with two large bedrooms on opposite wings and a large patio courtyard covered with greenery. We put a big patio table outside and it became our hangout spot. It was better than I ever could have expected. The prices back then weren't so crazy high. A struggling actor could still afford to "try and make it" and not live like a pauper in 1994. I think we paid $1,250 - so $625 each. That was actually considered expensive, but this place was a bit of a splurge. It included 2 parking spaces too! I don't know how someone can move to Los Angeles now (2024) without already having quite a bit of money. Are we getting the best actors or the richest ones? LA can chew you up and spit you out. Luckily for me, I was so naive that it played totally in my favor. I didn't know the rules and I didn't care.

Sadly, I bid Bill farewell. Sue and I got settled in The Summit. We had a rooftop pool that overlooked the Hollywood Hills. It felt swanky. Sue was a lot of fun to live with. She was motivated, smart and talented. I was wowed by her creativity. She was always up to something. She had her own cable access show that was super smart. Sue was blonde and bubbly and would best be described at that time as a young Goldie Hawn or Bernadette Peters. I had just turned 30, so I'm thinking she must have been about 26 in 1994. I mentioned she was on "ER" yes, the show with George Clooney, but she also would get TV credits that include: "The Office", "According To Jim", "Las Vegas" and "The King of Queens." She hadn't booked any of these yet, but it seemed obvious to me that she would sooner or later do even greater things. I was lucky to have her as my wingman.

That first night in LA, Sue had gone out and left Bill and I at her place to rest. I saw a paper on Sue's coffee table called *Backstage West*. It was a weekly trade paper similar to the New York-based Back Stage but with a focus on the West Coast acting community and casting opportunities based in California. Backstage West had just launched a few months before I arrived. I flipped through it and saw a casting for "The Falcon Cable Guy" with an address to send a headshot. All I had for a headshot was a whacky modeling card that I had used in Japan that was an odd size of 8.5"x 6". I had the pictures taken a year earlier while home on vacation by Pamela Mougin. Pamela became my go to person for all my headshots. She was a true force of talent right out of Indianapolis and later worked in London, LA and

Denver. She photographed Eddie Murphy, Donald Trump and reached international fame. I met her when she was just 19 and I was 22. She had already developed a reputation for being a genius with a camera in her hand. Like me, she didn't have a preconceived notion of what a Hollywood headshot was supposed to look like, so we just did what felt interesting. I give her a lot of credit for getting people wanting to see me. Getting in front of an agent or casting director is half the battle. I think surrounding yourself with talent can be a big part of success. I had Sue as my home motivator and was armed with Pamela's unique eye of me.

"I saw this ad in Backstage West," I said to Sue the next afternoon. "It's for a series of commercials for the Falcon Cable Guy," I mused.

"Most of that stuff is non-union. Do you have a headshot?" Sue asked. I handed her my odd model card. The front was a close-up of my face, the back had four photos (suit, topless, jumping and goofing). "You can't submit this, it's a comp card," she said. "This isn't an acting headshot. It needs to be 3/4 shot," she explained. Meaning the new Hollywood "in" photos that casting directors want to see are no longer just face shots. They wanted a bit of the body too, the photo should start at mid-thigh and end above the head. They can call them headshots but they were a lot more than a pretty face.

I shrugged, "It pays pretty well. It's four commercials."

"I'm not telling you not to try," Sue said with a hint of doubtfulness. I understood where she was coming from. As you can tell from my college interview resume and cover letter story, I'm into looking professional, but something about being in Hollywood made me feel that not being a cog in a machine might be a better way to go. I was hearing that I needed to taking acting classes, put on a showcase, invite agents, just a whole set of rules that I didn't want to follow. I did audit the Beverly Hills Playhouse and one other acting class but it didn't float my boat. I saw so many talented actors and I'd ask them if they had an agent. "I'm doing really great work and I feel maybe in a year I can try to go out on auditions" most of them were telling me. A YEAR? You've been here for three years and you haven't even tried to get an agent yet? I was thinking about getting an agent the first week I was there. That's why I came to LA.

I mailed my whackadoodle comp card, along with a cover letter, to whatever production company was doing the auditions for the Northwestern part of the US Cable Guy. A few days letter I got a call. I had my FIRST AUDITION in LA and I hadn't even been there a week yet. Other than trying out for IU Cheerleader, this would be the first audition in my life. I was excited but nervous. I had killed it in Japan. I was oozing with confidence, but this would be the first time that my acting chops would be tested against my fellow American-jin. The Spanish expression *mano-a-mano* means "hand-to-hand" combat. I couldn't fall back on being special simply because I was a foreigner. I really felt like this was going to be my litmus test. Before I could go on my first audition I had to figure out how to get there in my grandma's Oldsmobile Omega. Sue told me I had to buy:

The Thomas Guide

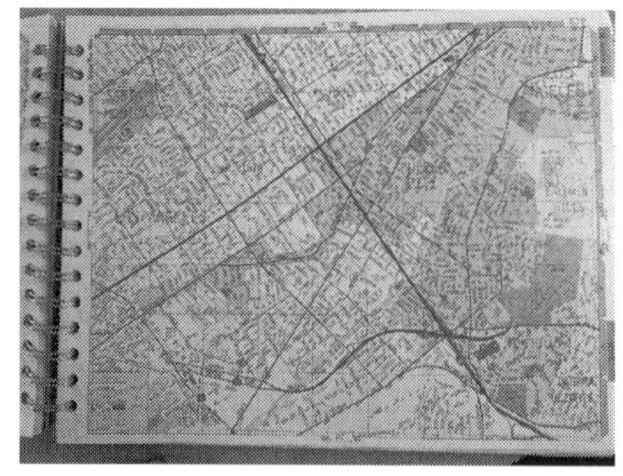

I'm including a picture of mine from 1994 because to any person who lived in LA before cell phones, they knew this was the holy grail of must have treasures. It was the only way you knew how to get anywhere. I read that the company started in 1915 and by the time I needed directions this was my most valuable tool. Everybody had one in their car. My method was to find the address I wanted to go to on this 15 ring binder and then use a highlighter to mark my path. I would also have a sticky notepad where I wrote out the street names and whether to turn L or R. People complain now about looking at your phone while you're driving, well that is nothing compared to flipping through your Thomas Guide trying to figure out your next turn. Even the Angelenos: a native Los Angeles, Californian, had to use maps. Every actor, you ever wanted to meet from that time period, has a Thomas Guide story. It was part of the fabric of survival.

My Falcon Cable Guy audition was in a production office near Santa Monica. Back then I didn't know much about SM because I was living up in Hollywood. All I knew was that I needed to drive down LaBrea to the 10W and get off on Lincoln Blvd. From there I don't remember exactly where I went but it was near Abbott Kinney Blvd. I do want to quote a writer I admire very much. I read his book on how to write a book, so there you go. Stephen King said,

"When it comes to the past, everyone writes fiction"

This is true for my book too obviously because no-one can remember an exact conversation, well except what Jesus said 2,000 years ago. Those were his exact words verbatim. But there are many stories I tell that are my balls & strikes, as I call them. They are how my memory connects and remembers the past. So I found my first audition location. I went inside and there were rows of chairs along the left side of the wall and a small table with a sign-in sheet. I printed and signed my name and waited. While I was waiting, two more guys that more or less resembled me came in and placed their names below mine. After about 10 minutes a door opened, a guy (like me) exited and a woman about 35 picked up the audition sheet and said my name.

Once inside the room there were three people sitting behind a desk including the woman who just walked me in. I later learned this was not the norm for an audition but this was my first one so I was going with the flow. There was a man with a beard who was also in his thirties who seemed to be in charge. There wasn't any script in the waiting room. I was all smiles and trying to show my friendliness, although truthfully I was a bit nervous.

"So we really just want to get to know you. State your name, your phone number and then tell us a little about yourself," he said casually. He then motioned for the same girl who led me in to start recording. One of my strong points is talking about myself. Or as my mother told me, "You talk about yourself too much!" She once gave me great advice about dating. If a girl talks about herself all night she's going to tell her girlfriends she had the "best date ever." I used this womanly witchcraft enlightenment all the time when I was single. I would ask my dates so many questions with follow-up questions. My dad's great advice was, "Son, think of dating like a smorgasbord. Go up to the buffet and put a little bit of everything on your plate. Taste it all. See what you like the best," he'd laugh, then he'd get philosophical. "You'll like the girl who brings out the part of yourself that you like the best," he'd explain. "With some women you might be the athletic couple, some the arts, the theater, others you may have great sex, spit on and choke each other..." he'd say. "Others may drive you crazy and you like that, some are money motivated, romantic, intellectual, you get what I mean," dad would proclaim. "Don't fill up on any one thing at the buffet until you know what you want a lot more of." The "spit & choke" thing is what I always remember. It seemed out of left field for dad. My parents divorced when I was four, as I wrote earlier, maybe this was something on his list that would bring out what he liked about himself? The other thing, my parents were virgins when they got married so this was advice maybe dad wished he'd gotten. Play the field son!

I tell the three production people that I'm new in LA. Had been in town only a week. That I had just come back from living in Japan. One of them asked me to say something in Japanese. I laid out all my entertainment jobs in Japan. Told them I was a Big Ten Cheerleader. I rambled on about myself and then they asked me a few follow up questions and that was it. The next day they called me for a "callback" which was a new word in my life that I wanted to hear again & again. At the callback there were only two of us. I had a 50/50 chance. They really didn't seem to know how to run the audition if I'm going to be frank. Later I learned there was a big difference between SAG and non-SAG auditions. They told me on set that they just wanted to get to know the future Falcon Cable Guy's personality and see if they liked him. Likability is a big factor in getting commercials. When I was called into the room again, we had general chit-chat. There were two chairs. They said that they wanted me to do some improv. They gave me the scenario of a girl I was dating, but not necessarily serious with, who had asked me to feed her dog while she was away on vacation. I was supposed to sit in the chair and pretend I'm driving. I'm picking her up at the airport. As she gets in the car she will ask about her doggy. I had completely forgotten to feed him.

Wow, this was fun. A girl I had not seen yet came into the audition room. I had my hands up like I was driving a car. "How was Hawaii?" I asked. Then her and I went on this wild ride of emotions. I had to tell her I had forgotten to feed her dog. He had most likely died a horrible death of starvation in her apartment. It actually took a serious turn. We both played it out as if it actually happened. There was no comedy. Finally the bearded guy, who I later learned was the director, stopped the scene. I left the room and I guess they did another, completely different scenario, with the other guy they called back. I could kind of hear his audition which is always fascinating. He came out and they asked me back in. They were very candid.

"We like you both," and then the third girl, not the one that was bringing us in & out, but the one that had been sort of quiet sitting next to the director on his left, my right, asked, "Tell us a joke!" I froze for a moment racing through the small catalog of jokes in my mind. I looked at her in silence and put out my hand and wiggled my index finger, motioning for her to move around the table to me. She looked a bit surprised, but after a moment, I wiggled my finger again and she stood up and started around the table towards me. I then threw up my hand in the universal STOP signal.

"That's far enough," I said. "I just wanted to see if I could make you come with my finger." The look on her face was priceless. It was a risky move. "I told you, he's our man!" she proclaimed laughing.

Needless to say, I did four commercials for Falcon Cable and it was a great experience. I wore a blue uniform with a name tag and I drove a van. The spots were all comedic situations where I would be interacting with Falcon customers. They'd bake me cookies. I hear that I was well known in the upper Northwest. They paid me $8,000, which was a lot of money - it would pay my rent for over a year! I have a copy of those commercials somewhere. That was a great start in Hollywood. Now I needed to set my sights on getting an agent.

Comp Card

Upper Left Suit Shot

The "Howe to Make It" *in Hollywood*

CHAPTER EIGHT

•

"May the Force be with you."
—Star Wars, 1977

THE CONCEPT of trying to "make it" in the entertainment field always bothered me. You really do need an outside "force" they say "a lucky break" someone in an upper position in the area of your dreams, to see something in you, to give you a chance. If you study to be a doctor you become a doctor. I've seen first hand that talent alone does not mean you're going to be a success in music, acting, writing, painting, dancing - basically in any of the arts. This always makes the arts elusive, it's like a moth to the flame. It can be painful and degrading to chase dreams at times. You have to be driven. You need thick skin. You also need to be realistic and level-headed, but the exhilaration of performing makes you forget all the hardships! The feeling of being chosen above all others for a part is addicting. I had a devil on one shoulder and an angel on the other, both pulling at me. "You only live once," one would plead. "You're throwing your life away at 30, you have a college education for Christ's sake," the logical dark side would counter. It's a tug-o-war that goes on & on. The phrase "Make It" is also vague. Do you have to be Brad Pitt to be considered "made"? Is surviving for years in a tough field "making it"? I suppose this idea of "Making It" rests in one's own mind. Now, one thing on my own mind was money. I always calculated how much I had and how long it would last me. I NEVER wanted my tank to be empty before I made a move to refill it. Probably out of guilt and not wanting to look irresponsible. I was on easy street with US Steel. I had gotten off the train track of corporate America. I definitely had doubts and pondered my future. Could I really make a living out in LA?

You may be wondering why I seemed to be stretching the almighty dollar. Why was I so thrilled to get my grandma's car? Happy as a lark to book the Falcon Cable Guy gig for $8K? It's true I did have money, but not as much as you'd think. The same reason I was able to pick-up the Varsity Villa Condos in Bloomington, IN during college was the same reason that I didn't make much when I sold them. Remember, I bought them for almost nothing. I assumed the seller's loans. They hadn't owned them very long before their sweet little kiddo was graduating from college, so I got them before any equity had built up. My 5 condos had not appreciated much after only 5 years either. I was having difficulty managing from afar. I had help, but the college kids were difficult to control. That's a nice way to say they can be destructive. I paid my cousin Susan Blackwell 20% of the total rent to do all the dirty work. I could sense she was over it too. The monthly income was decent, but my expenses would fluctuate trying to keep up with maintenance and paying Susan. I was making about $1,400 a month which was great but the pressure to sell and get away from this headache was too much. After the dust settled I walked away with $35,000 and quickly put that money along with $25,000 that I had been saving from Japan, into a house in Broad Ripple, Indiana. The house was $115,000 but I would only have a mortgage for $55,000. The mortgage payment was super low, like $375 a month but the drawback was I could only rent it for $850. I had most of my money tied up in that house. When I headed out to LA I had $7,000 so landing that non-union gig doubled my savings. Plus, I decided to park cars at the Indy 500, like I did every year, and I flew back home after only 2 months in LA to earn another $1,000 after paying for my flight. I was very cautious with my monthly expenses and always wanted to have a job so I wouldn't have to dip into my savings. Seeing money in the bank is security.

Money doesn't buy happiness but it provides the means to find it.

I kinda do that with my frequent flier miles now. I earn them and earn them and it kills me to use them. It's a funny mental block. I collect them to use them but then I horde my miles. I just like seeing big numbers in my checking, savings, stocks and frequent flier accounts. I still check all my accounts daily.

I think weaving your way through Hollywood is a series of steps and/or accomplishments. You start out in the bush leagues and you slowly move up the ladder. Better headshots, ,better agents, non-union to SAG, better commercials, better auditions, better opportunities. Better, better, better, but IT ALL STARTS WITH GETTING AN AGENT!

STEP ONE: "GET AN AGENT"

As I said earlier, right off the bat I decided I was going to try to get an agent. Landing the cable guy gig gave me confidence. Japan gave me confidence too. I didn't come out to LA to go to acting school. I came out to LA to dip my toes into the biggest pond and see if I could make a ripple. I had heard about Smart Girl Productions. She was a one woman operation that would help aspiring actors and writers make their pitch to agents and/or production companies. I made an appointment with Melody Jackson, the "Smart Girl", and quickly learned she was also from Indiana. We hit it off and I felt lucky that I had found her. She looked like Pat Benatar to me. She had short hair and a rocker physique. Melody was direct and confident. She definitely was all business. Her apartment was in Hollywood very close to mine, so close that I actually walked over for my appointment to meet her. Her livingroom was her office, but I still felt fairly certain she lived there too. She had a proper desk that was set up to do business. She interviewed me more than I interviewed her. I told her all my modeling and brief acting experience, that I just landed a 4 commercial deal here in LA and that I wanted to get an agent. I handed her my "Comp Card" and a resume that I had put together. There were a few places on it where I stretched the truth just a bit but for the most part everything was true. I felt reassured that coming to her was the right decision. She explained to me how everything worked and what she could do for me.

Shaking my comp card, "You know this isn't going to fly?" she laughed. "You're going to need a proper headshot." She liked one of the photos on my comp card, where I was wearing a suit. Pamela Mougin had taken that a little less than a year earlier in Indianapolis. I still looked like that I guess, is what I'm trying to say, because Melody didn't make any kind of comment that I looked younger because she would have. This would be my first Hollywood headshot! I needed it to be (8"x10") she instructed me. Smart Girl Productions would deliver to me 50 fresh new resumes all properly formatted as well as 50 cover letters with envelopes to match. She had the list of all the agents at all the agencies, along with their addresses. Each cover letter would be addressed personally to that agent, obviously it would be a form letter with just the contact info swapped out, and the envelopes would also be labeled. All of this really appealed to me. It reminded me of how I got my interviews in college. Melody explained she had A, B, C and D agent contact info. The A agents (THE BEST) were the likes of William Morris Agency, Creative Artists Agency, International Creative Management, United Talent Agency - she told me I'd have no chance at getting into any of these A list agents. For shits and giggles I asked her to throw in 3 of them (WMA, CAA and ICM) on my list of 50 which she laughed and agreed to. I'd have 3 (A), 15 (B), 22 (C), and 10 (D) agents. One of Melody's gifts is how she wrote my cover letter. It was hip & casual but gave me a mystic of talent with a fun demeanor. She nailed my personality. I think her fee was about $200 but I can't quite remember exactly what she charged back then. Whatever the price was it felt a bit expensive, but looking back now it was priceless. Smart Girl Productions charging that higher rate did that thing in your brain where you felt more powerful to be on her team. Made me feel special. I was investing in myself and my future. On my plus side I had Pamela's photo, Sue's energy and now Melody Jackson's marketing skills. I was excited to mail out my packets and see what energy the universe would spit back at me. It would take Melody about a week and all I needed to do was to get my headshots ready.

I asked Pamela Mougin to please send me the negatives ASAP so I could take them to the place everyone in LA takes their headshots to be mass produced. Although I only needed 50 for my mailer I hoped I'd need oodles more for auditions. I was being optimistic of course. Pamela wasn't responding as fast as I wanted her to and Melody had my marketing packet ready. I went to pick them up and it was magical. She gave me the beautifully printed cover letter. I only needed to sign them. I got 50 large 8.5"x11" white envelopes and the labels printed on a sheet that I would need to peel and place on them. I also got professional return labels. "Baby, you are so money and you don't even know it," Vince Vaughn said in Swingers in 1996. That movie rocked us "wanna-be actors" in LA at the time. It was so spot on. I loved it. Although Trent Walker did not utter those words, that lingo was out there in 1994 and I felt it, "I was so money" and I KNEW it when I walked out of Smart Girl Productions. I even thought that I might be that one in a million that got call from an A agent (aka - an agency who represents the likes of Tom Cruise). It's funny thinking back to that time and realizing I really DID think that. I took my papers of gold back to The Summit apartment and showed Sue (Susie). Still hard to call her Suc. I could tell she was not totally sold on my scheme. Was it a scheme? Not really, I just now googled "scheme" and it means: *putting a particular idea into effect.* I was definitely doing that but scheme doesn't always have to have a negative vibe.

Sue in 1998 was often eating at Chin Chin's on Sunset. It was a restaurant in Beverly Hills that was super famous for it's Chinese Chicken Salad. I worked there for a New York minute, but that's a different story. She ran into Jon Favreau (Swingers) and had a brief meet & greet with him. She saw how much he liked their Chinese fortune cookies. Half of them were dipped in either white or dark chocolate. They were decadent. She bought a dozen, half & half on the chocolate, and carefully pulled out the fortunes and inserted her own fortunes: "Today is your lucky day, Sue Nelson, actress extraordinaire wants to be in your next movie" or something clever like that. She made 12 different fortunes. She had them delivered to his production office. Nothing came of it but I loved her gumption. That was a move from my playbook. Quoting Swingers made me remember that story.

Anyway, back to my mailer. I was still waiting on getting my headshots from Pamela and it was eating me up inside. I was impatient and my creative juices were flowing on overdrive! I was out drinking a few days later and had this crazy idea of making my resume look like a TGIF menu. I already had Melody Jackson's beautifully produced resume waiting to be launched, but something inside of me said that I needed to do something different - something outlandish to make me stand out and bring attention to myself. The appetizers would be my commercial & print work. I had loads of appetizers because of Japan. However, my main course was skimpy. It was like the vegan section of most chain restaurants, non-existent or very few items. I had a few things from Japan that qualified as "Main Course" but I decided to stretch the truth a bit and added a couple of performances in plays that I had never actually done in order to look like a real thespian (remember it was 1994 and things couldn't be verified online like they can be today). Years later I heard a quote from Andy Dick that basically said in Hollywood, "Lie, Lie, Lie, and if you're lucky they might come true" and so I did tell a few little white lies. Desserts listed my skills. I wanted the whole back layout to look as if you were ordering from a menu. I had my comp cards from modeling and I could laminate those, create makeshift hinges, also laminate my "*resu-menu*" to give it the full TGIF affect. I think the only reason I was contemplating this, and then actually DOING it, was that I kept hearing warnings from other actors, "You'll get no calls. No one gets an agent from a mailer! You need to do a showcase," they said. I needed this or that on my resume. "You're wasting your money," I heard a lot of naysayers say and I guess I mostly believed them. But there's always that little voice in your mind "They are not me!" that "I am different" and so on. Your plane can be going down into the side of a mountain and in your mind you're thinking 'I'm going to survive this.' It's human nature to believe in yourself. The doubt -must have sunk in because I decided to go bold. I should have thanked my new acting friends for being negative (or realistic) because they made me do something outrageous.

I created the Resu-Menu and decided to go for broke. I didn't tell anyone I was trying this bold move. My mailer now had a Frankenstein design to it. The Smart Girl Productions presentation still looked, well - smart. My half of the mailer looked whacky, but I did a good job on making it look authentic. There is no doubt it was interesting. I thought if it didn't work, I at least had all the contact information for the agencies and I could re-submit a slightly different marketing plan that wasn't so outlandish in a few months. Once again, I decided to go big or go home. I had nothing to lose.

I finally got my headshots from Pamela printed, signed the cover letters, put all the labels where they belonged and stuffed everything (including *TGI Williamson* "Thank God It's Williamson") into the envelopes. I have to give some credit to Bill Niemann on calling myself "Williamson" instead of Will or Bill. I was thinking that the name Bill Howe was boring. It sparked no intrigue. "I'm just a Bill, just an ordinary Bill, sitting on Capitol Hill" was a song ringing through my mind from childhood Saturday morning cartoons. In Japan the Japanese called me William-san. It sounded a lot like Williamson. He suggested this and I was intrigued. I looked up William in a name thesaurus. William is a male given name of Germanic origin. It became very popular in the English language after the Roman conquest of England in 1066 and remained so throughout the Middle Ages and into the modern era. English variations include Will, Wills, Willy, Willie, Bill, and Billy along with the Irish form Liam. Scottish versions include Wull, Willie or Wullie and Williamson, as a boy's name, can be related to the Old German name William. The meaning of Williamson is "will helmet". There you have it, Williamson is actually an offshoot of William. I wasn't actually changing my name, I reasoned, I was just going with a different interpretation of it. I had already been Billy, Bill and Will. My grandfather was Willie. Now I would become Williamson.

So the mailer was mailed and I would officially launch Williamson Howe out into the world. It sounded ostentatious, which I didn't love, but maybe being a bit pretentious could get attention? It wasn't how I was, but I knew it was different than anyone else's name. Being unique can't be a bad thing, right?

Now it was time to wait for the phone to ring. I'd like to say my phone began ringing off the hook but that didn't happen - but it did ring. Six (6) agencies called asking to see me. Two of them were in the C category and the other four (4) were Ds. Obviously, I had hoped for one or two Bs and a few more Cs but I WAS NOT SHUT OUT. I had barely been in town a couple of months, my experience was minimal and yet I had meetings! I get a kick out of Hollywood because everyone talks about a "Meeting." I had a meeting with such and such, I have a meeting this week, I have a meeting next week, I had a meeting last week. I had a really great meeting - You rarely hear anything coming out of these "meetings" but they keep us all sane. They keep us feeling productive and busy.

I met with everyone who wanted to meet with me. The Ds were truly sketchy companies. They wanted money from me. I later convinced Melody to take one of the pushiest ones off her master list to save her future clients from the chance of being scammed. They wanted to charge me for their photographer to do my headshots. They had acting classes I needed to pay for. It felt like I was in a Holiday Inn conference room at a John Casablancas recruiting session, sans the 300lb moms dragging their beauty pageant daughters along to live the life they didn't. I did have one pleasant surprise on my list that I felt a kindred spirit to. *The Beverly Hecht Agency* (hooray! one of the C agencies!) had called and asked to see me commercially.

There's a big difference from getting a commercial agent and a theatrical agent. Hence to say, it's a lot harder to get a theatrical agent. Raf Dahlquist was the guy who called me. What I didn't know was that Teresa Dahlquist had purchased the Beverly Hecht Agency in 1993, less than a year before. Beverly Hecht had top clients back in the day like Sammy Davis Jr., Liberace, The Lennon Sisters, Debra Winger and now I was hoping to be part of their team. This was my most promising audition. Raf was somehow related to Teresa and he had come in to help her relaunch the brand. I don't think it was flourishing at that time. It felt like a start up when I walked in. Lots of energy, boxes laying around, shouting and phones ringing. Truthfully they seemed out of whack a bit, but I saw pure hustle. I remember Raf greeted me at the front desk. He looked like a larger than life leprechaun or someone Santa kicked out of the toy factory for being too big to be an elf. He was tall, barrel chested, with reddish hair and a scruffy beard. He was sweet but also looked like he could work as a long shoreman. I hope my memory of him is correct, but this is how I remember him. Nothing fancy, but he put off a great vibe.

"Hi, you called me in for an interview or to audition for commercial representation" I think I said.

Raf looks up at me during the chaos of the office, "What's your name?"

"Williamson Howe," I confidently said.

He smiles at me and goes into an office and comes back out standing in the doorway, "What the hell is this?" he laughed. He was holding my Resu-Menu and shaking it in his hand. I think I sputtered something about wanting to get his attention, and whatever I said in that moment, it worked! "Come on back," he said. I laid out my life to him, told him how "lady luck" had shined on me and said, "I promise, if you sign me I will make you money!"

Raf gave me sides for a commercial. "Sides" in acting is a small section of a script. For a commercial they probably aren't actually sides. It's the whole enchilada. I don't remember what it was for. I remember leaving the room, studying whatever I was to read and acting it out overtly. I was loud and unbashful. I think showing no signs of being nervous, "going for it" so to speak, played in my favor. The stars lined up for me. I landed The Beverly Hecht Agency. It was fate. They were willing to take a chance on me. They, themselves, were looking for a break, to dust off the cobwebs. I felt excited to be part of the new Beverly Hecht. Studio City was now where my agency was. It felt great to say I was with an agency. Someone believed in me. When Steve Martin's character in The Jerk found his name in the phone book he rejoiced, "I'm somebody now, I'm somebody!" Later they signed Shia LaBeouf when he was a little older than 10. He's got a good story to tell. I don't think he and I were ever with Hecht at the same time but I'm not sure. They handled a lot of kids so I may have met him. But going forward, I had an agent - mission accomplished!

STEP TWO: "Time to Prove Myself"

I had my headshots with my "Smart Girls" resume (not the TGIF Williamson one) stapled on the back and The Beverly Hecht Agency logo stamped on it. I was locked and loaded. Raf worked the phones and submitted me for commercials and I was getting callback after callback but hadn't booked anything yet. Raf was super supportive and told me that a call back was basically the same as getting the job. It meant I had talent. I had the right look, just not the look that particular client / director had in their mind at that moment, but he assured me it would come. In the meantime, I decided to join Central Casting. Central Casting is the King of Extras. I thought it would be cool to see behind the scenes. To be a background actor. One of my very first background gigs was for the show Melrose Place. The setting was in a posh country club up in the Hollywood Hills about an hour from Hollywood. They had given me a call time, directions, parking instructions and told me to wear a suit. I did not have designer anything back then, EXCEPT I did have an amazing Armani suit. It was freakin sweet. When I worked at Exiv in Nagoya one of the top executives took a liking to me. He had been a professional baseball player in his younger days. He was an awesome guy. One day he gave me this suit. It was gently used and it fit me like a glove. It was a rich beige color. Lingering over from my US Steel days I had a crisp white shirt, a maroon tie and very nice black shoes. Wearing this suit felt like Halloween for me now. It was definitely a costume at that time in my life.

I arrived at the country club. Us extras were herded together by the 2nd AD. She had a headset on and communicated with someone of importance quite often. They had all of us set up in a banquet room. There were just enough chairs for the 50 of us. Extras are an interesting bunch of people. There are quite a few lifers. They read their books and talked about the different experiences that they'd had on sets. There are a lot of great stories. I learned that the 2nd AD (assistant director) usually handles us. If you could be a featured extra you might be able to get a voucher. Two (2) vouchers and you could get your SAG (Screen Actor's Guild) card and be in the Union. If you got lines you might actually get "Taft-Hartlied" which is what people called it. It meant that the Taft-Hartley Act would require the production company to report that they hired you as a non-member. You would then not be allowed to do another union (SAG) job until you joined the Union. Joining SAG was the goal of nearly every actor I met. You'd have a few rebels out there that would boast they can get more non-union work, but if you wanted to make it in Hollywood you've got to become a SAG Member, period.

I noticed the 2nd AD was scrambling around. She looked like she had lost something important. She was talking via her headphones to someone in almost a slight panic. Another guy came into our banquet room. He was the 1st AD. There are so many positions on a movie set I had never heard of: Best Boys, Grip, Key Grip, 1st AC (Assistant Camera), 2nd AC, Gaffer, Line Producers... The 1st AD runs the whole set and is the liaison to the director, the big cheese. He's talking to his protégé 2nd AD and they are looking around the room. Maybe it was because this was my very first extra job, but I was paying close attention to their frantic gestures. I moved a bit closer to them. The 2nd AD then made an announcement to the room.

"Does anyone in here have any experience being a maître d?" she shouted.

"I do!" I quickly proclaimed, without missing a beat (or allowing anyone else to answer first). The 1st AD quickly looked me over. I, by far, had the best suit on in the house. Let's face it, a maître d's suit is half the battle.

"What does a maître d do?" the 1st AD asked me. Wow, this caught me off guard! I wasn't expecting a quiz. After all, I had never been a maître d, but it's common sense, right?

"They greet the guests with a smile, check their reservations - he's like a host," I surmised confidently. "Sometimes they walk the guest to the table and possibly oversee the wait staff."

"Come with me," he said. We stepped outside of the room. "Do you have any acting experience?"

"Yes, I've been in front of the camera many times."

"The director wants a maître'd to be in several scenes," he explained. "Are you in SAG?" "No," I reluctantly said.

"Okay, well you may have some lines, so follow me," he said as he turned toward the dining room. It was full of lights and there were power cords running all over the floor. There were train tracks for the camera to roll on. We walk up to a man looking through a small loop. "This is our director," he said. I'm sure he told me his name too but I don't remember. Gesturing to me, "This is our maître d."

"What's your name?" the director asked.

"Williamson Howe," I announced.

"Well, that's a maître d's name if I've ever heard one," he laughed. He didn't seem nearly as nervous about this small part as the 1st & 2nd AD's seemed to be and just like that, I was no longer in the stuffy banquet holding room! I was moved to another part of the country club that was more of a fancy lounge. There was a glorious craft services spread with the most amazing espresso machine I had ever seen. It looked like a copper steampunk engine but with the slight shape of a balloon from the 1800s. There was shrimp, gourmet cheese, fancy pastries and a chef that could make you something warm if you wanted standing in front of two burners. I felt like Charlie in Willy Wonka and the Chocolate Factory - I had just peeled open my chocolate bar and saw the elusive gold foil greeting me. "I've got a Golden Ticket" I was singing jubilantly in my head! So this was how the other half lived! One of the all-time great lines in a movie was from When Harry Met Sally, when Rob Reiner's actual mom said, "I'll have what she's having," as Meg Ryan (Sally) is faking an orgasm in a restaurant to impress Billy Crystal (Harry). I wanted what all these actors were having. Wow, what a way to live life.

Remember, I had been in Japan for the last 4 years. Melrose Place came out in 1992. I had never seen the show. I had no idea what it was about or who starred in it, but I knew it was a big deal. I was over at the fancy-dancy copper steampunker coffee maker and a cute little button of a girl comes over with pink slippers on. I figured she was an actress. She had tissue paper around her neck.

"This is quite the spread, this coffeemaker is ridiculous," I said making small talk.

"Are you in this scene today?" she asked.

"Yes, I'm the maître d," I confirmed. She didn't seem to have much reaction to that and before I could continue, the coffee guy ruined my moment with Heather Locklear. I didn't realize it was her then, but I've got to tell you, I did realize that she was smokin hot. It's amazing in life how you can go from the crowded, no air-conditioned banquet room (sweat box), to luxuriously munching on Chocolate Éclairs and Raspberry Macaroons while sipping the best coffee ever, talking to a beautiful woman. This was Hollywood. Anything really can happen in a heartbeat! I was like Cinderella and the glass slipper was placed on my foot. Grandma's Olds Omega, sitting in the parking lot, was still my reality, but it felt great to get this look into a crystal ball of what could be. It was motivating. I had an agent, I was getting really close to landing a commercial and now I was about to be Taft-Hartleied, SAG eligible baby! Things were moving fast for me.

My mom's phone began ringing. People I hadn't talked to in a long time were calling her to ask if their eyes were deceiving them.

"Was Billy Howe on Melrose Place last night?" they'd ask surprised.

Proudly mom would say, "Yes, that was him!"

"When did he go out to Hollywood? Last time I heard he was in Japan modeling." That whole sentence makes me laugh.

"He got the crazy idea of acting and went out there almost a year ago," she'd explain. Truthfully, I don't think mom thought I had a chance but to her credit she never discouraged me. After she passed away I found a sort of diary she kept of all our phone conversations. She logged all my auditions, my close calls and my wins. She had always been an odd bird that way. As kids, she'd call us into her bedroom, one by one, if me and my two sisters had been fighting. She would secretly record our explanations of what had happened from our own individual points of view. I think she studied them. She told me much later in life that us kids would say, "I didn't say that" or "Mom, you said - this or that" and she wanted proof she wasn't crazy when she knew we were wrong. I feel like her little diary on my Hollywood escapades was her way of tracking my truthfulness and also she had that business side to her that liked to take notes, in corporate America they're called minutes. They've been helpful in writing this book. As far as Melrose Place, I did get a couple of lines, broke up a cat fight on the dance floor and earned enough screen time that mom was getting calls.

The Beverly Hecht Agency wasn't submitting me for too many non-union jobs but I remember I told Raf that I had been Taft-Hartlied.

"You'll have to join SAG before you do a Union job, they'll make you," he explained.

"How much is it?"

"I'm not sure, you'll have to call them but it's probably close to $2,000." This was a big surprise for me. That's expensive.

Raf thought, "You might have lost some of those callbacks because you're non-SAG. It's a pain for the production company to go through the paperwork." This was news to me that I didn't know about.

"The good thing is that now we can submit you as SAG eligible," Raf proclaimed.

I had been out in LA for a little more than a year now. I had gotten a job at Yamashiro restaurant in Hollywood to help me not spend all the money I had in the bank. I'm going to tell you the Yamashiro story in the next chapter (its a good one), but I can't wait to tell you one of the TOP 5 STORIES of my life first. I had booked a few smaller gigs and knew I was getting close to getting a "big break" again.

I got a *callback* for a *Coors Light* commercial that would superimpose John Wayne and the Bonanza cast into it. This was new and exciting technology! I had my first audition for this commercial just off LaCienega somewhere near the Beverly Center, basically close to my apartment, although in LA it's never easy to get from point A to B. Thank you Thomas Guide maps! After stating my name and agent, normal protocol, the scene was for me to walk up to a table and say, "Excuse me, those are our beers." It was fast and easy. Wham-bam-thank-you-ma'am and I was out the door. The more you do auditions the more comfortable you become. I was super relaxed at this point.

On the day of my *Coors Light* "callback" I also had a *Bud Light* "callback" as well. What was going on with me and beer? Two callbacks in the same day, that was a first. The *Bud Light* was in the San Fernando Valley area at 9:35am and the *Coors Light* was in Venice Beach on Abbott Kinney at 11:15am. I don't remember the exact scenario of the Bud commercial but I remember that I thought I did really well. Now it was time to head to Venice Beach. It was just after 10am so I had an hour. I jump on the 101 to the 405. The traffic was hell that day. When you get on the 405 from the 101 you climb a long lumbering hill. It was bumper to bumper, starting and stopping. I'm looking at my watch and I'm starting to think I'm going to be late. I had my Thomas Guide splayed on my lap. I had never been to the Abbott Kinney area before and without this map I may as well be driving blind in the Indy 500. I was so pissed off in my car, cussing and flailing my arms about, mad at the world.

"Pressure is a privilege"
—Billie Jean King

This was the title of Billie Jean King's book with the tag line "Lessons I've Learned from Life and the Battle of the Sexes." Somewhere deep in my pissed off soul I knew I was privileged to get this callback. I was a damn lucky soul to be chasing these dreams and this is why I came out to LA. I actually remember getting in the far right lane and contemplated getting off on Sunset Blvd, but just then the traffic lightened a bit and I rolled onto the 10W, the next exit was Lincoln Blvd and I weaved my way down to Venice Beach. Of course, parking was a bitch but I finally got in the door late at 11:25am. I was frazzled. The chairs in the waiting room had only one guy (he looked like me) and two pretty blondes in their 20's sitting there. I found out the girls were actually 35 minutes early. I signed in, grabbed the "sides" to refresh my memory on the few lines I needed to recite and took a seat. Within a minute a fellow actor exited and the casting director assistant picked up the sign in clipboard and looked at me.

"You're late," he said.

"I know, I had a call back for Bud Light in The Valley. The 405 was a nightmare," I was babbling. I could tell he totally had sympathy for me. Anyone who has spent time in LA knows that anyone, at anytime can be late. The traffic is unpredictable. You can NOT plan for it.

Pointing - "He's last audition before they break for lunch, but let me see if I can get them to see you?" he said with a look of doubt on his face. He took the other guy in for his 11:30am call. As I'm wondering if I'm going to even get to audition, a delivery guy came in with a shitload of food and drinks. I thought, "How many people are in there?" The last guy, except me, came out of the interview room and smiled,

"Good luck!" I couldn't tell if he said it sincerely or more like "you poor bastard!" Soon I'd learn it was definitely the latter.

The catering guy went right in and I could hear them scattering the food among themselves, "Who got the Caesar Salad with chicken - blah blah blah." After a few minutes the assistant casting director came out.

"Let me see if they'll see you?" he meekly said. I could tell he was scared to ask. He left and came back and said they'd see me but that they were going to be eating.

"That's totally fine," I said, feeling I had nothing to lose at this point. I must say I went in there with a little internal anger. Not at them, but at the ordeal of getting there. I can relate to the Michael Douglas movie Falling Down. I don't know if you've seen this movie but it's about a man caught in traffic, his AC is broke, he's frustrated and he gets out of his car on the freeway and starts walking through LA. During his trek, loads and loads of negative things push him to the brink. The movie should have been titled "Breakdown". I had this tinge of foreboding in my gut. I felt carefree too, with a bit of an "I don't give a shit" attitude as I walked into the audition room. I might be sounding like I was a tough guy but I was actually only feeling this way inside. I was still the nice, Midwestern boy outwardly and they had no idea I was feeling extra loose. There were 6 people munching away: casting director, 2 ad agents, Coors rep and the director. The assistant casting director introduced me, "This is Williamson Howe," he said. I didn't know who he was at this point in time, but a very tall man, with mangy long shocks of gray hair and a gruff voice barked at me.

"What kind of fucking name is Williamson?" he sounded angry. This man was intimidating. He could play a great Frankenstein or a mad composer from the 16th century. I later heard his bloodline might be Ukrainian, but he was in fact born in Pittsburgh, but he called it America's Liverpool. More about Joe Pytka later because I didn't know who he was yet.

"Well, Williamson comes from...," he cut me off.

"Aren't you nervous having all of us stare at you?" he asked oddly. I thought that was a weird question to ask an actor. We live for that, right? Besides, they were all chewing away.

"No, not really. I lived in Japan for 4 years and people stared at me constantly, everyday," I said nonchalantly.

"You lived in Japan for 4 years? You like to fuck Japanese girls, don't you?" he said, staring at me. Everyone had been eating, hardly looking at me. I think they didn't want to look at me as he spoke to me like that. For some people that could be awkward or embarrassing, but not me. I shot it right back at him.

"Yeah, I fucked one last night and I fucked her good." Now, everyone stopped eating and looked at me. I had everyone's attention including Joe Pytka's.

"Where are you from?" he asked, now interested in me.

"I'm from Speedway Indiana," I responded. I had no idea where this was going.

"Speedway? You're a fucking Sparkplug?"

"Yes I am," I said proudly. Sparkplug was the mascot for my High

School. Not everyone knows that so this guy must have spent some time in Indy I was thinking.

"Did you play basketball for the Sparkplugs?" he was baiting me.

"Yes I did, two year varsity starter," I said, but actually I only started full time varsity my senior year. There were a lot of good players in the class of 1983.

Joe Pytka peppered me with some more outrageous questions. I couldn't tell if he liked me, hated me or just enjoyed harassing people.

"You know, you're interesting enough but you're not right for this commercial. Get the hell out of here," he said while biting into his Stromboli, waving me off. This guy loves Primanti Brothers, for sure.

"Ok, well thank you for the callback. I really appreciate it," I said sincerely. I was not being sarcastic. I knew I had taken a chance by saying I "fucked a Japanese girl last night", but I was following his lead. I didn't want this casting director to blackball me or tell my agent I was rude. I politely left and started back up to Hollywood in pre-rush hour late morning traffic. There's always traffic but it's broken down into minute segments. It all sucks! You plan your day around driving, or not driving, certain roads at certain times.

Raf called me about 3pm to tell me I was "on avail" for the Bud Light commercial (my first audition of that day).

"What is avail?" I asked him.

Raf explained excitedly, "They want to confirm your availability to work on a specific day or date range. This doesn't mean you have the job but it's probably you or another person or two and they want to make sure you're available."

"That's great," I said. "I thought I did really good." I was standing up in my apartment pacing around like a panther. I was pumped. Then Raf dropped the bomb.

"But you're "on hold" for the Coors Light commercial too," he smirked. "Hold means you're definitely someone's top choice. It's basically the same thing as 'on avail' but I think it's a little better. I talked to Bud Light earlier and told them you're available, but when the casting director called for Coors Light I told him you're currently 'on avail' those same dates for Bud Light." I'm actually not sure Raf told them the other product I was "on avail" for, but knowing Raf, it seemed like something he would do. Battle of the beers is always a good thing.`

The next day Raf called and said Bud Light released me from "avail" meaning I did not get it. I was bummed. So close again! Coors Light knew I was not officially booked with Bud yet. Raf called to let them know I was officially available. I went to the gym and my pager went off. In the mid-90's technology advances were making life better. Everyone had pagers or beepers, some of them even scrolled messages depending on how much you were willing to spend monthly. A few people had car phones but they were seriously expensive. I found a phone booth and called Raf. He had great news.

I BOOKED MY FIRST NATIONAL COMMERCIAL

This was a big deal. I could not believe it. I told Raf that I was actually kicked out of the audition! They didn't even have me read the lines. Life has some crazy twists & turns. I learned that the director was Joe Pytka. He later directed Space Jam with Michael Jordan. This commercial would be a full minute long and premiere on the season finale of Seinfeld, which was the #1 show in the country. 35M+ people would be watching. I was the star of this commercial with John Wayne and the Bonanza cast. Me, John, Hoss, Little Joe, Adam and Ben all together on the same screen!

Raf (Beverly Hecht Agency) called with my schedule. They were shooting in Culver City Studios. I was needed for two days. Raf told me that under no circumstances was I to play basketball with Joe

Pytka. Do you remember the Field of Dreams commercial where the dad comes walking out of the corn crop asking for a Pepsi? Well, I was told that the actor playing his son cried on the set. Coincidentally, I was told he was from Indiana too. The urban legend is that he played basketball with Pytka and things didn't go well. I was under strict orders, no basketball. Remember, he asked me if I played.

If you see the commercial, which you can find on YouTube by Googling "Coors Light and John Wayne", you'll see an amazing bar. That entire set was built inside one of those large studio hangers. It was impressive. Every detail was perfect. There were at least 50 extras. As I'm escorted to my trailer I see a basketball goal setup just outside the 40' sliding doors. I meet the two bad guys who will steal my beer. These guys were perfect casting. They looked scary but in all actuality were anything but scary. They had both worked with Pytka before. We were standing around talking and the 6'5" director comes up to us and tells us not to rehearse our lines and not to get too chummy. I doubt he used that word, but it was something like that. He wanted whatever fear or reaction we have to be natural, not overly practiced. Let it be on film.

I'm called to the set for my first big time scene. I'm nervous. All the extras are staring at me. They all want my job. I know they felt envious because I had felt that way when I was doing Central Casting. This crew was big enough to shoot Braveheart. Lighting was everywhere, a wheeled dolly on tracks was used to smoothly move the camera along the bar. There were sound people, a fog machine to emulate smoking and Pytka was using jargon I wasn't sure the meaning of. The 1st AD also was calling out things. I was faking it and praying I make it. I pretended this was all old hat to me, but in reality my heart was pounding out of my chest. Imposter syndrome was a huge spotlight shining on me with 10,000 points of light. I felt like I had gotten myself in over my head. I was trying to remind myself that I did that Yamaha Piano show in Japan feeling the same way and I ended up killing it - hey, at least this was in English!

The two bad guys come strutting in. They were perfect. I was studying what the 1st AD and Pytka were saying to them. The lingo of when I'm supposed to make my move was all I was worried about. On my very first take....

"Roll camera, roll sound, background..." and I think I may have heard "Speed" too but I'm not sure. The scene number was called out, "Take One" and a clapperboard was slapped down in front of the camera as I walked up behind the bad guys who had taken John Wayne and I's beers.

"Excuse me, those beers are ours," I said pointing my finger at the beers.

"CUT!" a deep female voice said from far across the room. She came walking towards me. Pytka was just a couple of feet away. "The line is 'Excuse me, those are our beers' not those beers are ours," she explained. She had a script in her hands, glasses hanging off her nose.

"You got the fucking line wrong on the first take," he yelled out. I was embarrassed.

We did a few more takes and Pytka just seemed unhappy with me. He gestured to the room of extras, "Does anyone think they can do better than this guy?" Before anyone could answer he said, "Back to one" which meant do another take. Even thinking back on this now hurts my soul. We had several more takes and scene changes. This commercial was extra difficult because of the green screen and superimposing John Wayne and Bonanza into it. There was an actor who played John Wayne in all the Coors Light commercials that was his height and build. If you'd see a side shot of Wayne it would be him. He told me at break that I was doing a good job. That I was handling Pytka better than most. Right before that first break Pytka bumped into me hard, "Have you been on a fucking set before?" he said "fuck" like most people use every other adjective. That word was woven into the fabric of his colorful tongue.

Over at the fancy craft service I saw one of the Coors Light ad men.

"How did I get this commercial?" I asked. "I didn't read my lines."

"You were the only actor who stood up to him all day," he mused. "We saw your 1st audition and liked you. That's why you got a call back. We knew you could handle him on set." he explained. "You're taking it like a champ in there, like we knew you would." Believe it or not, I needed that little pep talk to get through the day. I now knew I had been cast because they liked what I had done in my initial audition. I was ready for round two. Looking back, I know now that the traffic, running late and feeling frustrated were all good factors that helped me get this commercial. If I had been on time I would have been just another actor. I wouldn't have stood out or been given the chance to show my moxie, stand up, go toe to toe with this director. That day's "bad things" turned out to be a blessing for me.

After speaking to the ad man, I left the hanger to take a break in my trailer. There was Pytka shooting hoops. He was waiting for me.

"Sparkplug, get over here and play me one-on-one," he demanded. Normally, I'd think that maybe I could win him over with some guy stuff. I really wanted to get him to like me but I had been warned not to play basketball with him. I was pretty good at basketball. I mean, I could play and I felt confident I could beat him by watching him take jumpers. Don't get me wrong, he wasn't bad and he was 6'5", but I was crafty. But I didn't know how to say no. Why would I say no? I decide to just tell the truth.

"My agent and everyone have told me not to play basketball with you," I said honestly.

"What the fuck, you're gonna let them tell you what to do?" he yelled. "I'm telling you, get over here and play me one-on one!"

I wasn't sure how to address him? Mr. Pytka? Mr. Director? Joe? So I decided to just leave the formalities out, "If it were up to me I'd play, I promise." Luckily he didn't push it anymore but it just furthered his dislike of me. The next day I'm headed to the fake mountain they built inside this large hanger that I need to climb up. It was just he and I, so I tried to thank him for casting me.

"I didn't want you!" He said curtly. "I got out-voted by the suits." Then, as he walked by me, he hit me with a really hard shoulder slam, so hard that for a moment there I thought he'd dislocated my shoulder. Wow, this guy is a tough cookie. The rest of that day's shoot went well enough. It would be only me and one of the female actors on set for day 2. When I got home at about 4pm (Pytka didn't like shooting late I'm told), Raf called me and said good job on not playing basketball. Apparently, Pytka was not happy someone had gone around his authority and told one of his actors not to do something with him. I still wonder to this day what possibly could have happened that could have been that bad if I had played him. Would he have won? Would I have won? Would I have cried? I don't think so. A great "What if" in my life.

The commercial came out and it put my face on the map. My family and friends were so proud of me. I especially remember my dad really getting choked up when telling me how proud he was that I was acting alongside the legendary John Wayne. I had to pay my SAG membership dues which took a big bite out of the day rate for the Coors Light commercial. If I remember right, I actually got paid less for the two days of acting than what I had to pay SAG. But don't feel sorry for me - the big money would come in when the commercial ran. I would get residuals every time it played! Back then if you had a Class A Commercial in major markets you would get about $120 every time it was on TV. That number slowly goes down the longer it runs. The formula they use no one knows. It's locked away in Al Capone's Vault.

Once your commercial airs you get paid in 13 week increments. Believe it or not, the Coors Light gig did not end up being one of my most profitable commercials because the John Wayne Foundation put a limit on it's run. I think I made close to $75,000 over the next year. I was thrilled. That was my take after my agent's cut.

Me in the middle of the bad guys

Director Joe Pytka shooting over Michael Jordon

Me on the right, John Wayne and the Bonanza Family in the background (Hoss & Ben Cartwright)

"Excuse me, those are our beers!"

STEP THREE: "Time to Move Up"

I booked several more commercials with The Beverly Hecht Agency but by now, I had a couple of close friends who were experienced in the industry, telling me that I needed to get better representation and a manager. The thought of facing Raf and telling him I was leaving was hurting my soul. Beverly Hecht took a chance on a nobody. However, I was assured that this was the normal protocol in Hollywood. You jump ship, you climb the ladder by moving up to better and better agents. Beverly Hecht didn't have the pull that a bigger agency would have. I was told that I could be going out on 10 auditions a week. I was getting maybe 10 a month. I started looking around and putting my feelers out there and I got an appointment with Kazarian Spencer & Associates (KSA). They are now Kazarian/Measures/Ruskin Talent Agency (KMR). I'll refer to them as KSA because that is who they were when I met them. At that time, they were considered one of the top three commercial agents in the city. Landing them wouldn't just be a step up, but would be one giant leap forward financially.

I remember very well meeting the decision makers at KSA. They were all women. I was brought in, placed in a chair in front of them and they began asking me questions. It was like a firing squad. They were intimidating and ALL BUSINESS. I don't think they gave a hoot about a pretty face. It's Hollywood, a pretty face is a dime a dozen. They drilled me about what casting directors I had been in front of. They tested me to make sure I wasn't bullshitting them. They wanted to know what I had booked and better yet, what I had gotten call backs for. You weren't getting into KSA unless you had clout. There was no audition. They knew I had booked some really big commercials and also knew that I had beaten out a couple of their actors for many of those jobs. I nailed that interrogation. Once again, I told them the magic words as I was leaving (the same words I told Beverly Hecht at our first meeting), "I promise you, if you take me on I will make you a lot of money!"

My new agent would be Alicia Ruskin. I really liked her as my agent, I still like her today when I run into her. Even to this day, I still pop in to KMR now and then. The R in their name represents her. She is a full partner and I couldn't be happier for her. Back then it was KSA and I still needed to tell Raf that I was leaving Beverly Hecht. I don't remember the exact details. I think the brain blocks out things it doesn't want to recollect later. I do know they were graceful and didn't show any anger towards me. I think it's part of being an agent. You lose talent to other agencies. It's all part of the sucky game and unfortunately I had to do what was best for me.

On top of signing with KSA, I also signed on with a manager. I landed The Dora Whitaker Agency. Dora comes from a famous acting family. Her brother is Johnny Whitaker. If you don't recognize his name he was a famous child actor, most notably for playing the small boy Jody on Family Affair. It was a popular show from 1966-1971. I saw him in the office all the time. Rumors have it Walt Disney's desk was sealed the day he died and Johnny Witaker's name was opened on his planner to star in the next Disney movie. I dealt with Dora mostly. She was a hustler and someone you want on your team. I was hoping to get theatrical auditions. KSA was only representing me commercially and I was beginning to land quite a few big commercials and my callback ratio was impressive. The great thing about commercials (aka CM's in Japan) was that they make you money. More importantly, they gave you freedom to be creative. To have the time to think outside the box and that's exactly what I did.

Dora and my agent were getting me some auditions and small hosting gigs but I wanted a chance at something meaty. An opportunity came my way. There was murmuring among my fellow actors that there was a way to get the "Breakdowns" illegally. The Breakdowns list all the auditions (meaning the parts they are casting) from every casting director. The casting directors are hired by the movie studios, commercial production companies, TV Networks - basically any entity that wants to hire actors uses the Breakdowns. Some of the parts listed didn't even go through a casting director but were placed directly by the production that was shooting something.

All the agents and managers get the Breakdowns daily in the morning at about 7:30am and go through them looking for parts their talent might be right for. This same system must still be used in some form today but probably encrypted electronically. Back then the Breakdowns were faxed out. Through the black market I could get them faxed to me every morning for $400 a month. That was a lot of money and rumors ran rampant that people were getting busted for doing it. My thought was "are they really going to throw me in acting prison"? I highly doubted it. That's like believing that the Beverly Hills Playhouse will really kick you out of the class, that you're paying a high monthly fee to go to, if you don't book something within two weeks. HORSECRAP! My old roommate drank that Koolaid. He'd come home from the playhouse and tell me, "Oh my god, they put me on terrorist theater," he would bemoan frightened.

"What the hell is that?"

"If I don't book something within two weeks I'm kicked out of class," he would explain to me. He totally believed this poor economical business decision on their part.

"They will not, I mean it, they WILL NOT kick you out," I'd profusely explained. "They love the money you pay them every month."

"No, they will."

"Brian, if they kicked out every actor that didn't book anything then they'd be broke. They're not kicking you out."

Milton Katselas, a well know Scientologist and Jeffery Tambor were gods to their pupils and I thought it was freaky. They also seemed to push nudity back then and leave people psychologically scarred.

"Have you ever seen anyone kicked out?" I asked.

"Well, I heard a girl was and...," blah blah blah - he tried to come up with someone but he actually had no concrete evidence anyone ever had.

Anyway, the BS of being put on the "terrorist theater" list and potentially getting kicked out of your acting class put things into perspective for my own situation. No paying student is getting kicked out of his class and I would NOT actually get arrested for paying for the Breakdowns and submitting myself for acting jobs - well, I hoped not. I mean, I'll admit I was a little worried that I could get busted, but jail time was never a thought. I bought a fax machine, met my "Breakdown Dealer" who was on the down low because I paid a drop-off person in cash who then paid someone else. I never met the true kingpin, which I preferred. If something ever did go down I could honestly say I didn't know who the hell was sending me those classified breakdowns every morning via fax. It's exhilarating to be part of a clandestine operation, well, as long as it's not too heavy.

Trust me, I was sleeping like a baby - except it was expensive. On top of paying the $400, I also needed to pay for my submissions to be sent to the casting directors at the studios and production companies that same day before 11am. Each submission cost $2.75. That actually sounds cheap but when I'm pouring over 50 pages of potential acting jobs there would be 20 parts I wanted to submit for.

Measures Take	Casting Director: John Smith / Universal
Feature Film	Location: Belize
SAG/AFTRA	Start Date: 06/28/1995

[**ANDERSON COLLINS**] (25-40) Former marine and current middle management for a commercial real-estate developer. He's grizzled and tough, but he tends to buck convention and go against the grain. Coming back from a trip to Central America he loses chunks of his memory and must return to Puerto Rico to learn what happened. Has a rocky relationship with his wife, Eva. (LEAD)

[EVA COLLINS] (25-40) Anderson's wife of 7 years and ambitious professional in her own right. She works as a photographer for the LA Times, but also dreams of starting a family. Knowing that he has cheated on her in the past, Eva is very suspicious of Anderson's recent shady activities.

[**ROGER COLLINS**] (20-30) Anderson's younger brother. A bit of a hotshot, Roger was able to scam his way through college and now works as a low-end psychologist. He never takes it seriously, however, and when Anderson tells him everything that's been going on with him, he jumps at the chance of an adventure and goes with him to Puerto Rico.

[KERRI LORD] (20-35) A blonde bombshell and Anderson's direct supervisor. They had an affair in the past which Anderson ended, but Kerri clearly wouldn't mind starting up again. She goes with Anderson to Puerto Rico to make sure he stays on task, unlike last time...

[OSVALDO ROSADO JR.] (20-30) As a teenager, he and his best friend were attacked by a Chupacabra immediately after witnessing a military facility being bombed. He tries to forget the experience while raising his younger brother and running a bar in "downtown" Canovanas, Puerto Rico.

[**STU HOLLENBECK**] (18-25) A youthful hippie and leader of a protest to fight the development within the forests of Puerto Rico. But when Anderson comes to town he gets sucked in way over his head.

I could see myself as Anderson Collins or Roger Collins, hell I could play Stu if I grew my hair out. These casting opportunities were actor's crack. You wanted to audition for them all! You'd see a pizza delivery guy (28-32) to be on Friends or Seinfeld. How could you not submit yourself for that?! If you do the math and I submitted 10 day that's nearly $30 dollars a day. I started out like gangbusters. I would submit 20 some days. I was going broke and not getting any auditions. I had developed a slight flirt with one of the girls who worked in the courier company that was delivering my submissions. She was about 24, light brown hair and had a hippie vibe. Fatefully, I asked her to lunch one day.

"They aren't opening any of your submissions," she blurted out over a Fatburger. She had the look of pain on her face.

"What do you mean?" I said. "Why aren't they opening them?"

"When we deliver them to the studios, the casting directors have their assistants go through all the envelopes," she hesitated. "They only open the envelopes from agents they like or have some sort of relationship with."

"You've seen this?"

"Yeah, when we drop them off I see them going through piles of submissions looking at the agents and just dumping the rest in the trash." "Oh fuck, no wonder I'm not getting any calls," I bemoaned. "Then what do they do?" "They take the stack of agents they like, then pull out all the headshots & resumes and go through them. To me, it looks like they're just looking at the headshot," she eked out

"Then they take that stack to the casting director?" I asked.

"That's pretty much what I think they're doing," she sighed. "Then they will go through them, pick the ones they like and have the assistant call their agent."

This obviously bummed me out, but I wasn't ready to throw in the towel just yet. Getting the Breakdowns was still a major coup. I quizzed my courier date a bit more on the mechanics of the delivery and asked her to gather more information. From what I learned, it seemed likely that if I had the RIGHT AGENCY NAME on my envelopes they would pull my headshot out and put it in the "good stack". They'd go through that stack and look mostly at the headshots. Then, they'd take their dwindled down pile of potentials to the decision maker. My new goal was: How could I get MY envelopes opened? I knew someone who knew someone and learned that William Morris Agency used the printing company Prints Charm'n for all their corporate labels. That got my brain working overtime and I came up with a risky, diabolical plan.

I put on my Armani suit, the same one that helped me land a part on Melrose Place, and headed down the Prints Charm'n in West Hollywood. I said I wasn't nervous about getting the Breakdowns, but what I was going to do now sis make me feel almost criminal - almost.

I cased the joint with three drive-bys in my UNstealthy 1984 Omega. This car stood out in Beverly Hills for all the poor man reasons. I found parking just off of Rodeo Drive which is not easy. I could see the Prints' front door from my car. My heart was pounding. I felt like a bank robber mustering up the courage to go in guns a blazing. My weapons were my beautiful suit and a lucky thrift store Mark Cross briefcase. I walked in looking like a million bucks. I had done some homework and had a name at the William Morris Agency (WMA). I walk up to the counter hoping the guy I was approaching didn't have any sort of relationship with WMA's normal pickup person. I feel fine bending the creative rules but I've always followed the rules of society.

"Yes, I'm here from Mark Shapiro's office to pick up some mailing labels." I don't remember the name I dropped but Mark Shapiro is the current president of WMA (Endeavor now) so I'll use his name just for fun. The young guy behind the counter didn't seem to suspect a thing. Why would he? My suit was impeccable. I had confidence.

"How many do you want?" was a question I wasn't prepared for. I didn't know the increments they usually bought them in. But I didn't want to put myself in this position again so I decided to jump right in and go big or go home. I hesitated just a moment...

"You want the whole 1,000?" he said, bailing me out. "You want all the logos too?"

"Yes, I'll take them both," I blurted out, my heart was still pounding. I was prepared with cash. He disappeared, for what felt like too long, was he calling William Morris, the police? He emerged with two boxes holding the entire Holy Grail. I paid and quickly turned to get the hell out of there. He shouted, "HEY WAIT!" I stopped in my tracks, feeling sure that I had been caught. I felt like raising my arms. "You're going to need this receipt," he said. I turned back around, grabbed it and left as quickly as possible. Thinking back, why would they have those labels pre-printed, did they always have them available? Would someone from WMA come in later that day and wonder who the hell picked up the order? Oh well, those weren't my concerns now. I had what I had come for and as Arnold Schwarzenegger said in Terminator 2: "Hasta la vista, baby."

I was speed walking back to my car thinking, "I just landed 1,000 labels and mailing stickers." Way more than I ever expected. "If I submitted 5 a day, that's 25 a week," I quickly added it up in my head, "Hell, I'd have enough for a year!" I surmised. I'd make sure when I went through my morning ritual of sorting the breakdowns for acting gigs I used my WMA labels on "Sponge Worthy" parts only. I became choosier in a good way.

My courier friend gave me a sample of the WMA envelope to duplicate. I had the presentation down pat. The tricky part was that if my submission was opened, and if the assistant liked my look (as well as the casting director), sooner or later they were going to review my resume on the back and see The Dora Whitaker Agency printed in the upper right corner. The jig would be up. I wasn't with one of those top agents, despite my mailing labels! My hope was, that they'd think it was some sort of clerical mixup and decide to call me in anyway.

The More Chances You Take the More Luck You'll Have!

Luck (or not), the much wished for "inevitable" happened. The first sign that my master scheme was working was when I got a call from Dora at The Dora Whitaker Agency. There was confusion in her voice.

"What the hell are you doing?" she asked directly. "I've gotten two calls today from castings that I didn't even submit you for."

I took a deep breath, because I knew this was going to be tricky. "Let me come in and talk to you," I said. I knew Dora was a Latter Day Saint (LDS) or some say Mormon, but she never spoke about that as my agent. I'm bringing this up because I don't think she wants to do anything sketchy, but coming from a long line of family in the entertainment industry she also knows that it's a dog-eat-dog world. I think someone she's related to even worked for Walt Disney (besides her brother) and helped create Donald Duck.

Suddenly Dora was like Sergeant Shultz, "I know nothing, nothing!" she said with dismay (and I'd like to think with a bit of pride). I admitted to her that I WAS submitting myself for parts. I didn't go into any of the specifics of HOW I was getting the Breakdowns, but she must have known it was unusual (if not illegal) that she was getting calls asking for me. I did NOT tell her I was using the WMA labeled envelopes to get my submissions opened, which I knew would have been a deal breaker with her and the reputable business she was starting to build. No offense to Dora, but my little trick was likely getting my headshot looked at more than she ever could have at that point. Her agency was new and she handled a lot of children back then. Fast forward 28 years, and now she has a lot more pull. I am fortunate that she was willing to close one eye as I bent the rules a bit. At the end of the day, she fielded the incoming calls for me and I had a lot more auditions.

This was the THIRD STEP along my journey in Hollywood. I started with no agent and then slowly working my way up the ladder to success. In an ironic twist, I was later actually signed by William Morris Agency (WMA) in their commercial division! I had left KSA with hopes of doing well commercially with WMA and that I might lead to a chance at their theatrical division. "Theatrical" in LA agency jargon didn't mean Broadway - it meant movies and television shows.

Landing a couple of high profile commercials with WMA could pave the way towards me getting parts like the "pizza delivery guy" on Friends. I learned a valuable lesson that I did not understand until it was actually happening to me. William Morris Agency "Hip-pocketed" me. To be hip-pocketed means that an agent signs you and then puts you in their pocket. They don't send you out on auditions. To hip-pocket is to take someone OFF the market. Hide them away. This is a cruel thing to do to a person who is trying to make a living and work their way up. Sadly, WMA signed me because they had 1-2 other guys who you would consider my "type" that they liked. By eliminating the competition (ME) - their go-to guys would have a better chance at booking something.

I was going on a minimum of 2 auditions a week with KSA, but often 5-7 times. I had booked a Ford commercial which also included a photo spreads in big magazines like Sports Illustrated (see insert) and Time Magazine. I also booked a big Acura campaign that got me a lot of attention as well as commercials for State Farm, FTD Florist, DirectTV, Kaiser Permanente, Vidal Sassoon and so many more. After WHA hip-pocketed me, I stopped getting any auditions. ZERO, for 3 months. My agent looked straight out of Central Casting. She was in her 50s, had bright unnatural fluorescent red hair, along with blue rimmed glasses that hung on the end of her nose. I think she felt this look gave her a youthful vibe or an artistic mood. She used words like "Honey and Darlin'" as she sat behind her stacks of papers. Friends fans might conjure up Joey Tribbiani's agent. It would have been comical except my fate was in her hands. I went in and begged her to let me out of my year contract. I mean I begged and begged. Whatever I said, it actually worked! William Morris Agency let me go - I was set free. I then crawled back to KSA and Alicia Ruskin with my tail between my knees. They were gracious enough to take me back, which I think they did because I was sorrowful and honest when I left. I explained why I was leaving them, I wanted to branch out into movies and television. Despite their lack of theatrical support, I still needed to provide for myself financially. My experience with William Morris was eye opening and I was so thankful KSA took me back. I felt confident that I could continue my commercial success with their partnership.

Cover of SI with my ad inside

Page 1 of 2 page spread

Eisaku Yoshida and I getting some Ramen

Eisaku, his Wife Anna. Myself
and My Wifey Jill Kelly

"The LA Hustle"

CHAPTER NINE

•

"There comes that mysterious meeting in life when
someone acknowledges who we are and what we can be,
igniting the circuits of our highest potential."
—Rusty Berkus

THERE WAS MORE going on in my life than just getting agents and booking commercials. I've been highlighting my path in acting, but during much of that journey I was also dipping my toes in the water of other business opportunities as well. Before I landed the big Coors Light Commercial with John Wayne I was working at Yamashiro Restaurant just up the road from the Magic Castle in Hollywood. It was nestled in the Hollywood hillside and has a special and fascinating history. Brothers Charles and Adolph Bernheimer (German-Americans) had it built in 1911 by Japanese artisans & craftsmen from Japan. It's an exact replica of a Japanese palace in the "Yamashiro" provenance mountains outside of Kyoto. It was extravagant and built to house their Japanese art collection. In the roaring 20s, this was the place for Hollywood elite members called the 400 Club. However, during WWII it lost it's luster. Being owned by Germans and looking like a Japanese Castle (our two biggest enemies) didn't help its reputation. It was vandalized and it was rumored that the Japanese were signaling submarines from one of it's towers! By the time I got a job there it was a restaurant, the roaring 90's were in full tilt bookie.

Their wait staff back then was predominately female and Asian. I got a job in the catering division but really wanted to be a waiter. That was where the money was. I became friends with a guy named Hiroto Uehara. He was the front house manager/host. Hiroto was 23 and I was still 30. We really hit it off. I missed Japan and liked hanging out with him. I eventually got a job as the first male cocktail waiter they had ever hired. I think knowing Japanese helped. During this time I had gotten an agent and was going on auditions, but had not landed anything significant other than the Falcon Cable Guy. I do remember during one of my catering gigs at Yamashiro (which I kept doing along with cocktailing), a big group of Indiana University alums, about my age, came in for the night before their wedding dinner. There were about 40 of them. As I'm leaning over to fill one of the guy's waters he says to the guy next to him, "Have you heard about Jimmy?" the guy shakes his head, "No" and he continues, "He's just a waiter!" Just then, he looks up at me with horror. Maybe not "horror" but with an "Oh shit" look meaning I'm sorry. He starts to apologize and I cut him off, "Don't worry about it. I actually graduated from IU in 1988, I'm out here chasing the acting thing," I said straightly. Obviously, I still remember this story because it must have bothered me. Maybe it's that the truth cuts closer to the bone? I did likely have some doubt. I'm 30 years old, I had worked as an elite recruit with US Steel. I lived in Japan for 4 years. I had traveled a lot of the world, but here I was filling water glasses as a waiter in a catering position. OUCH!

Sue and I got along really well, but I do think she liked living alone. I was a lot to take in and she hinted that she could get a one bedroom in The Summit. Hiroto was looking for a roommate and the next thing you know, he and I are roommates. This pairing with him was a particularly good turn in my life. I had missed the Japanese culture. Although I had dated non-Asian women since coming back to the US, I did want to meet more Japanese girls. I liked their disposition, their mannerisms and it felt comfortable. I got to speak Japanese a little, eat Japanese food and still have that special connection that had made Japan seem so wonderful to me. Hiroto wanted to date Japanese girls too. He was born in Kumamoto, the countryside of Japan, and had come to America to study English. His English was definitely better than my Japanese. We'd go out together to Japanese spots and had some luck meeting Japanese girls but nothing to write home about.

TeaTime Asian Dating Personals

It wasn't too long after he moved in that I booked that life changing commercial with Coors Light. I was experiencing some financial freedom and I was able to leave Yamashiro. Keep in mind, at this time the internet was still rudimentary. There was Love@AOL and Match was just launching in 1995, but classified ads were still the popular way to date. The LA Weekly had a well known, highly successful, full page spread in the Weekly promoting their 900# dating phone lines. Someone would place an ad:

> **NO COUCH POTATO PLEASE**
> Outgoing, adventuresome, 27, good shape, SWF who is looking for fun-loving, mountain biking friend or more to enjoy life. No smokers. Leave a message, maybe we can build a fire. BOX 1234

It would be free to make an ad, but you'd have to pay $1.99 a minute to listen to and leave a voicemail. It's a man's world in many respects, but when it comes to dating women they are by far the superior race. They are in the driver's seat. Women could call a FREE line. Basically, everything was free for them. This got me thinking. I asked Hiroto if there was any type of dating system like this in the few Japanese papers published in Los Angeles. He did some research and said, "No!" and that's when we started our own company called *TeaTime* and *AsianDateline.com* which we later morphed into One World Intercultural Dating.

www.AsianDateline.com

SEEKING
• Non-Asian Women
• Non-Asian Men
• Alternative

ONE WORLD Dateline

SEEKING
• Asian Women
• Asian Men
• Special

"The BEST Asian Personals in LA by far!" -LA Weekly-

12 (December)

Welcome to TEA TIME & ONE WORLD the best "Asian Dateline" in California. We have put together these personals in hopes to bring a diverse group of Asian Singles from a wide range of backgrounds together. They range from American born Asians to those who are new in this country. Our singles also include non-Asians who are interested in meeting people of a different heritage from themselves. This is an unique opportunity to make new friends and maybe find that someone special.

ONE WORLD Intercultural Dateline

How it works: The system works like any other voice personals. You can place your ad FREE by calling (323)830-6577. You'll receive your confidential box # and pin code. You can retrieve your messages FREE too! To respond to the personals below you must be at least 18 yrs old and the cost of the call is $1.99 a minute. Get connected now call (900)844-1111 !!! We hope our service is a great success!

ASIAN FEMALE SEEKS MALE

This is the front page of our mailer. There would be 6-8 pages. It was very popular!

ASIAN FEMALE SEEKS MALE

ASIAN MALE SEEKS FEMALE

NON-ASIAN MALE SEEKS FEMALE

NON-ASIAN FEMALE SEEKS MALE

ALTERNATIVE

ティータイムでたくさんの友達をつくろう!

1-900-844-1111
18 and over

Bridge USA Japanese Paper.

Hiroto & I many years later!

We found a 900# programmer and explained to him how we wanted the call system to work. In total, we decided to both put in $5,000 making our budget to launch $10K. We needed to purchase a 900# and attach it to a bank account. We also needed to set up an LLC to protect ourselves in case someone sued us or had a bad experience with someone they met via *TeaTime*. My college education was paying off. It took us about 2 months to get the system up and running and we had a monthly fee of $700 for the company that maintained the computer program and voicemail system. How do you create Publication #1 when you haven't had it out there for people to see and create voicemail? We decided to place 1/4 ads for Tea Time in the LA Weekly ($400) and two ads in the Japanese paper's Bridge USA and Vogue. It was free to create a profile.

Here is how it worked. You would call a free (213) number to place an ad. You would be prompted to sex (M or F), Race, Age and what you were looking for. The computer would then place your VM in the correct section of the program. The "Single" person looking for love would get a Box # and PIN code that was unique to their box. They could call in for free to see if anyone had left them a message. It was pretty straight forward and user friendly. We ran the smaller ads for 6 weeks. Hiroto and I would listen to the VMs and type out what they said they were looking for. We'd come up with cute tag headings for each one based on their wants. In the very beginning we had them give us their mailing address and we would mail out each month's newest edition of *Tea Time*. Our first mailer was beyond our hopes! We had about 400 people requesting our dating pamphlet. We had 104 people create ads but we also had 300+ people wanting a copy of *Tea Time* as well. We printed our ads, folded them, put them into envelopes, applied stamps and took them to the Post Office. It was a lot of work. I typed up all the ads with both of us brainstorming on how to word everything.

Page 164 you'll see our categories along with an "Alternative" section may include Gay or someone who was looking for a Stripper or anything exotic that didn't fit into our standard categories. *Tea Time* took off like a ROCKET SHIP! It was great because Hiroto and I had a business backline that only we could track, that would let us know the total number of hours people had used our service. The first monthly mailer was a big money maker. The 900# ($1.99 a minute) brought in a little more than $10,000. We were ecstatic! That paid off everything we had invested into it. As I often say, Winner winner chicken dinner! However, after 6 months of mailing out our dating pamphlets, our numbers began to dwindle (sales). We kept placing 1/4 ads in different papers in attempts to attract new people. We had some new free personals via VM but not enough new customers were requesting the pamphlets. Without the ads in front of them, no one would call the 900#. Our sales dropped below $5,000. We had expenses and taxes to pay. By the end of the our eighth month our balance sheet was inching towards the red. To try and regain our initial momentum, we rolled the dice. We placed our pamphlet directly into a FULL PAGE ad in the LA Weekly. That was pricey at $3,800. For me, that put us on the map. This free paper was the gospel, everyone read it. Buying a full page ad in it was incredible.

TeaTime is an expression in Japan for picking up someone. The actual word for picking up or hitting on someone is "Nanpa"(ナンパ) or "Nampa" but that term is used only for men trying to meet women. For women trying to meet men it's called "Gyakunan" (逆ナン). Obviously, the male version nampa, is much more popular. Using this word is like us (Americans) saying booty-call, it's a silly fun phrase. Japanese are quite shy in many ways when it comes to the art of dating. If you meet someone and you'd like to ask them out on a date, the Japanese typically ask them if they'd like to have tea. "Ocha shimasen ka?" is a common phrase, "Ocha" means tea, the rest of the sentence is 'to do'. We decided to use this polite way of asking someone out as the name of our dating service *Tea Time*. Another cultural expression, that I think is adorable, is if you are having a great night with a girl or hanging out at a bar and you want her to spend the night with you, you need to be sneaky by asking, "What would you like for breakfast?" and if she says she prefers "Toast" then you know you can just lead her straight to your futon. If she says "I don't really like breakfast" or "I'm not eating breakfast right now" then you know it's not happening. I always thought this expression is/was a great way to save face.

The full page ad in the LA Weekly had some success and inspired us to place full page ads in the Japanese papers as well. We were going for broke. Our numbers peaked at $15,000 for ONE MONTH, but then they leveled off and slowly declined again. I think there was a certain stigmatism for the "900#" that left a bad taste in some people's mouths. We tried having parties and were treading water near the end. *Tea Time* definitely had made us money but suddenly the effort wasn't making enough dough. As mentioned Love@AOL had come out in 1995, and other dating sites were popping up as the internet was starting to become a thing. We tried launching *AsianDateline.com* to keep up with the times, but our platform was still using the 900#. Even if someone went to our website, our revenue was only generated through our phone calls. You could see the ads online, but could only reply to them via the 900#. We didn't have the sophisticated programs that soon became the modern way of dating like Match.com, eHarmony.com, PlentyofFish.com - I often think that if Hiroto and I had invested in technology, we might have been filthy rich. Coulda' Shoulda' Woulda' gives me regretful goosebumps to this day. We were ahead of the curve. I had approached a programmer in 1996-97 and explained to him what we wanted to do. He said we'd need a minimum of $75,000 to setup that kind of interface! Our experience with *Tea Time* had been so up and down. That kind of risk seemed financially reckless. We had a Korean guy offer us $20,000 for our phone system and our crude internet site. I think overall, we made decent money with *TeaTime* but technology was moving faster than we had the money to keep up with. We sold it with sadness and relief. Seeing where the internet is now, we definitely lost a massive opportunity to be one of the pioneers of the social media dating scene.

The Exchange Asian Talent Agency

I was a busy boy back then going on auditions via KSA and Dora Whitaker. I was getting the Breakdowns everyday. Up early going through them, then submitting my "William Morris Agency" envelopes and I was about to create another company called **The Exchange**. My youthful mind was on overdrive back then.

My sister Jacque, my mom and my step-father came to stay in LA for a week. There was a band called the Booty Quakes that played at The Viper Room every Friday, they were the resident funk and disco band. They would dress full-on disco with fake afros and 70s jumpsuits. I went to their "Suck My Dick" New Years Eve party one year. They were the "it" band to see back then. Four groovy white guys gyrated, spun and got funkalicous while dressed in the best possible nod to Soul Train. I personally loved them. The Viper Room was located in the heart of Sunset Boulevard. It brought in all the young Hollywood elites. Johnny Depp was part owner at that time and, on a macabre note, it's well known that River Phoenix died of a drug overdose the night before Halloween there in 1993. There's also a story thrown around that Courtney Love was given CPR by Johnny Depp after an overdose inside the club. I mean, this place oozed with fame, it was truly infamous. Adam Duritz, the lead singer of the *Counting Crows*, worked as a Viper Room bartender in late 1994 and early 1995 to escape his newfound fame. I am a super Counting Crows fan, so that just blows my mind. *Back to my story...* my sister Jacque and I headed to the Viper Room on a Friday night. I want to show her all my favorite hip haunts. We aren't there too long and I see one of the most famous actors from Japan named Eisaku Yoshida. When I was living in Japan he was everywhere. I saw his face on TV, commercials, billboards, trains, magazines, like I said - EVERYWHERE. He also had a very famous songs that every Japanese person can sing by heart. I would compare it to "Sweet Caroline" or "Jesse's Girl" - but actually it may be even more famous than those two songs over there. Eisaku was with Risa Hirako who was beautiful and would later become famous in her own right after becoming his wife.

"Anata wa cho ūmei, deska?" I asked him in Japanese which means - you're really famous aren't you?

"You know me?" he answered in English. I was surprised how well he spoke my native tongue. He was like the Tom Cruise or Brad Pitt of Japan. I was in awe of him - he had the "it" factor and was known for his cool look of jeans and a v-neck white tee shirt.

He and I hit it off. Eisaku said he was taking a sabbatical from Japan to get away for at least a year. To take a breather from fame. Eisaku Yoshida was born in 1969 making him 4 years younger than me, so when I met him he must have been 26 or 27 years old. He's nearly 6'1" which is quite tall in Japan. He was voted the "Best Looking Man" and "Best Looking Man in Jeans" in Japan - which is hilarious that they have labels like these. His hairstyle back then was so popular that young men would tell their barber, "Give me the Eisaku Yoshida" and they knew what that meant. I can only compare that to the Dorthy Hamill cut that all the girls wanted growing up in 1976. Remember, I have a special connection with that name, Dorthy Hamill was my grandma's name too. His cut be might comparable to the craze of young girls asking for the "The Rachel" from Friends in 1995. Needless to say, he was very famous.

Since that first meeting with Eisaku Yoshida at the *Viper Room* he has been one of my best friends. We've now known each other 25+ years and are as close as ever. We've taken trips all over the world and still talk all the time even though he's back in Japan. When he married Risa Hirako, the girl he was with the night I met him, I stood up as his best man. Japanese paparazzi helicopters were buzzing above us and his marriage became big news in his country. Years later, he was part of a show called "Another Sky" where they would ask Japanese celebrities to name a place, other than Japan, where they spend part of their life. He chose Los Angeles and had me featured with him running all over town to our favorite spots. When I asked my wife to marry me in Kyoto in 2015, we had stopped at a ramen shop to escape a downpour of rain and get some lunch. We were the only ones there because it was a bit too late for lunch and early for dinner. The owner of the shop gave me a strange look as I stood there drenched from the rain clutching my "gomi" umbrella and asked me if I was on "Another Sky" with Eisaku Yoshida. Wow, I guess I had a tiny bit of fame in Japan too! Later that night in a 250 year old Japanese ryokan called the Kinsai Inn I asked my wife, Jill Kelly, to marry me. She was quite surprised. I had told her I could be with someone for life but no god or government would tell me that I'm married. She said, "Yes!" It was the best decision of our lives! I highly recommend checking out the Kinsai Inn if you're ever in Kyoto, Japan. I also strongly recommend marrying the love of your life.

Since I was still booking commercials, I had freedom. Eisaku was on his American vacay in LA, which lasted three (3) years, so we had a lot of time to hang out. He had a connection with some tennis courts associated with MGM in Santa Monica. We played tennis a couple times a week. It was like our job. He even traveled back to Indiana with me a few times and experienced an American Thanksgiving Dinner in the Midwest with my family. I remember once we went up to

Seattle to meet a big Japanese production company called Toei and several Japanese girls recognized Eisaku and we were literally running down the street to escape them. We ducked into a restaurant and he bolted into the men's room where he stood on the toilet so they wouldn't see his feet under the stall. I remember on one of our trips I came into his hotel room and he was washing his underwear in the sink.

"What are you doing?" I asked. "Why don't you use the laundry service?"

"I never do that," he explained. "Someone might steal them!"

Now, I highly doubt someone in America or the Bahamas, or wherever he and I were traveling, would steal his underpants, but he had gotten into the habit of washing them himself because it was a real life possibility in Japan that they would end up on ebay.jp. Things you learn while hanging out with someone famous! Eisaku grew up in Hadano, the Kanagawa prefecture of Japan. It's a beautiful town nestled between the mountains and the beach which leads to a variety of outdoor activities such as hiking, mountaineering, sea kayaking, rock climbing, and para-gliding. Jill and I traveled there once and it's an idyllic place to grow up. Eisaku formed a band in high school (he sings & plays guitar) and headed to Tokyo at 18 to pursue a music career. He got a job working in a coffee shop called Fuglen and rented a sparse room nearby with a shared bathroom and no phone. A talent scout came in one day for some coffee and told him he should enter a contest called "Nice Guy of Japan" or something along this line in 1988. It involved a talent, which I'm sure he sang, and the winner would get ¥1,000,000 ($10,000) and a chance for a spot on a Japanese TV drama produced by Toei. He won that contest and it launched his career to super stardom. I have to say, that lucky bastard is living an amazing life. I've been blessed to be around quite a few "celebrities" and it is an extraordinary life. The other thing is, they are just flesh & blood believe it or not, but most of them are talented and very driven. Does the fame fuel that continued drive? That, I'm not completely sure about, but the few famous people I've gotten to know have a story to tell. They were broke, they were sleeping on a couch, struggle after struggle, but somewhere in their story was the "NEVER GIVE UP" attitude and a lucky break, and a discovery happened. They put themselves in that spot, in that time, to be ready to accept that 'hand of god' that shined on their blessed motherfucking soul. We walk this planet one time, there's no second chances, and to get to live at that level is a gift. The celebrities I admire and like to be around are the ones that know that. Once they drift into the '*big me, little you*' mindset, it's a sad sight to see.

Eisaku is one of the good ones! He's always been completely grounded around me and is one of the most dedicated and hardworking people at his craft that I have ever known. He is even picking Jill and I up at the airport this July when we travel to Japan.

Let's go back to Eisaku and I enjoying LA during his three years living in Los Angeles. I'm still going on auditions and getting the Breakdowns every morning. I asked Eisaku if he'd ever thought about trying to get into American movies? I started to think maybe I could submit him via the Breakdowns. If an American movie would put him in their film they would have a built-in revenue from higher sales in Japan. They'd love to see one of their own on the big screen. He didn't seem against it, but he wasn't doing cartwheels either. Regardless, this gave me the idea for yet another new business venture. I decided to start my own management company that would specialize in acting Asian talent. I had written a screenplay about a Japanese police officer that came to America on an exchange program to try and find a serial killer who was targeting Japanese girls. The title was The Exchange. That's what I decided to call my new talent agency. *The Exchange Talent Agency* was launched and my first actor was Eisaku Yoshida which was pretty darn good. I had been running around with him for over a year and he had done a few concerts for the LA Japanese community. We'd go to Cafe Muse that was owned by a Japanese musician named Hideki on Sawtelle Boulevard. Sawtelle is on the Westside area of LA and is known as a Japanese district. We'd meet up there often and I got to know a lot of Japanese people in the industry. Hideki is an amazing guitar player.

I put the word out that I wanted to try to help Asian actors, mostly Japanese, get auditions. I quickly signed 5 (actors) talent, then 10... and I think I peaked at about 25. I had approximately 15 women and 10 men that had all entrusted me to help their careers. Being an actor myself, I wanted to be more generous and understanding with my actors, therefore I told them that whatever they booked through their agent I would not take a percentage of. I would only take 10% of bookings they made through me. My manager, Dora Whitaker got 15% of all my booked gigs (including my commercials), even if they were booked by my agent. That never seemed completely fair to me, but I know it's the normal protocol in the Hollywood world of business. I was out 25% off the top plus Uncle Sam. Some managers take more than 15%, but I was ONLY asking for a paltry 10%. My talent would not pay me a single penny unless they booked something that I sent them out on. Oftentimes their pay would go directly to them and I would collect my fee once they were paid. This removed the headache for me of cashing a large check and then turning around and writing them one for 90% of it. Occasionally, I would collect their full payment but that's not how I preferred to do it. I had to keep track of it more carefully and a higher level of trust was needed, but that's how I rolled. I hoped The Exchange could be profitable but I also enjoyed it.

I was already getting the Breakdowns so opening my own agency wasn't going to increase the cost of my side hustle. What would cost me were the daily submissions. I couldn't use the "William Morris" switcharoo for *The Exchange*. I created a logo and added "Asian Talent Agency" in hopes that specializing, narrowing down my focus, could possibly make me the guy to go to if they needed Asian actors. I knew there was a chance that my envelopes could be tossed in the trash and I'm quite sure many of them were, but I was determined. I printed on my submission envelopes that the couriers would deliver daily the words: "**ASIAN TALENT ONLY**" in 4" block letters. It was an attention getter. Melody Jackson (Smart Girl) also had a list of casting directors big & small. I put out another mailer asking them to look for *The Exchange* if they were casting an Asian actor. I can't say how successful this *intro mailer* was but my talent did slowly begin to book commercials, hosting and small parts in lower production films that I sent them out on. It always felt so good to call them and tell them they had been cast. Twenty years later I was at a Jeremy Buck & the Bang concert at a live house in Hermosa. You'll read later how I met Jeremy but for now let's just say he's a good friend from Indiana who transported his life to Southern California. I had something to do with that. He and Eisaku Yoshida became good friends too and they even collaborated on jam song called "Smokey Smokey Smokey".

To this day, nearly every year Eisaku comes back and they do a concert called *Tokyo Sunday*. It brings an eclectic crowd of Eisaku fans along with Jeremy's crowd of followers. Eisaku may have left LA 20+ years ago like me, but he tries hard to come back yearly for three (3) weeks to reconnect. At one year's *Tokyo Sunday*, held at Saint Rocke in Hermosa Beach, I had an actress that I hadn't seen in a long long time come up and thank me for helping her get her SAG card. Truthfully, I didn't remember but she was one of my talents at *The Exchange*. Those years have become a blur. I was working hard and had so many stimuli firing in my brain that things got lost in there. When I say "Stimuli" I do NOT mean drugs. It was more the drive. The experiences that were being thrown my way. It was an overload of trying everything I could to make something of myself in Hollywood. I can regurgitate things and spit them out. I could tell that my blood, sweat & tears over the damn Breakdowns had paid off for her. It really felt good. I think she bought me a drink and I moved on mingling and a couple of minutes later an Asian woman and a tall white guy approached me.

"Are you Williamson who started Tea Time?" the Asian woman of about 50 years old asked.

"Yes, yes I am," I stated with curiosity. "And who are you?" I said kindly.

"I'm Kumiko and this is my husband Tom," she said.

"Nice to meet you. How did you know my name?"

"Oh my, we met 21 years ago," she smiled, pointing at her tall hubby named Tom, "From Tea Time!"

"Wow, that's amazing," I said. "We've been married for 19 years," Tom said.

"We are so thankful to you for helping us meet, thank you," she said slightly bowing. No matter how long a Japanese person lives in America they still bow to show gratitude or respect. I think I broke out some of my Japanese language skills with them and they told me their story.

"I'm blown away, thank you for introducing yourself to me," I beamed.

"I've heard there are quite a few couples who got married from Tea Time," she said.

All of this put a big smile on my face. I have to admit I was walking on a bit of a cloud. Two businesses that I felt had sort of failed (because I eventually walked away from them due to the lack of revenue), had affected people's lives in the best possible way. Hiroto and his wife Yumi came to see Jeremy Buck and Eisaku's show that night too and when I told Hiroto that a couple told me they met via

TeaTime and got married we laughed and we reminisced about those good ol' days. Later I saw him talking to them.

Eisaku was still getting acting offers from Japan but he was enjoying laying low. I was trying hard to get him auditions in America but wasn't having as much luck as I had hoped for. I had NO CLOUT, NO CONNECTIONS. We had several close calls with big studios and some interested independents but nothing ever panned out. I was amazed at his professionalism and how hard he worked at music and learning his lines when he did have an audition. We worked together to improve his English pronunciation, he is a consummate professional, a true perfectionist. I could tell that in America, his first true love was making music and that was bubbling back to the surface. He had gone to Tokyo at 19 to be in a band but had such success as an actor that it took over his life. Throughout it all though, he's continued putting out albums and still has a large fan base. His story reminds me of Johnny Depp. I recently read the highly entertaining book Age of Cage about the life of Nicolas Cage. He apparently met Depp via a stylist and a friendship was launched. Depp's band was waning on Sunset Blvd and Nic Cage said, "Why don't you meet my agent - cause I think you're an actor - You could be an actor -" "I said I'll meet anybody. I'll do anything at this point," Depp told Cage. I think Eisaku, like Johnny Depp, has multiple creative talents. Both are musicians who became massive actors.

"I'm a great believer in luck, and I find the harder I work the more I have of it"
—Thomas Jefferson

I have had luck, no doubt about it, but I also had helped to create the opportunity to get that extra kismet of fate. You need to stay relevant, you need people to believe in you. It's rare for someone to be truly a "Self Made Man" because it takes people around you to get to the top. No man is an island. I remember when I first got KSA, (that's the really good agency) and Alicia Ruskin was sending me out on auditions, I wanted to be in their head when the *Official Breakdowns* rolled in. I did two things to accomplish this:

1) I bought beautiful Sunflowers - you know the big yellow flowers with the daisy like flower face? I got a strong vase and then cut out my face from my headshots and pinned them on each flower. It was a bouquet of me!

2) I went to Costco and bought a large plastic barrel of oversized pretzels. I peeled off the product logo and glued my face on it. It was funny.

I can tell you these both worked. The Sunflowers were cute, but I only did them one time. However, the pretzels were a bonafide ongoing hit that I kept fully stocked for them. A free healthy snack in the break room is always welcome. They couldn't avoid my face!

My first headshot on the (L) and about 5 years later (R)

Both of these were Successful!

Me, Dyanna Lauren (2nd Season Host)
and Bridget Spurgeon on Promo Cover

ENTERTAINMENT WEEKLY coined me the
Bob Saget of The Playboy Channel.

(I did not love that but I made EW)

PLAYBOY MAN

CHAPTER TEN

•

"Life is too short to be living someone else's dream."
—Hugh Hefner

IT'S SUPER HOT at the top of the impressive staircase inside the *Garden of Eden* nightclub. Suddenly a spotlight hits me square in the face and Bill Maher is on the mic, "Ladies and gentlemen, Mr. Williamson Howe, the host of Playboy's #1 show, along with Miss December and February!" I was wearing Hugh Hefner's personal pajamas that had been autographed in silver ink by the legend himself. They had sprayed the sides of my hair with gray paint to give me Hef's mystique. This was the *25th Year Anniversary Party for Playboy TV* and was part fundraiser. For an added thrill, it was a pajama party too, of course. Hugh Hefner attracts controversy, not unlike Bobby Knight, and he also had a big heart. I know recently there has been some dirt coming out about him that I don't know much about. I do know he took every opportunity he could to assist, donate money or raise funds for those less fortunate. He was big on the First Amendment rights too. I'm sue he had demons, but I didn't see them.

I was given very little instructions on what I was supposed to do that night. I was sweating bullets. The room was filled with celebrities and I was the main attraction for the auction. People killed to own one of Hef's custom robes. This was the maroon style with a black lapel, the classic. Tonight's robe would also include a pair of his maroon monogrammed slippers. The two Playmates on my arms were dressed in gorgeous bustiers covered completely in colorful candy. Mostly Lifesavers, Skittles, Twizzlers and Starbursts. Miss December had an extra Christmas theme with red candy canes and those round red & white mint twists. They hadn't been given any instructions either. We asked each other what we were supposed to do? Once our names were called, the spot light shined on us, and we started down the stairs. The girl's instincts kicked in and they started treating this like a runway show and I guess it was. They were turning, pausing, stopping, glamming it up so I just followed their lead. I oohed and ahhed over them, "acted" suave to give the Hef persona and did my best to not fall down this massive wooden bannister. It felt like they had brought in the staircase from the Gone with the Wind set just for this show. Who knows, they might did? Once we got near the bottom of the stairs there was a two foot high elevated runway (36" wide) that snaked through the nightclub. I had Miss December in front of me and February behind me, not a bad sandwich. Bill Maher was still announcing something, cracking jokes, as we continued our strut through the club. At some point, the focus was squarely on Hugh Hefner's robe, meaning ME! Thank God people bid on it. They had asked Mr. Hefner himself if he would wear it for the bidding but he refused. I felt if it didn't raise much money it might be blamed on me. I was trying to act cool, spinning slowly, grabbing the collar, playing with the robe belt (what are those called?). I looked at Hef and pointed. It was like we were bros. Was this really happening to me? Bill Maher brought down the gavel, "SOLD for $13,000!" he gleefully announced. He seemed close to Hugh Hefner back then. I always thought they had a slight resemblance to each other. I had heard Hef hoped the robe would go for at least $5K so it went well. The whole night was a serious surreal moment, a reality that remains a mystery to me of how I was the one lucky enough to live this dream. Growing up, Playboy was a boy's dream. The mansion was sacred ground I never thought I would set foot in. It became a place I often went to and the staff eventually knew me by name, including the big cheese himself, Hugh Hefner. Hef would see me, "Williamson, I hope you are enjoying your self," he'd smile. Just knowing, he knows my name was pretty cool. They had NAHV on all the TVs 24/7.

Puberty

I'll get into how I ended up being the host of Playboy's #1 show worldwide, *Naughty Amateur Home Videos,* later in this chapter. When I think about Playboy, I think about growing up and reaching puberty. Your balls are dropping, your voice is changing, your socks turn crusty yellow and can stand up by themselves. Somewhere wedged in these changes for most men are the thoughts of women. Lots and lots of thoughts of women. My own personal puberty took some time. Not necessarily my attraction to girls, they weren't women just yet, because I did like girls a whole heck of a lot. I did all the things my generation fondly thinks back on; Spin the Bottle, Truth or Dare, 7 Minutes in Heaven and lots of make-out parties. This was all by the time I was out of 8th grade. Speedway was active in the young love experimental years. My issue was: body hair.

I was tall in 8th grade and heavily into athletics. I pretty much started on every basketball, football and baseball team I played for. Not only did I start, I think I was considered one of the better players on the team. What I didn't know then was testosterone plays a big role in your hair growth. I'm 59 years old while I'm writing this book and I have a full head of thick hair. I'm NEVER going bald. Hair is a funny thing, if you have a hairy back you're going to be bald, period. If you have a hairy chest & legs your chances of going bald go up tenfold. To this day I have no hair on my arms or chest. I have the perfect swimmer's body. No waxing needed.

Starting in 7th grade you are forced, for the first time, to take showers after practice in whatever sport you are participating in. Humans at the age of 11-14 are at vastly different scales, or should I say timeframes, of reaching puberty. Going into the summer after 7th grade, my twig & berries were bald as a cue ball. It was worrying me to death! I was heavily into FCA (Fellowship of Christian Athletes) and MYF (Methodist Youth Fellowship). I asked God to give me pubic hair every night in my prayers. It's hilarious now to think back on that but it was catastrophic to me then. I was terrified I might be be called out for my lack of "Manhood" by my fellow teammates. That summer (June) I was on a houseboat at Lake Monroe. I was 14. I went into the bathroom to pee and the sun was shining just right through the small window - the beam of light, like the bat signal, hit directly what I was holding in my hand. There it was - my first pubic hair. It was a sign to me that God had been listening to my fervent wishes. I couldn't believe it. The rest of the summer I was like a Chia Pet down there with little baby blonde peach fuzz sprouting in. There was some hair on my balls too but the most important place was above my junk. By August, I had decent growth but it was barely visible to the naked eye. Two-a-day 8th grade football practices were starting in a week and I really wanted to feel confident hitting those showers this year.

Remember, my mom and dad were divorced when I was 4 years old. I was being raised by my mom and my two older sisters. That's when I somehow came up with the "brilliant" idea to use my mom's waterproof Maybelline Mascara to help the appearance and definition of my pubes. I tested it secretly, I mean very, very secretly, and the commercials were true! It lengthened, colored and even seemed to add volume to my sparse patch of baby buds. I remember looking at myself naked with my full(ish) tuft of dark manly pubic hair. I was over the moon! Even to this day when I hear the Maybelline theme song (cue music "Maybe it's Maybelline...") I chuckle to myself.

On the first day of football practice (two-a-days), that hot August, I was relieved that I had finally "appeared" to be a man. I could shower with confidence. When I got back to my locker and pulled down my sweaty jock strap I saw a black smear of a mess. It was a train-wreck down there. My skin was stained all around my penis, not so "waterproof" after all. It looked ridiculous. At that very moment, I knew this could affect the rest of my life. God only knows what degrading nicknames would be attached to me for eternity, i.e., Mascara Man / Bald WeeWee Boy. There was no way I could take a shower, impossible. I remember seeing other boys had become even more manly than they had appeared in 7th grade and I felt I was still falling behind. The coach had a strict rule that everyone had to shower. It was part of growing up. It's a cruel tradition to force young kids to get naked together at a time in their lives when their bodies are all developing at different speeds. I went into the coaches office and put on an award winning act of not feeling well. I'm not sure he completely bought it, but I was off the hook. I skipped the 2nd practice that day to be consistent and believable.

As with most things in life, the conjured up fears I created in my head were not as bad as reality. Yes, I was still behind most of the boys that 8th grade year, but by High School I was par for the course.

Landing Playboy

I had submitted myself for the Playboy gig via the Breakdowns and Dora Whitaker fielded the call from Willenborg Productions. It was for hosting a new show that Playboy TV was putting together. I remember when I saw it I felt a strong spark of interest. It didn't involve me doing any nudity and I was practically weaned on Playboy. In 1970 I was 5, so in 1980 I was 15, my formative years for sure. i grew up in the 70s, man! My buddy Tony Parker's dad always had Playboy hidden around the house for us to find. We would look at the naked girls for hours. It did something to our souls. The same summer my pubes were finally showing up I went on a mission trip to Mountain Top, which was a Methodist Church Camp in the Cumberland Mountains of Tennessee. We built fences, repaired porches, painted, cleaned and overall helped people's environment become more livable. It was an amazing spiritual experience. I went several summers. We usually took a bus called The Nightcrawler. It was a charter - the name always stuck with me. We had just pulled over at a truck stop for a quick bathroom break and I needed to get something out of my bag from under the bus. As I was rustling around under there, I found a bag full of nudie magazines! It was the Holy Grail. It had Playboys of course, but also the harsher Penthouse & Hustler along with a few Forums for the cerebrals. In this grab-bag of smut there were a few new ones to me; Juggs, Club and the amazing High Society which might have a photo of a naughty celebrity. I stuffed them all in MY bag knowing that whoever owned them couldn't make an announcement "Excuse me, whoever stole my porn magazines give them back" so it was the perfect crime. Later I saw the bus driver super pissed off - that mystery was solved. So what I'm saying is when I saw Playboy TV in the Breakdowns, I didn't hesitate.

My Breakdown trickery worked and I had an audition at the *Improv Comedy Club* on Melrose Ave for Playboy TV. The *Improv* is legendary and back in the day performers such as Judy Garland, Bette Midler and Barry Manilow would meet up there to play & party. Comedians the likes of Richard Pryor, George Carlin, Eddie Murphy, Robin Williams, Jim Carrey - basically all the greats, have stood on the stage I would be "performing" on for my audition. My agent got me the sides (script) and I could tell the show would be along the lines of *America's Funniest Home Videos* - but with nudity. Someone might be at a wedding and their top fell off or an amateur might have a hidden camera that usually involved nudity and laughs. The *sides* were two pages long and laid out like a monologue. It made sense that the auditions were at the Improv because this script seemed like a standup routine. Two pages seemed like a lot of dialogue and when I went through it I didn't find it all that funny. I decided to *punch it up* with some of my own brand of sick humor. I knew it would show my personality more and it was a gamble I thought I needed to take. I wanted to show them who I was and just reading their script didn't cut the mustard, as they say. Now, if it was a movie or TV gig of course, I would read the lines as they were written but this was hosting. A completely different ball of wax. I had watched Carson and Letterman walk out and deliver their opening monologues for years and I had often pretended to be them in the mirror.

I added a Richard Nixon impersonation with my shoulders crunched, my arms up above my head giving the double peace sign with both my hands, "I cannot tell a lie, that woman's boobs were flopping in the wind..." or something along these lines. I changed 50% of their jokes to be a lot more edgy, meaning dirty. I rehearsed for this audition more than I usually do. I had a girl I was dating come over and sit on the couch as I performed my shtick over and over again. She loved it. I felt good about my material and had it memorized. I knew we could take our lines in with us during the audition but I wanted to be more than prepared. I didn't realize the audition was at the *Improv* until I looked up from my Thomas Guide and saw the address below the marquee. This was different and exciting. I went in and there was a sign-in sheet as usual but the waiting area had those little tables you often see scattered throughout a bar area. My fellow auditionees (not a real word) were studying their lines, mouthing the words of the script to themselves. There is always one or two who are standing up facing a corner doing their bit. I had typed out my "new" version of the original sides and had them in my hand but knew once I walked through those curtains I was going to be script-free. You could slightly hear the other auditions which I loved and hated.

"Williamson Howe," said a good-looking guy named Jeremy. I raised my hand slightly and stood up. He motioned me through a velvet curtain and we entered the room from the back as a customer would who had come to see Jerry Seinfeld. I was led to the legendary stage and stood there in awe. Three people had set up shop with papers and headshots spread out before them on a portable table.

"You're Williamson Howe?" a man I later learned was Greg Willenborg asked me while holding up my Pamela Mougin headshot.

"Yes," I said.

"Williamson is my middle name," Greg proclaimed. He seemed to like me right off the bat. Maybe it was the connection with the name? I mean, how many people have that name? Greg was about 40 years old, had a light beard and a friendly confidence about him. I could tell he wanted to like me. Willenborg Productions had done some big shows including live events with Ray Charles, Oprah and had created original content for ABC, NBC, PBS, Disney and soon would add Playboy TV to it's resume. Greg was well known in the industry. I didn't know him from Adam at this point but I could tell he was in charge.

"You can go up on stage," he said. "Go ahead and start anytime."

My added jokes instantly paid off. As soon as I began I heard a laugh! Then I heard another laugh, then another. It felt good to hear them reacting to my jokes. I killed it. My audition felt great!

"Great job," I think Greg said with a small clap or two. "We'd like you to watch a few amateur videos and give us a play-by-play." His assistant Jeremy rolled a TV set from side stage to the center and angled it so we could both see the monitor. He hit play and the one video I remember best was a 300lb+ black woman, wearing a very small Teddy, coming down a flight of stairs. She was in a small apartment and trying to look sexy for the camera. I presumed she was performing for her man and I took over his persona.

"My oh my, here comes my sexy tons of fun, oh yeah baby, I'm gonna roll you around in flour to find the wet spot," was the first thing that came out of my mouth. Then her feet slipped out from underneath her and she began to bounce down the stairs on her butt. Her boobs flopped out the top of her Teddy. It was funny.

"Come to poppa, those delicious chocolate chip nips are as big as saucers," I blurted out. "Big daddy's going to treat you like a farm animal tonight." I heard gasps of joyous shocked laughter from Greg. They were loving my comments. I looked like a good "milk & cookies" kinda boy but I could talk like a sailor and my sense of humor was sexual and raw. To host a show on the *Playboy Channel* they needed someone who was not a "prude" - not shy. I knew I had passed this first test with flying colors. Sir Francis Bacon made me wonder...

I'd like to think that a man's fortune is in his own hands, but this is not true. Nothing can change a man's fortune faster than another man's folly. You can often get fortune faster from another man's error and this is exactly what happened to me. The wheel of fortune spun in my favor!

After that initial audition I had five callbacks. They weren't even auditions, they were more like meet & greets. I went to Playboy's headquarters in Beverly Hills, very close to Rodeo Drive, three times to meet executives or see how my chemistry was with certain girls who were "would be" co-hosts. Sometimes I'd be in someone's office and they would film our interactions. It was all very strange but I was thinking that I must have the job because they seemed very concerned with who I would bond with. I met Playmates, pornstars, E! Entertainment hosts and a plethora of other beautiful, talented women. I went to Greg Willenborg's office twice and he put me on camera with fun interview questions. I remember it was a Tuesday and Greg said that the President of *Playboy TV*, Jim English, was in Europe putting together a DirecTV deal and he was scheduled to look over the footage when he returned Thursday. He would make the final decision on the hosts by Friday, that's in three days. They all said I was their guy. Friday comes and goes, NO CALL. I'm beside myself with dread. It's the weekend so I can't call Willenborg's office to see what happened. Finally, Monday at 10am I call them. Jeremy, Greg's assistant, answers the phone.

"Hey Jeremy, it's Williamson. Greg said he'd call me by last Friday about hosting Naughty Amateur Home Videos and...," he stopped me.

"Oh Williamson, Greg wanted me to call you today. He's upset about it but Jim English looked at all the footage and just didn't want to go with an unknown person," he said. "We all wanted you, you were the only host we recommended."

I was heartbroken. I was so close to hosting my own show worldwide. I decided to go back to my business sense and I wrote two "Thank You" letters. One to Greg Willenborg and the other to Jim English personally. I told them both that getting this close gave me the confidence and reassurance that I'm out here in Hollywood for a reason. I now knew I had what it takes to make it. I used 100% white linen paper (highest quality), the best envelopes and signed each letter with a good quality pen. I had told a lot of people that I was super close to getting the Playboy job. I called my sister Mary that Monday afternoon feeling dejected.

"Hey Mary, I didn't get it," I said sadly.

"You're going to get it. I was in the shower and had this vision. You're going to be the host of the Playboy Channel," she assured me.

"No, I didn't get it. They want someone with a name," I explained.

"You're going to get it, I know it," Mary said. She didn't know how Hollywood worked. She persisted with her premonition, "You'll get it!"

- Perseverance is one of the keys to success. In tough moments most give up. Right when you're about to give up is often when magic happens.
- Show up! Not the best in school? Not all that book smart? Showing up and trying is 9/10 of success. Don't be lazy for your own dreams.
- Skills can be learned- especially now with the internet. Most pursuits don't require talent, it's learned skills and drive. Drive is king!

Jim English and a slew of Playboy executives were on set for the 1st day of filming the launch of *Naughty Amateur Home Videos*

(NAHV). The host was a B-level standup comedian along with Bridget Sturgeon and Nici Sterling. They had a lavish display of food from a top craft services company which included lobster, shrimp and champaign. From what I later heard, it was just before a break at lunch and the new male host was asked to do a few commercial tosses that would promote NAHV on Playboy TV to let viewers know where they could find the show. To me that seemed like a no-brainer part of the job, but this guy said it wasn't in his contract. He wanted more money to do the promos. Apparently, this didn't sit well.

"Get Williamson Howe on the phone PRONTO!" I'm told Jim English screamed. "That's the guy you all wanted anyway!" he fumed. 'Ring, Ring, Ring' my phone sprung to life. I was sitting at my desk looking over my recent submissions. A (213) number popped up - LA!

"Hello, this is Williamson," was how I always answered the phone.

"This is Greg Willenborg," he said with urgency. "We just fired the host of NAHV and Jim English says he wants you! Can you get over to Culver right now?" I said something like...

"I'll be there in 20 minutes," my heart was racing.

Promo party with Playboy execs along w/Bridget Spurgeon and June Playmate Carrie Stevens

Self Starter

With its own soundstages and distribution system, Playboy TV has become a ministudio.

BY ALAN WALDMAN

Hollywood Reporter had us on a full page spread. I wasn't laying low.

My fortune was another man's misfortune. A year later I'm at Gold's Gym in Venice Beach, California and the Rock, yes Dwayne Johnson, just asked me how many sets I had left on the vertical benchpress. I loved working out there because I saw celebrities all the time and the photos of ex-bodybuilders were cool. The place had an old-school vibe that motivated me. A guy came up to me soon after the Rock and said with a Spanish accent.

"Are you Williamson Howe?" he seemed surprised. "Yes!" I replied.

"I do your voice in Spanish," he declared excitedly.

"What do you mean?" I blurted out. "Naughty Amateur Home Videos, I dub your voice for Spanish speaking countries," he grinned.

"Wow, really? That's great," as he shook my hand.

"I know the guy who does your voice in German. He's gonna freak when I tell him I met you," he gushed.

Hosting for Playboy was an amazing experience. There can be repercussions to being part of something that can be controversial for some people but you just need to take the good with the bad. I didn't love ENTERTAINMENT WEEKLY comparing me to Bob Saget, I mean he's pretty cheesy but I guess so was our show. It was #1 worldwide and seeing my name in national magazines felt good. Plus, my picture was in each issue of Playboy Magazine.

The Mansion

The number of mansions in Los Angeles is uncountable, but from 1974-2017 if you uttered the words "I'm going to the Mansion tonight" people knew you were going to The Playboy Mansion. When I tell people I worked for Playboy one of their very first questions is, "Did I ever go to the *Mansion*?" The answer is, "YES, MANY TIMES!"

The first time I went to 10236 Charing Cross Road I remember pulling up to the gates and gave my name to a guy on an intercom,

"Oh hi, Williamson. We are excited to meet you," he casually said. My mind was blown as he said that. He knew me?

The two gates slowly swung open and I began driving my Jeep Cherokee through the entrance and up the plush green driveway peppered with a few Roman statues. I got a kick out of a yellow traffic sign warning "PLAYMATES AT PLAY". It's uphill through a luge of bushes and trees towards the entrance. When you first see "*The Mansion*" it's stone exterior is impressive with a Gothic-Tudor architectural vibe. You pass a circular fountain sitting just outside the front door and the valet takes your car through a stone entryway that goes between the main house and possibly an extra kitchen area. It all resembled a medieval castle with it's thick sturdy walls - very manly and strong in stature. From there you can walk directly into the main foyer and just like that, you are inside the world famous home of Hugh Hefner. There is the famous pool, a zoo, a separate building that housed a top notch game room with a pool table and several Playboy themed pinball machines. The floor was soft, I mean like cushion soft. It's like you're walking on a couch. It was almost difficult to walk around certain areas of the game room. I guess having the entire floor padded means you can "get busy" anywhere, at anytime, which I think was the point to having it that way. The well known grotto is a craggy cool cave that is attached to the pool. You can swim in through a rocky opening that gives you the aura of spelunking in Belize. There is also a small ledge around the inside of the grotto that would let you go inside without actually getting wet. It was a favorite place for party goers to chill out at night and imagine all the past, present and future debauchery this cave will inspire. What I didn't expect was the size of the grounds. You're driving in from Beverly Hills, so space is at a premium but this feels vast. It's 5.3 acres which best can be visualized as a little more than 4 footballs fields all laid out side by side. The walk from the pool to the zoo is a hike through the woods. The three (3) licensed zoos are a whacky addition to the adult playground. You will hear strange hoots, screams, howls and coos and that's just from Hef's bedroom! No, but actually "most" of those exotic sounds are the monkeys, cockatoos, peacocks, ducks, African cranes, parrots, toucans, pelicans and doves who were enjoying life. I saw them all on my numerous visits. The birds would have a run of the place which made it magical.

I mentioned that when I pulled up to the *Mansion* gate the guy who buzzed me in knew who I was. I was a mild celebrity there. At some of the bigger events I would be brought in by limousine and when I stepped out I would be hit with hundreds of flashing cameras. It was staged paparazzi but hey, I'll take it. I was new to this attention and I gotta say, "I liked it" and took it all in. The reason the staff, including Hugh Hefner himself, knew who I was is because they had Playboy TV playing on <u>all</u> the TVs 24/7 throughout, everywhere, inside & out. NAHV was the new #1 show so my face was a constant all around the *Mansion*. I also went to a lot of corporate events there, many during the afternoon or weekday evenings. Big companies would throw "thank you" parties for their top muffler salesmen or whatever they were hocking. Everyone was always excited to go to the *Playboy Mansion*. Hef would often make a guest appearance along with "props" (meaning girls hanging around the pool) to keep the mystique alive. If you go on Disney's Pirates of the Caribbean boat ride you expect to see skeletons and booty, right? Well, Hef gave you both! His skeletons were the old Hollywood stars, I mean the real oldie but goodies. Red Buttons was often there, Tony Curtis, James Can, Jack Nicholson, Warren Beatty and many other older legends came to his parties. Don't get me wrong, the young guns like Leonardo DiCaprio, Rihanna, Eminem, Snoop Dogg, and Quentin Tarantino to name a few, were there too. It seems that everyone who has or had a name in Hollywood has been there.

Other than the corporate events or fundraisers, getting into the real *Playboy* parties was almost impossible - especially for men. Hef had a team that worked on his exclusive guest list and being invited was a symbol of success. I would say the parties were as wild as you expect. Yes, there were orgies in the Grotto and people were amped up sexually, but during my time there it was a somewhat more tamed *Mansion*. Hefner married Kimberly Conrad in 1989 and they had two kids together. The parties were still great but less cray-cray than they were in the 70s & 80s. I heard they got back to being naughtier in 1999 after Hef & Kimberly split. *Playboy* cover model Pamela Anderson told FHM of her time at the Mansion. "It was all wild, but respectful." While she says "a kiss-and-tell is not my style," the star did offer up one tidbit of the overall vibe. "The men were elegant, and you wanted to badly get the most charismatic man to notice you," she said. "Girls were everywhere, giggling and laughing." This was my experience too. It had an intellectualness about it. Hef would have jazz bands, violinists, harps along with a sophisticated looking staff dressed in tuxedos. He had his famous “Movie Night” three times a week. Friday & Saturdays brought classics and Sundays were for first-run movies with actual 35mm prints supplied by the studios. It was amazing back then that someone could have movies at their house that were playing at the theater. Hef’s first love was the classics. Vintage films consumed his life on a daily basis, whether he was watching, cataloging, discussing or writing about them. Besides hosting his beloved movie nights, Hef was a serious force in the world of film preservation. He donated millions to the UCLA Film and Television Archive and George Eastman House to preserve such classics. I guess my point is, the Playboy Mansion was unique for many reasons and it was because of the eccentric life Hugh Hefner brought to this world.

Conventions / AVN / Fame

The hosting of Naughty Amateur Home Videos was only part of my *Playboy* experience. It was surprising back then how many people recognized me from *Playboy TV*. The problem is that when you're below even a B-grade actor, your "fans" (or at least the people who recognize you) give you no space. You're the ultimate "Bro" to them.

You've watched naked women together. Most people who came up to me assumed I actually lived in the basement of the Playboy Mansion, which was the show's premise. Guys would bear hug me, punch me, treat me like a long lost frat brother. On the other side, a side I find humorous, people would recognize me for something but they couldn't quite place how they knew me. I was in St. Elmos Steakhouse in Indianapolis. It's famous for it's steaks but even more so for it's insanely spicy shrimp cocktail sauce. Peyton Manning made St. Elmos his personal hangout. I'm sitting in the main dining room, "Excuse me, I don't mean to bother you, but I know you from somewhere," a guy of about 45 said while leaning over me. Then his wife joined alongside of him.

"Sorry, he kept telling me he knows you or maybe went to high school with you?" she said smiling suspiciously.

"Hmmm, I grew up in Indy on the Westside," I said. "You don't look familiar to me, but people always think they know me. I have a generic face."

"No, I recognize your voice, your face, your mannerisms," he insisted. We went through a few spins on the wheel of fortune but his luck was not shining on him. He could not remember where he knew me and would not let it go. I figured it must be Playboy TV. With his innocent wife at his side, I asked him in a way you may tell someone their fly is undone. Half whisper, face tilted and speaking a bit from the side of my mouth.

"Do you ever watch Playboy TV?" His wife gave a look like 'of course not' but he gave me a stare that said it all. Recognition had slapped him in the face, but it was apparent his wife did not know they had the Premium Channels. This sort of interaction happened quite a bit in one form or another. I learned that a lot of people watch *Playboy TV* secretly.

The conventions were a blast. They were often in other cities and everything would be comped; flight, hotel & food. We were treated like celebrities. In my first season with NAHV I had two co-hosts - Nici Sterling and Bridget Spurgeon. Nici was a Brit, born in Surrey, England, and from what I heard her family was quite well-to-do. Her socialite status may have taken a hit when she entered porn, I'm not sure, but I remember going to her ranch in LA and she had horses. She seemed a proper lady to me all the time I spent with her. Bridget Spurgeon was much like me, in that she didn't do nudity, no porn but was openminded and liked the energy of *Playboy TV*. Bridget was the sweetest person and aways full of great energy. She resembled a cross between Pamela Anderson and Jenny McCarthy to me. Her personality was electric. I heard she married a well known comic book artist, publisher and creator which makes me extremely happy for her.

She deserves all the best that life can shower onto someone. When we went to these conventions there would also be a group of Playmates and pornstars. I got to go to dinner with Victoria Silvstedt Playmate of the Year 1997. She was stunning and driven. She was a competitive skier in Sweden and placed fourth at the Swedish national alpine youth championship, in the giant slalom event. She was a pleasure to get to know. I met Lexus Locklear at a particularly wild convention in Nashville, TN. Nici Sterling couldn't go to that one because the authorities had threatened to arrest her at the airport. She had done an anal scene or something that the conservative bible-belt felt was an act against God. Lexus, dare I say, almost seemed to be pursuing me in Nashville. She introduced herself to me and I was gobsmacked. She had a shyness about her you wouldn't expect. I think she gravitated towards me because I was an outsider and not in the porn industry. There were rumors swirling about that she was going to be the lead in the new *Debbie Does Dallas* so there was that buzz going on around her which was exciting. I felt flattered that such a beautiful woman seemed smitten with me. We went to lunch and she spilled her coffee across the table and apologized.

"I'm so nervous," she squeaked out. "I'm so sorry." I remember I felt awkward around her too and I'm not sure why. I could theorize that I didn't like the idea of dating a pornstar and that's probably it. I was dabbling in the "forbidden fruit" side of life and I wasn't completely comfortable with it. My character on NAHV was the gullible nice guy. It wasn't that too far off of who I really was, or at least who I hoped to be. I knew hosting Playboy TV could help my career, but also more likely hurt it. The money was decent, regular and I was gaining more & more confidence in my acting. Hosting *Playboy* definitely helped my commercial auditions - meaning I was better on camera.

It was either at the Nashville convention (or maybe Atlanta) where I had some crazy fans and the girls (Playmates & pornstars) were teasing me about it. We had security assigned to us and I remember one wild woman got up to me and thrusted her vibrator in my face.

"Oh my god, Williamson will you sign my vibrator?" she begged.

"Look, I wrote your name along it's side and I masturbate with it every night." Then she tried to slip me her room key. I actually got to slightly feel what it must be like to be a star. I can't even imagine, well I can imagine, what it must be like to be Brad Pitt. I want to introduce something that has always intrigued me: *ENERGY.* Remember back in the day when you would pick up your phone and your mom would be on the other end? It took exact timing for that to happen. You hadn't spoken to her in a week and then this happens?

We emit a flow, a power, a spirit from our bodies that others can sense. I wanted to mention this earlier when I was talking about the *Playboy Mansion*. If you were standing with your back to the door and a huge star like Tom Cruise walked in - you would sense it. It's hard to explain, but a life-force emits from them. I'm writing about Tom Cruise right now, you're reading about Tom Cruise right now. How many people in the world, AT ANY GIVEN MOMENT, are watching his movies, reading about him or throwing his name out in a conversation? Tom is probably sitting on his couch in Beverly Hills chillin and all the human electricity of thought is beaming towards him. How could he not glow? Big stars have a coloring, a flavor, an aspect or ambience about them that puts them in a different atmosphere. I mentioned my movie star friend in Japan named Eisaku Yoshida in Chapter 8. He was coming to stay with my family and in Indianapolis, Indiana for his first American Thanksgiving Dinner. I had just finished my first week of shooting for Playboy. I was the big cheese all week and I felt powerful. When I met Eisaku at the airport in Indy he looked at me.

"You got it, man" he said smiling.

"I got what?"

"You have that look, you are shining. Hollywood man!" he smiled. "I know," he said leaning in laughing. "I'm fucking famous in Japan." He was kidding, but he is famous in Japan. He was basically telling me that I had a swagger, an aura of "I'm somebody" and he could sense it or see it on me. The night before Thanksgiving is a big bar night in most cities. I took Eisaku to Broadripple in Indianapolis. We headed to a new place called Eden. A girl came up to me, "My girlfriends and I are having a bet that you're not from Indianapolis," she flirted.

"No, I grew up here, on the Westside, Speedway," I told her.

"Really, wow. We all thought you weren't from here," she confided. I had been to Broadripple many many times. Never had a group of girls approached me me like this.

"Well, I live in Los Angeles now. I'm home for Thanksgiving," I confessed.

"I knew it, there is something about you that just didn't seem like you were living here," she proclaimed. I looked over at her table and waved. The girls were giddy. I bring up this story, not to brag, but to confirm there is some kismet, some forces in this universe that we can't explain. I was wearing the same old jeans and t-shirt but I was putting off a new energy. We all do this at times in our lives when we are beaming with an accomplishment. I think movie stars beam this energy at nuclear levels because they are given so much. I was in a Nightclub in Gôteborg, Sweden and I was recognized from Playboy and then again the next day on the street. The powerful force of TV was shining on me. This was incredible. I was being recognized in Europe.

We were obligated to do personal appearances at the *Mansion* and represent at conventions, but also Playboy wanted to be recognized at the Adult Video News Awards, which most people call AVN. It's in Vegas every year the same week that CES (Consumer Electronic Show) goes on. CES is the most influential tech event in the world. It's the latest and greatest in breakthrough technologies, and an incredible mashup to have both AVN & CES there at the same time. It makes for an interesting weekend of people watching. The AVN is an adult expo with novelties (vibrators and such). It is also known as the "Oscar for Porn" in the Adult Industry. My best memory of attending was when it was being held at Caesar's Palace. The red carpet event was outlandish. The fashions that sauntered down that red carpet were eye-popping. The wilder the better. I was assigned to work the red carpet to interview the stars as they made their way into Caesar's. I was in a sweet tux and my handheld mic had Playboy TV's logo attached to the end. All the stars wanted to be interviewed by *Playboy* and *E! Entertainment*. I might have had Brooke Burke next to me, or it was another one of E!'s well-known female hosts. I felt a sense of pride battling E! for the interviews. E! seemed more legit and I was doing just as good of a job as they were. I knew I could hold my own. Suddenly, I see Ron Jeremy. Some call him the Hedgehog for obvious reasons. He was in a tux and dragging a wannabe pornstar with him. He's basically in prison for life now, but back then he was a big deal - no pun intended. He was launched to stardom for sucking his own dick, I guess that is a "big deal" to say the least! I was given a cheat sheet to help me know which awards the stars were up for. I didn't know who any of them were so that was challenging, but I did know the Hedgehog and he was coming my way. Before I get into my brief Ron experience I thought you might want to hear some of these categories

• All-Girl Performer of the Year • Best Amateur Release
• Best Anal Series • Best Big Butt Release • Best Comedy
• Best Director Parody • Best Drama • Best Editing • Best MILF
• Best Oral Release • Clever Title of the Year

There are over 100 Categories. There's best body, best boobs, best webcam and it's a big deal to the winner's lives. Winning an AVN Award can lead to product endorsements and larger contracts with bigger production houses. There was NO WAY I could know what awards or categories all these stars were up for. When I saw Ron Jeremy I looked on my list and saw that he was up for 87 and Still Banging. It never crossed my mind that he had sex with an 87 year old lady.

"Ron, Ron... Williamson Howe here with Playboy TV," I got his attention. He's only about 5'8" and had put on some weight so he looked even shorter. He cuddled up right next to me. He was very comfortable in front of the camera.

"So Ron, you're up for 87 and Still Banging," I stated. "How in the world did you manage to have sex with 87 women, that's impressive!"

"No, no, no, I had sex with an 87 year old woman!" he laughed. Then he grabbed my face and turned it towards the camera. "Look at this face, this is a good looking guy," he said. "I have to bang 87 year olds!" He was cracking jokes left and right. He let my blunder go and was enjoying the red carpet. I felt bad I had made that mistake but it wasn't like I was on the Oscar Red Carpet and asked George Clooney how it was working with James Cameron on Titanic. Who could know all these titles? I was flying by the seat of my pants trying not to let the cat out of the bag: that I hadn't seen ANY of the films these people were starring in.

I mentioned novelties were a part of the AVN Awards. Doc Johnson is one of the leaders in sex toys. Some of their stuff is very realistic. They've been an innovator in this industry for 40+ years. On NAHV we would sometimes leave the studio and go to places like the famous Club Chateau in Van Nuys. Male patrons pay for "submission and dominance" sessions with women employees that can include being bound with chains and whipped. Oh the stories these girls can tell.

Apparently, some rich power movie executives like to be spanked and spit on. To each his own I guess, but it was a fascinating place to see and our viewers loved to get a look at the darker side, it was good TV. We also did segments at several dildo, vibrator and doll factories. We toured the places that made sex swings, lube manufacturers - basically if they made sex stuff, then *Playboy* wanted us there. A couple of interesting things came out of these visits. First, I was offered $20,000 for them to create "The Williamson." I believe it was Doc Johnson, but I'm not 100% sure. "*The Williamson*" would be a realistic penis molded from my you-know-what. They created a prototype box with the face of yours truly on it and WILLIAMSON written vertically along the side of a clear plastic window that let's us see my faux-member. I instantly turned them down. They countered saying they could use another man's anatomy if I didn't feel that mine was up to par. Trust me, that was NOT the issue. I mean, sure if I was actually going to do it then why not stretch the truth a little? But if I kept true to myself, I could hold my head high. Second, meaning the 2nd interesting thing, was that while hosting a visit to Doc Johnson I did let them cast my nipple, YES, MY NIPPLE! They made a silver money clip out of it. For a New York minute they wondered if they could sell that too, but women don't use money clips and the gay market was not Playboy's strength. I still have my silver nipple money clip in my nightstand. It's fun to pull out now & then. (see page 205)

The real issue coming to life was that my two different worlds were beginning to cross paths with one another. I was at one of my convention jobs signing autographs and a guy leaned in, "Does Acura know you host this show?" I was starting to become one of those "Commercial Stars" - you know, the ones you see over & over again hocking different products? I was also becoming known for hosting *Playboy*. These two worlds were going to collide and I knew that corporate America would drop me like a bad habit. Casting directors would dry up. Stopping "The Williamson" or a nipple money clip from getting into the open market would not save me. I was getting noticed on two completely different platforms and I was worried.

It wasn't too long after the encounter with that guy a big break came my way. My agent called me and said, "Oh my gosh, Marc Hirschfeld, the head of casting for NBC wants to see you for a development deal," she screeched. NBC had seen my Acura commercial where I drive all the way from LA to San Francisco, over the Golden Gate Bridge, and into a restaurant to meet a girl on a blind date. I drove all this way not for the girl, but because I just love to drive my Acura. In the spot I say, "LA" in response to her asking me where I drove from. It was a popular commercial. It aired during the Oscars and several championship sports game. My agent had seen the request to meet the guy in that commercial. This is the break all actors dream about. The hand of God was plucking me up to the top. That lightening in a bottle we all need to succeed was lit. Nearly every actor that made it to the top has a story to tell. It usually involves a lucky break. I had followed the best pattern possible. I had been hammering away going to auditions. I worked smart when dealing with the Breakdowns, I was diligent and focused. Booking commercials is one of the proven ways to get noticed. I had always treated going to Hollywood like a job. I did everything I could to move myself forward. I always knew that taking the Playboy gig could taint me, but I ignored that gut feeling. Jenny McCarthy was butt naked in *Playboy* and she got her own show "Jenny" on NBC at the exact time Marc Hirschfeld was requesting to see me. Tim Allen has a checkered past that makes me look like a choir boy - but he gets to play Santa. I never felt what I was doing was bad. I kept my clothes on and played the Jack Tripper part to Janet (Nici) and Chrissy (Bridget). It was all pretty innocent, especially after experiencing the AVN Awards.

I had a meet and greet with NBC. I remember sitting in the waiting area and there were large posters of Seinfeld, Friends, Jenny, ER, Fraiser - I mean, NBC was king. According to my agent they wanted to talk to me about being one of the leads in a new sitcom they were developing. I honestly don't remember much after going into Marc's office, but I know that *Playboy* came up and I never heard from them again. Of course, I will never know why I wasn't called in for a screen test. In my heart I felt it was Naughty Amateur Home Videos. Being associated with that level of nudity was a gamble NBC did not need to take. The fresh faced guy they saw on the Acura commercial was interviewing Ron Jeremy. I honestly cannot blame them. It hurt me though. I started to think that I had run my course in LA. One person who I felt truly accepted me was my mom. She was a hard working Christian woman and she seemed genuinely proud of me - even with

Playboy on my resume. She and my stepfather drove down to Nashville, TN and booked a room in the same hotel I was staying at with the *Playboy* crew. I was able to get her 2 passes into the convention and I think she had a ball. She waited in line for close to an hour to get her picture taken with me that they put inside a promotional booklet. Funny thing about parents, they are usually not as nerdy or conservative as you think. They were young and wild once and maybe still are. When I was living in Japan, I had mom record a bunch of commercials to use in my classes as teaching material. I let one of those VHS tapes run a bit longer and low & behold - I saw old school porn. So you never know who will accept you and who won't. I sure wish NBC would have given me a chance. I deserved it. On to bigger and better things. Well, I'm not sure about better...

A couple of things happened soon after my disappointment with NBC. At one of our conventions, I think was in Long Beach, I got into an elevator at about 12:45am. I thought I was the last person still out, but boy I was wrong. When the door dinged there was Doria Rone, the host of Night Calls. Her and Juli Ashton were the wild dynamic duo who fielded live phone-in listeners to discuss sexual issues and a lot of fantasies. They had a famous red couch that I'm sure had more DNA on it than a comforter at the Chicken Ranch. I was a guest on this popular show several times. I let viewers know that I studied at the Kinsey Institute in college and did so well, I became an AI and ran my own discussion group. I was trying to add some street cred to my advice. I wanted to be Dr. Drew so badly. I remember on one of my guest appearances, I bowed to the red couch to show respect because many of the Night Call guests would treat that couch like a wicked stepchild. Anyway, back to running into her on the elevator. Doria was drunk and yelled my name.

"WILLIAMSON!" and she raised her dress up to her boobs and showed her whole world to me.

"What are you doing?" I asked.

"Come on, we're going to a party in the penthouse," she mumbled. We went to the top floor, she marched out like she knew where she was going. We walked into a suite and it had a party going off. Girls were naked, girls were jumping up & down on the bed, people were dancing, but the thing is - IT WAS ALL GIRLS! Then I see one of the top executives of *Playboy*. Not *Playboy TV*, *Playboy Inc.*: the big cheese. He sees me and instantly beelines towards me.

"Williamson Howe, what are you doing here?" he asked annoyed.

"Doria grabbed me on the elevator," I explained innocently.

"You shouldn't be here," he said and then grabbed my arm and took me over to a table that had a lot of cocaine on it. "You're going to do this right now," he said while handing me a rolled up C-note. I knew what he was doing. He wanted to have something on me that would help keep my mouth shut. At the time, I didn't know things like this went on during these conventions, but I thought if they did, who cares? Why was this executive worried about me talking? I mean guys have "guy code" and he should be worried more about these girls than me.

"Ok," I said, bending over and doing a toot. He then got right in my face.

"Did you see Men in Black?" I nodded. He then lifts up his hand and pretends he's holding that instrument in the movie that makes everyone forget everything, the neuralyzer, the little device that makes a super bright flash and erases people's memories. He made a sound like paper tearing as he fake clicked his fingers.

"I won't say a word to anyone, I promise," and I didn't, until this book and I won't included his name. About three months later I'm at the *Mansion* for a violinist promo and I see him across the room. He comes over to me and says, "Don't fuck me!" and then put his hand up and repeated the neuralyzer gag along with the tearing paper talk. He then directly led me over to his wife and introduced me to her. I heard later they were having some issues and his extracurricular partying was on the highest down-low. I will say, after that incident my Playboy days seemed numbered.

Soon after that, *Playboy* brought in a German woman from Disney named named Dieta, who would be in charge of programming. She couldn't understand why my character on NAHV wasn't getting naked or at the very least, fondling the co-hosts. She said that 30% of Playboy viewers were women and that I needed to step up and strip down or they were going in a different direction. I was toast. *I walked away. It was a helluv a ride. Now what?*

Promo Cards: I'm here with Lexus Locklear and 1997 PMOY Victoria Silvstedt and unidentified Playmate.

My mom, stepdad Bruce and Bridget Spurgeon at my booth.

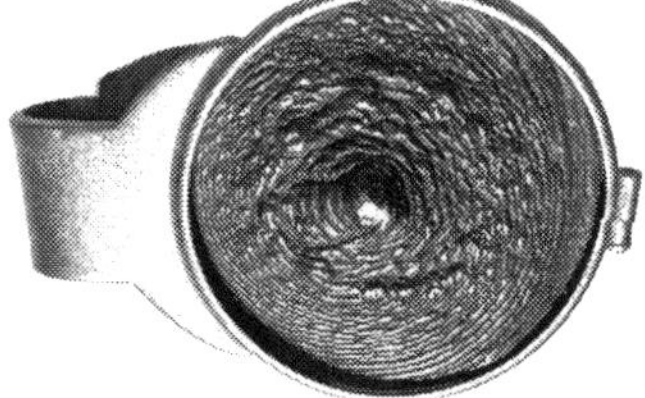

My Nipple Money Clip

Ric Payne

CHAPTER ELEVEN

•

"Run to the woods, Ricky!"

—Carl "Moose" Payne

FREEDOM, I'M SITTING in the *Cow's End* coffee shop in Marina del Rey, CA, about 1/2 mile from the boat Ric Payne and I share, writing his chapter hoping to be inspired. Back in 1997 I often came here to write in solitude but I also loved the energy of the people that drift in & out of this place, it kept my mind buzzing. The 2nd floor was, and still is, my sanctuary. It really hasn't changed much in 26 years. The other coffee shop I often squatted at was Novel - off of Main Street in Santa Monica. In 2017 I took my wife there to reminisce about my past Hemingway days and it had changed names to 212 Pier Cafe, but it still had the same old school charm. Michael Keaton was sitting at a table reading a script minding his own business when we walked in. It's these moments that only LA & NYC can provide. "I'm Batman" or "It's Showtime" from Beetlejuice, shot through my head. I've been around many movie stars in the last 20+ years and it makes me appreciate the magic of Hollywood. These people rose to the top in one of the hardest industries to "Make It" in. I know, I gave it a real gung-ho effort myself. Nostalgia always feels good to me. To come back to this coffee shop (Cow's End), this many years later, and basically do the same thing, WRITING, is a blessing and a real joy. The energy is still flowing. I'm still not tied down to a 9 to 5, thank god!

Meeting Ric Payne, and working with him and his brother Kerry, has a lot to do with this freedom. Ric and I met in LA in 1998 and he soon funded my screenplay *Back Home Again*. Unbeknownst to me then, we were creating a lifelong friendship which has lead to successful businesses in the entertainment field, bars & nightclubs and several successful inventions. How did this fateful meeting happen?

It's Season 2 of *NAHV (Playboy TV)* and I'm looking over my script when there's a knock at my dressing room. My dressing room was nothing fancy but I did have my name on the door and some shrimp cocktail chilling on my makeup counter. I looked legit Hollywood. Little did I know when I opened the door that I would meet a man who would change the course of my life.

"Hi, I'm Ric Payne," he said putting out his Andre the Giant size paw to shake my hand.

"Oh, great! Bill Niemann said you were going to stop by," I said. With Ric, was my future roommate Brian Nahas. Ric had gotten my number via Bill Niemann. Remember, Bill's the friend I drove my grandma's Olds to LA with & he lived in Japan for three months.

Ric was in the bar & restaurant business in my hometown (Indianapolis) and Bill worked for Sysco Foods as his reps. That connection and our mutual love of creating stuff got us off to a good start. Ric had grown up only about two miles from my house but went to Northwest High School, not Speedway and he's 4 years older than me. Northwest HS students called Speedway "Home of the Comb" and we referred to them as "Northworst." They thought we were "rich, clean cut preppies" as Ric always says, but in fact we were just barely middle class. In our Westside bubble we didn't know about the real Richie Riches on the Northside of Indianapolis; Carmel, Zionsville, prep schools, private schools. When you're a kid you don't know what you don't have. To Ric's crowd we were a bunch of Donald Trump Juniors - spoiled rotten. Our high-schools were only 1.2 miles apart so Ric and I basically grew up "*universe brothers*" on the world scale of things; our experiences, the places we ran around, the weather, the Indy 500, Long's Bakery, cruising the same McDonald's and lets not forget girls - lots of connected experiences. We also had plenty of mutual friends.

Ric & Kerry (his brother) owned Eden Dance Club in Broadripple, Indiana along with one McGilvery's Pub & Eatery in Greenwood when I met him. These business partner brothers had owned another

McGilvery's in Speedway, but had sold it. This McGilvery's Irish Pub was a favorite hangout on my side of town. Everyone went there, it was THE PLACE to go! Many teachers from my high school hung out there too. It's always a trip to share a beer with one of your ex-teachers. It's a right of passage. I had gone there many times but had never met Ric or Kerry, they were lay-low owners. They still are all these years later.

Ric & Kerry had sold that McGilvery's (Speedway) to open Eden Dance Club (circa 1991-2001) which left them back down to only one pub when I met Ric. Eden Dance Club took Indianapolis by storm. In my opinion, it's still considered the most popular dance club in the history of the city. If not by everyone, then by the ones who experienced it's magic. It put a lot of money in their pockets and was the reason Ric could knock on my dressing room door and later fund our movie. He was riding high on his bar & restaurant success, but had an itch for Hollywood.

Ric had gone to New York City with his wife Madonna, no not <u>that</u> Madonna, and they headed to the famous dance club - The Palladium. This was around 1989. At this time, he and Kerry owned two McGilvery's and as usual, Ric was hungry for more. Lack of motivation was never on his radar, it's still not. Ric heard the house, techno/trans music pumping. It was blowing up in NYC. The Palladium planted the seed and Ric went on the hunt for the perfect space to build his own monster dance club in Indianapolis. Kerry was looking through the paper one morning and saw: **Old Masonic Lodge** *for rent* in a tiny little ad. It was laid out perfectly for what they wanted to bring to Indy. This would be a whole new type of entertainment. The music was hypnotic and Ric's decadent decor brought out the masses. Each of the three floors had a different sexy vibe. The main room had 30' ceilings, a huge dance floor, booming bass, electric light LED displays throughout the club and live performing go-go dancers brought sexuality and excitement. The 2nd floor had pool tables and swinging chairs and the top floor was a cushy VIP lounge with it's own private bar that looked down on all the action. The show-stopping thrills were the DJs they brought in from around the world. Eden had a big city vibe that many in the Midwest were jonesing for - high energy fun. It had everything you'd expect to see in Vegas or NYC, but this was in Broad Ripple, Indiana. It almost felt out of place, like a bar in the middle of the desert. I'm talking about Ric & Kerry's bar/club experience because it ends up becoming a big part of my future too, but I didn't know that just yet.

The quote below the title of this chapter "*Run to the Woods*" refers to the woods just past the end zone at the Little League Football field where little Ricky played as a kid. Ric's dad, Carl Payne, knew something about winning and he instilled that drive in Ricky early on. *Run to the Woods* is motivating, never give up, see your goal and GO FOR IT! To understand Ric Payne you need to know his family history.

His mother and father were two of the most famous Roller Derby stars that ever lived. I know that's a big claim but it's true. Carl's nickname was "*Moose*" because for that era he was unusually tall and strong as oak. Their mother, Monte Jean, was a superstar's superstar as well. Both were captains of the New Jersey Jolters which had both a men's & women's team. Moose & Monte were becoming the darlings of America's fascination with sports. Starting in 1949 the Roller Derby had a contract with ABC to have their matches televised live all across the US. Promoter Leo Seltzer had made a couple million dollars creating "*Walkathons*" which is what they called Dance Marathons back then. He now was working his barking magic with the Roller Derby. Ric and Kerry's parents were his stars. They were a big deal. TV was just starting to take off and roller derby was one of the first sports to capture an audience. In 1950 the New Jersey Jolters won the Roller Derby World Series and their championship matches in 1950

& 1951 broke all attendance records at Madison Square Garden. They were sold-out for five (5) consecutive days with between 77,000 to 85,000 fans in attendance. New Jersey had a ticker-tape parade for their champions. Ric's mom and dad were true celebrity athletes back then. They were up there alongside Joe DiMaggio, Jim Brown, Ben Hogan, Rocky Marciano - I'm trying to help you understand a lost era in history. It happens. Famous people are forgotten. Roller Derby was a big deal in the 40s & 50s. His mom, Monte Jean, was the first woman to be promoted by Wheaties Cereal. His mom and dad are in the Roller Derby Hall of Fame and their story is being developed into a screenplay. I hope one day we can all go to the movies and see this slice of history.

Carl "Moose" Payne getting the championship trophy from Leo Seltzer

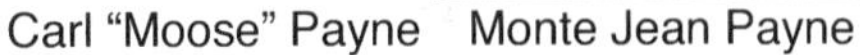
Carl "Moose" Payne Monte Jean Payne

I got a bit off track - Ric is talented and had dabbled in commercials along with acting in several independent movies back in Indianapolis. He had the acting bug. With the success of Eden Dance Club along with his *McGilvery's Pub & Eatery,* he was doing well. He had gotten an apartment in Hollywood with a fellow Hoosier named Brian Nahas. Brian was with Ric when they knocked on my dressing room door. Ric would fly back & forth from LA. He had a manager, but he wasn't booking anything much in LA. I had a story idea I thought Ric might like. I had written a few screenplays, one had Eisaku Yoshida (Japanese Movie Star) signed onto called The Exchange. I told Ric that Tom Benko from Paramount, who was an accomplished TV director/

editor, was interested in it. He had worked on shows like *MacGyver* and *Star Trek the Next Generation* and liked the script. TV directors are always looking for a project that can lead them to film. I had another one titled The Soup Story that I got a phone call about one night from Christopher Lemon, yes - Jack Lemon's son! He and his wife were reading it in bed and liked it. It is a father/son story and Christopher gave me instructions on how to get it to his dad. He said he had always wanted to do a movie with his dad and this might be the right story. I was trying to let Ric know that my writing was getting some attention. I told him about another script that Suge Knight from *Death Row Records* had optioned, *Yes, THAT Suge!*

I need to tell the Death Row "option" story! Suge was in prison at the time, later he got out but went back "home" again. I say that because he's been in & out of custody so much that prison probably felt comfortable, homey. I heard he was thinking about creating *Death Row Pictures* and through a connection, he wanted to read a script I wrote that is racially motivated called Torn. The plot centers around a serial killer who hates one-half of his own self. It's a twisted psychological thriller. I got the idea from an Oprah Winfrey episode - when she still did controversy. It also mimicked some of the racism I saw & experienced in Japan. It was around 1998 and I had a meet & greet with a man & woman from *Death Row Records* at the Cheesecake Factory in Beverly Hills. I gave them the script along with my inspiration for it and two weeks later I got summoned to Death Row. The few people who had read Torn had told me I should let an African-American read it to see if it's offensive, "get notes" they said, "Feedback from the race it's about." I hadn't done that. Oprah & Japan were my guiding light. Torn represents inner racism. I felt confident in my story, but I must confess I didn't want to piss off the bigwigs at *Death Row Records*. By this time, Tupac Shakur had been killed in Vegas (1996), Dr. Dre had left, Snoop Dog bailed on Death Row too in 1997. Death Row Records seemed to be in a decline and I think Suge thought movies could be the ticket to continued success. The brand "Death Row" was powerful. Everyone knew the players; Dr. Dre, Suge, Snoop, Tupac, Dick Griffith and "Harry-O" Harris.

The thought of going to their studio made me nervous. It was out of my comfort zone. In 1994 Suge Knight had been convicted of beating two musicians with a telephone inside this studio. That's when telephones could be a weapon - big & heavy. These studios had history, the type of history I didn't want to be a headline for. I distinctly remember hoping they weren't upset with this "white boy" handing Suge Knight a script to read in prison, a script that describes black racism, where 1/2 of a serial killer's DNA drives him to murder. He's racist against half of himself. He developed a hatred for his mother, who was black, because she created him with a white man. It's very controversial and could be taken the wrong way, but these types of "Torn" feelings exist. The black panel on Oprah were honestly discussing it, I saw mixed race discrimination firsthand in Japan. The truth isn't always pretty. This script shines a light on a tough subject.

My meeting wasn't at their polished 8200 Wilshire Blvd headquarters, it was at *Can-Am Recorders* in Tarzana. It's a legendary *Death Row Records* recording location that looked a bit dodgy from the outside. I remember sitting in my car looking at the front door. The windows were blacked out. The exterior walls were grey cinderblocks with a terra-cotta awning hanging over the front door and a rollup garage to the right of the entrance. I mustered up the gumption and went inside and I'm hit with the sweet smell of weed, no surprise there. No one was at the reception desk and I looked around awkwardly. I saw a long hallway to my right and a couple of black guys were sitting very comfortably on a couch to the left. There were loads of gold records and photos on the walls. I felt completely out of place but then I saw the guy from my first meeting at the Cheesecake Factory coming down the hallway towards me.

"You made it," he said smiling. "Follow me back." We went into an office.

"So did Mr. Knight like Torn?" I asked. I used 'Mr' because I wasn't sure it was acceptable to call him Suge, or even Suge Knight. The guy I was meeting for the 2nd time was young, about 26, well dressed casual preppy and mature beyond his years.

"Would you option the script for 3 months?" he asked.

"Absolutely," I blurted out. No playing hard to get from me. "Did he read it?" I asked again, hoping for an answer. The thought of my script going through prison security and to Suge's cell had an element of excitement to me. Suge was a big name and my ego wanted to know if his hands had flipped my pages while hardened criminals possibly screamed bloody murder in the background. I never got a direct answer from him, leading me to believe Suge likely didn't read it, but someone must have because they are talking options. Maybe the "Death Row Pictures" idea wasn't Suge's? No matter, I got a stipend for their exclusive *First Right of Refusal*. Unfortunately, none of this story materialized into them making Torn but it gave me confidence in my writing, and what a story to tell my grandkids or at least give me mad cred to Ric Payne.

After initially meeting Ric on the set of Playboy, we began hanging out. As mentioned, we both grew up on the Westside of Indianapolis and quickly learned we knew loads of the same people and his girlfriend back in the day was from my high school. We were both motivated and I'm sure he could see I was a go-getter too. I was getting the Breakdowns illegally daily, I had my own Asian talent agency *The Exchange* along with the Asian dating service *Tea Time*. Most importantly, I was consistently booking acting & hosting gigs. I brought up my script history to him to convey my "near misses" as clout. I pitched him my storyline for "*Back Home Again*" in hopes he'd like it. It was about four high school buddies from Indiana. The title seemed perfect because *Back Home Again* is basically the state song in Indiana. Jim Nabors sang "Back Home Again in Indiana" at the Indianapolis 500 Mile Race for 36 years. Every Hoosier knows this song and the title of my future screenplay said it all. Here was my pitch:

Back Home Again (*Synopsis*)

Four high school buddies graduate and go different ways. They all leave Indiana except one. Fifteen years later they are all back together for the holidays and go out running around like the good ol' days. The Hoosier who never left could see that none of them were all that happy with their lives and he convinces them to move "Back Home Again" where they would all open a bar called Dillingers. It's a heartfelt buddy comedy.

I got an encouraging green light from Ric. He loved the concept of the story and would be interested in making a movie called *Back Home Again*. It was the perfect project for two Indiana guys to dip their toes into the movie making waters. The four leads would be Ric as Gary, me as Decatur, Ric's good friend Brian Nahas could play Tipton and we could cast the remaining characters in Indiana. I started hanging out with Brian a lot more and developed his character Tipton around his amusing ticks and unique personality. We eventually became roommates in Santa Monica. All the characters in the movie would be named after Indiana towns as an added Indiana secret.

"Freedom is just another word for nothin' left to lose"
—song Bobby McGee

Kris Kristofferson wrote this song and Janis Joplin put it on the map. Great relationships, great collaborations - create greatness. Ric was a outstanding receiver in football. He went to Georgia in 1979 as a walk-on freshman and made the traveling squad which is unusual. He had phenomenal hands, he could catch anything thrown anywhere near him. He had wheels too, running a 4.5/40. That's fast. His family's DNA has a lineage of greatness. His older brother Randy played 7 years in the NFL catching passes from "The Scrambler" Fran Tarkenton when he was with the New York Giants. I bring this up because Georgia's 1980 season was magical. Led by Hershel Walker - they beat Notre Dame in the Sugar Bowl to claim the National Title.

What trips Ric Payne's switch? I'll play armchair psychologist - he LEFT Georgia football after having the best first year one could ever hope for. He was homesick and a bit too cocky. He transferred to Indiana University football and sat at home New Years Day 1981, watching the guys he ran circles around play on football's biggest stage. Many of them went on to play in the NFL. That decision was a gut punch. Ric missed that stage. The drive for glory is still in his blood. Today, he continues to chases big dreams and the sting of Georgia may or may not have anything to do with it?

Don't get me wrong, he's living a phenomenal life. He's figured it out. Freedom is our middle name, but Ric is still striving for greatness. He's never quite satisfied. Not that this is always a perfect quality but it's worked for him. When he does something he pushes all his chip in. He's very motivated to succeed and that drive has carried over into all the business shenanigans we've gotten ourselves into in the last 25 years. We continue to create new adventures.

Ric, Kerry & I have a great partnership that I'm thankful for.

The Moo Brothers
The Bar Kings

Myself and Ric
2024

Back Home Again

"The Movie"

CHAPTER TWELVE

•

"The only safe thing is to take a chance."
—Mike Nichols

IT'S HARD TO look at the above quote and not love it. Mike Nichols won all four of the major entertainment awards: Emmy, Grammy, Oscar and Tony (EGOT). I was thankful that Ric Payne was willing to take a chance and invest somewhere in the ballpark of $50-75,000 to make Back Home Again into a feature. Remember an earlier quote, "*if you want more luck take more chances,*" a life force that I definitely know Ric and I both subscribe to.

I had gotten the idea, or should I say the vibe, for BHA from a 1996 movie called Beautiful Girls. Eisaku Yoshida and I went to see that movie in Westwood (UCLA campus area) and we loved it. The spirit, the environment of that film called out to me. The words "back home again" just set up the whole idea of friends all returning home for some function, be it a wedding as it was in *Beautiful Girls*, or the Christmas Holiday as my script did. At this time I was doing my writing at the Insomnia Cafe on Beverly Blvd which is in the Fairfax District. Not too far down from the famed Farmer's Market. The original working title for the hit TV sitcom *Friends* was *Insomnia Cafe*. Marta Kauffman, co-creator of *Friends,* said she'd often drove by the cafe and it sparked the idea for one of the most seminal shows in television history. I didn't know any of this at the time. Apparently loads of celebrities liked this caffeinated place too: Tim McGraw, Mel Gibson, Sharon Stone, the genius Robin Williams, Leo DiCaprio - but I never saw any of them because I was there too bright and early. It had a creative energy flowing inside along with the coffee, so maybe I felt the presence of greatness there?

Getting there right when they opened at 7am actually helped create a funny scene in *Back Home Again* (BHA). I liked to set up shop in the front window. Usually I'd be the only one there for about the first hour besides the few customers who double-parked and ran in for a cup of Joe to take to the office. One morning a stunning young girl of about 25 came in right at opening. She unloaded a stack of books from her backpack and set up her own little shop too. She had the girl next door look, but with a splash of Ivy League and hippie thrown in. I had seen her one other time and she more than caught my eye.

We were both sipping our coffees and did small acknowledgements to the existence of each other. I'd like to say those brief eye contacts were flirting but it might have been creepy too. She got up and headed to the bathroom in the far back left. Insomnia only had one unisex bathroom. I waited a minute or two and thought I'd go back there and pretend to be perusing the bulletin-board. I could break the ice and say, "Hi" or something clever "You're an early bird this morning," but I never got the chance. When she exited the toilet I turned towards the opening door and the look on her face was terror. Well, terror might be a bit strong, but "horrified shock" might fit the bill best. An alarm went off in me that said *'this is not the face of a person who wants small talk'*. She blew past me and avoided all eye contact. I waited a beat, to not look stalkerish, and went into the bathroom to kill time. What I didn't know was she had already killed that room, something died in there. The funk was nauseating - you could almost taste it's thick foul fumes on your tongue. It was hard to breathe. The toilet still had a muddy, soiled splatter decorating it's once white porcelain bowl. There wasn't a toilet brush in there so there would have been no way for her to wipe away the damage and the smell would just take time to dissipate. I gasped for clean air as long as I could and got the heck out of there. I heard the little bell at the top of the front door clatter, she had gathered her mammoth loads of books and boogied out of Dodge faster than I would have thought humanly possible. She was GONE!

I instantly saw the humor in what had just happened. I wrote a scene where Tipton Riley, played by Brian Nahas, had a stunning blonde checking him out in a restaurant. Encouraged by the attention, he went back to the restroom to groom himself. He's bald, so that in itself was funny, he had no hair to fix. When he got back there, the men's room had a little yellow caution/closed sign on the floor in front of the entrance. He wiggled the women's room door and it was locked but just then a little old lady came sauntering out with a satisfied smile on her face, seemingly oblivious that she had left him a big surprise. Tipton steps inside to witness the same bomb as the "*Insomnia Cafe* HiroSHITma Scene" that I had experienced but with an even greater exaggerated mess. He goes to get out of there as fast as he can but when he opens the door the blonde bombshell gives him a big "Hi" and a smile. He can't speak. He goes back to the table and tells Gary (Ric Payne) and Decatur (me) what had happened. The blonde comes marching back, quickly gathers her things and heads to the door. Gary says, "What the hell happened back there bro?" Tipton points to the little old lady, "See that little old lady? If the Germans would have had her they would have beat us to the bomb!" Gary teases, "She thinks that's YOUR funk stinking up the joint" and Decatur barks, "You've got to go tell her that wasn't you!" Tipton chases after her with success. He convinced her it wasn't him who destroyed that toilet and better yet, he gets her number. I took this comedy one step further. On their first date we see them kissing goodnight in Tipton's car. She steps out of the car to leave and as she shuts her door Tipton releases a stinker he had been holding in for an hour. Just then, Marion (Jody Rasp), realizes she left her purse in the car and yells, "WAIT!" It was clear Tipton saw & heard her plea but he still sped away in a panic. While circling the block, he rolls down his window trying to fan the smell out. He pulls up and she's angry.

"What the hell's your problem," obviously annoyed. "Did you step on the gas or what?" she says as she's leaning in to grab her purse.

"Yes, yes my foot got stuck, I'm sorry Marion!" Tipton promises. Just then you see her nose crinkle up.

"Oooh, that WAS your butt gravy stinking up the cafe, yuck!" she proclaims while slamming the door. Tipton rolls down her window and pleads to her.

"It's wasn't me, I swear!" She turns again before storming off, "YOU'RE A LIAR, TOO! He had lost this beauty forever. I never had forgotten Lee Mann using the phrase "Butt Gravy" when I accidentally put my hand where it did not belong during IU Cheerleading tryouts. It's a great scene in the movie with loads of one-liners and throwing that phrase in there still makes me chuckle.

It's June and I had the *Back Home Again* script just about finished. Ric and I were in constant communication. We'd need to start shooting around the end of November and then finish up just before Christmas. It's set around the Holidays, so we wanted it cold and the city decked out with holiday joy. This gave us only 6 months before we were to roll film. That was not very far away for everything we needed to do, but we didn't want to wait another year. We were under the gun but sometimes a deadline gets the lead out. We figured it would be about a 20 day shoot. There was still loads to do and mentally we were going over locations we thought we could use. We needed an impressive Hollywood mansion to pull off a big scene with Brian's character Tipton and Auburn. We were fortunate to have Heather Kozar, Playmate of the Year 1999, whose character is a wanna-be actress named Auburn, as part of the cast. Heather and I had become friends through Playboy and she is simply stunning inside and out. I was thrilled to have her as part of this project.

Around July I'm talking to Pamela Mougin, the photographer, about getting more headshots and telling her about the movie I'm going to be shooting In Indy. She said she had a connection to Jim Irsay - the owner of the Indianapolis Colts. I asked her if she thought she could get my script to him? There was an interesting part in it for a Hollywood Producer who lives in a big fancy mansion. The movie being called "*Back Home Again*" added some clout to my fellow Hoosiers and I had heard Mr. Irsay was generous and liked helping out the artist. I thought I could kill two birds with one stone: cast him as the Producer and use his house as a location for the audacious mansion. It was a Tuesday morning in August and the NFL Pre-Season was in full bloom. I was sitting in LA drinking coffee when my phone rang. Irsay's secretary is on the other end asking me if I'd like to fly with Jim, his family & friends on their private jet to New Orleans and be his guest when the Colts play the Saints. Wow, what a surprise! Unbeknownst to me, Pamela had gotten my script to him after all. I don't even think SHE knew she had actually finagled it into his hands. Of course I said, "YES!" as fast as I could. She told me that Pamela was welcome to come too and that she would send more details in a couple of days. I needed to be at the Indianapolis Int'l Airport that Friday, late morning. My mind sprung to action. This is incredible, I put good energy out there and it's flowing back to me at light speed. I booked a flight to Indy and was officially "Back Home Again" on Thursday, the day before my adventure.

Friday morning, Aug 20, 1999, I drove out to an area of the airport I didn't know existed. It's the private hangar area where the bigwigs store their toys. There was a small gathering room with coffee and snacks where I was meeting my fellow passengers. It was me, Pamela Mougin and her assistant Carrie-Ann. I adored her. Dr. James Steichen and his wife Joan were on the plane along with Jim Irsay and his family, which included his wife Meg and two of their three daughters. I think it was Casey & Carlie because Kalen would have been quite young, but I'm not sure. It was a great group of people and Jim Irsay was very accommodating, welcoming, generous and kind to me. He had just inherited the Indianapolis Cots in 1997 and I got the feeling he was really enjoying the freedom of being "The Man" in charge. I say that in the best way possible because he was giddy with happiness, a playful love for living the dream. This was my constant experience with him. He was a big kid enjoying life. He genuinely loved / loves the Colts. This was his team now and he had a fire in his belly to win. Winning seemed to be his passion but with a flare of fun. He has an oddity about him, but he felt like my kind of odd. I liked him from the minute I met him.

When we landed in New Orleans there was a police escort that whisked us downtown in a blacked out mini-bus. It was all very incognito. I didn't realize "the rich & famous" could get police escorts for basically no reason. I mean, there was no emergency, no safety threats, so why would we "deserve" an escort other than the amazing feeling of swinging our dicks around? I loved it but it felt undeserved, at least to me it was. We were staying at an elite hotel, luxury baby, even my itinerary was neatly typed up and laying on the bed. The whole group was invited to dinner at *Antonio's* which was established in 1840 and claims to be the country's longest family-run restaurant in the US. It's absolutely one of New Orlean's finest places to eat. I was told to bring a collared shirt and this place was the reason why, swanky! Dr. Steichen, I'll call him James, was a true aficionado of wine and Antonio's is known for having one of the best collections in the US. The wine master (keeper), Mathew Osset, offered to give James a tour of the cellar and I eagerly volunteered to tag along with him and Mr. Irsay. Just us super successful men choosing our gazillion dollar libations, like you do. I'm kidding, but hanging out with a billion & millionaire felt important, privileged - although obviously MY bank account was not in their stratosphere. I was the welcomed screenplay boy from Hollyweird because movie making carries it's own glow of power. They made me feel like one of the guys.

The wine cellar was impressive, hidden away in the bomb shelter basement. It was a long & narrow, a dimly lit hall that begged for a bowling ball to be tossed down it. There were close to 20,000 wine bottles stacked from floor to ceiling. Many of the bottles had a thin layer of dust coating their aged bottoms. James was like a little kid in a candy store but Jim Irsay and I just nodded a lot. Three bottles were chosen; a Bordeaux, a Pinot Noir from Burgundy and I think a Cabernet Sauvignon. I'm not a wine guy but I try to fake it whenever I can. We returned to our table and I learned that these three bottles were rare and expensive choices. The red liquid gold added $20,000 to our bill! They poured them into carafes to let them air out ("let them breathe" as they say) after being corked up for decades. The genie was out of the bottle and ready to serve her purpose, alter our minds and stroke our egos. It was fun for me to play rich. I appreciated every minute of it. James asked for the empty bottles to be wrapped in foil so he could keep them as trophies. I knew I was experiencing something special through his genuine excitement. Dr. James Steichen founded the Indiana Hand Surgery Clinic. It's one of the top facilities in the world. He set a high standard for everything he did. I later heard he had an impressive collection of antique cars, art, watches, canes and of course - wine.

The next day we were up in the visiting owner's suite at the Superdome and being treated like royalty. The buzz that season was rookie Edgrin James. He was selected 4th and Irsay signed him to a $49M rookie contract. There were some naysayers suggesting the

Colts should have picked up Heisman Trophy winner Ricky Williams instead, but "The Edge" proved them all wrong and was the NFL Offense Rookie of the Year. Impressively, he also won the rushing title as a rookie. How often is that done? Before I move on, I have to plug Jim Irsay one more time. Edgrin James left the Colts as their All-Time leading rusher in 2006. The following year they won Superbowl XLI. Irsay sent The Edge a Superbowl Ring. That's a class act in my opinion.

The Colt's won the pre-season game in New Orleans 37-7 and Irsay was in a giving mood. There were no bodyguards, no protectors with us, as we marched down Bourbon Street through the thick crowd of misfit toys (overt partiers). Jim Irsay was handing out $100 bills to strangers. It was wild. He always kept moving. We marched into an oyster shucker joint and Irsay went down the line handing all the staff C-notes over the counter. He put smiles on people's faces everywhere we went. If my memory serves me right, we walked into a shelter, cold off the street, and he wrote them a check bigger than our wine bill the night before which sounds pretentious, but was $20K+. We finally sat down to eat at another Or'lens place, as they say, when Irsay jumped up and wanted James and I to truck back to the hotel with him. We bulldozed through the crowded streets again and headed to his room four blocks over. He had forgotten 3 boxes of Colt's gear (shirts & hats) in his room that he wanted to give away. He was beaming from the ass whoopin' we gave the Saints. We proceeded to toss out Colt's swag as we pied piperied back to dinner. We finally emptied the cardboard boxes with a final toss of shirts to the restaurant staff. If you look up *Grab the Tiger by the Tail* in the dictionary, Jim Irsay's picture should be in there. He was lightening in a bottle in 1999. I will always remember and appreciate that trip. He was experiencing YOLO before YOLO was a thing.

Ultimately, he decided to pass on playing the Hollywood Producer in our movie *Back Home Again*, but Dr. Steichen's wife Joan was at the gym, not too long after that trip, and she ran into Richard and Donna Deer. The trip to New Orleans ended up adding a lot to the movie and my life after all. I didn't have a clue who the Deers were but they just had a spread in the *Indianapolis Monthly* featuring their home. It was gloriously gaudy. Through photos it looked like Hollywood on crack. It was more Hollywood than Hollywood because it fit the fantasy. Joan had told them about me and the project. James called me and said the Deers seemed interested to meet. Richard & Donna Deer made their money through BDI Marketing which sold *Mini Thins* as dietary supplements jacked with caffeine for truckers. BDI was legit but walked a fine line with the Feds because the pills also had ephedrine in them which wasn't allowed to be marketed as a diet pill. Calling them *Mini Thins* implied weight loss but they didn't market them that way, genius or diabolical? I'd vote genius. The Deers were riding the wave.

It was obvious they were rolling in dough. Their garage was filled with extravagance; Rolls Royce, Vanilla Ice's $250K Porsche and their own private limousine. THE HOUSE was a sight to behold. I showed Ric the magazine spread and he was like, "Holy shit, we've got to meet these people!" In the article Richard Deer had the loudest jacket on I'd ever seen - which I don't say lightly. It was silk with large colorful boxes on it with either a red drum, gold bugle or a golden royal crown placed inside them. He ended up wearing that jacket in the movie.

Joan Steichen got me the Deer's phone number and when I reached out to them they knew who "Williamson Howe" was from Playboy TV. I'm not saying they were fans, but I'm not saying they weren't. They did have a room completely decked out in bondage that was better than Club Chateau's in Van Nuys. Did they see the episode when I went there? Possibly, but anywho, I know they were a fan of Playboy and flirted with the dark-side. Richard and Donna Deer were two of the most interesting people I'd ever met. They were ostentatious, cocky, funny and just a blast to be around. Richard had worked at Allison's Transmission while moonlighting his idea of selling uppers, through magazines and then ultimately truck stops and convenient stores, all across the country. He walked out of Allison's factory a rich man. His story should be a movie. If ever the term *nouveau riche* was appropriate it was for these two. They were newly rich, extravagant and liked to show this publicly by spending insane amounts of money, they were flashy mofos. Personally, I don't see anything wrong with enjoying the spoils of your hard work. They earned it with their own two hands and if living larger than large flips their switch, so be it. There's no doubt they were! Living high on the hog made them unique. Having a chance in life to experience these types of people adds a special sauce to your own life.

Ric and I scheduled an appointment to meet them at their mansion in Carmel. That's the rich area of Indy on the Northside of town. We were blown away by the opulence. Pulling up, the grounds were immaculately kept. There was a large fountain in the front yard that a wraparound driveway hugged. The roof was a maroon-ish red terracotta that made the white walled exterior pop. Four pillars held up the grand entrance. Knocking on the door felt like we were thrust into the old Hollywood movie Sunset Boulevard. Richard Deer would be Norma Desmond. "Alright Mr. DeMille, I'm ready for my close-up," she declared. If you know the movie, you'll know the sense of spooky grandeur we had walking in. When you entered this behemoth home there were two sweeping staircases on each side of the foyer that met in the middle on the 2nd floor. A giant crystal chandelier hung in the center. It was a grand, baroque style I guess you'd say. Greek statues, avant-garde artwork, high ceilings, white and gold walls, fountains, indoor balconies, outdoor swimming pool with a clubhouse bar and a basement setup for fantasy & entertaining. When we took the elevator to B1, we entered a large room with a French outdoor cafe setting, along with casino tables scattered around to mimic Casino de Monte-Carlo. Another area has been described as an 'urban speakeasy' - in the style of Chicago's Rush Street nightclubs. There was a 4,000sf ballroom, a home theatre (of course) and a huge gym but the creme de la creme was the Star Wars game room / bar with life-size Storm Troopers and Han Solo in Carbonite (Harrison Ford) frozen in concrete. A full size Darth Vader battled the Predator alongside the futuristic neon bar. A lovely red billiards table was smack dab in the middle of this Galaxy. The place was amazing. Everything was over the top in the best possible way. Richard and Donna were no nonsense smart and didn't take crap from anyone. Their home may have been a fantasy, but they were real. You always had the feeling Richard would try and kick your ass if you did him wrong. He grew up on the Westside of Indianapolis, like Ric and I, and there is always that small edge of hillbilly in us that we just can't shake. Fully refined we are not although we can fake it really well.

They earned this success and obviously enjoyed being exorbitant. Soon after we got our tour, Steve Hilbert and his wife Tomisue stopped by to meet Ric and I. We were blown away. Steve Hilbert at the time was one of the richest men in the US. He founded Conseco, an insurance holding company, and his name was plastered all over Indianapolis. Notably, the Fieldhouse where the Indiana Pacers played (Conseco Fieldhouse) and our most ornate theatrical theater on The Circle (The Hilbert Theatre) had his mark on it. He was very well known, if not infamous. He looked conservative but he also had a side to him that people whispered about. He met his wife when she apparently popped out of a cake for his son's birthday party. No judging here - these types of experiences and these types of people, make life less boring. *See - The DiVona Factor Chapter 19*

I had been hobnobbing with the Colt's owner, flying on private jets, now Steve Hilbert is yucking it up with me and I'm learning they are all envious of Richard Deer's eccentric free way of living. He didn't follow rules, he broke them. Ric and I had met the perfect guy to help us make our movie better. Richard and Donna agreed to let us use their house for the big Hollywood scene and Richard would play the Hollywood producer. He fit the part perfectly. We needed a visible manifestation of a megabucks lifestyle and it had fallen into our lap. Richard could portray the sexist vile Hollywood producer while standing on his head! Sure we wanted to use his house but he got that part because it was written for a guy like him to play the villain.

If you're going to write a book about your life and you rub up against such success and meet extravagant people you need to look to the great philosopher ***Plato***:

Q1. What are the behaviors of people who surprise you?

They get bored in childhood and hurry to grow-up,
but then they miss their childhood.

—•—

They lose their health to earn money and worry
about tomorrow. They forget about today,

—•—

In the end they live neither for now or tomorrow
They live as if they will never die yet as if they never lived.

Q2. What do you suggest is the most important thing in life?

It is not to have the most but to need the least.

—•—

Don't try and make anyone like you, the only thing
to do is leave yourself open to be loved.

—•—

Reality is created by the mind, we can change
our reality by changing our mind.

Armchair quarterbacking the previous quotes from 2,500 years ago and applying them to my new acquaintances is a fun experiment. For the most part, I see them living their lives to the extreme and I could

NEVER say they will die without having lived. Maybe it's the *nouveau riche* aspect in them that puts the childhood in their adult lives? They are big kids at heart. I saw it firsthand. Jim Irsay is not newly rich so it's hard to put him in the "nouveau riche" category like the Deers and Hilberts, but he didn't have much control over his finances until his father passed away, so in a non-traditional way he's new to his own family's money. I think *"it is not to have the most but to need the least"* is a philosophy everyone who suddenly becomes wealthy falls victim to. When I first started making big money from my inventions I was gravitating towards wanting the most. This is a hard trap to not fall in. *Plato* was an older man when he came to these conclusions and I myself can see reason and strength in his words. You realize you need less to be happy. Success becomes more about freedom, about relationships, not objects. This wisdom comes with age. When Plato talked about being liked I've noticed that people who really know you are the ONLY ones who can evaluate if you are "like" worthy. If you are living your life the way you should, meaning treating others with respect, being generous with your love, and just overall being a good person, then those around you will like you because they know you. If you are living this way then don't fret about the ones who seem to not care for you. Who cares! That's not a question, that's a statement. Don't care, because you can't make everyone like you and most often it's the ones who don't even know you. The bad energy wondering why someone doesn't like you will get you nothing but frustration. 9 out of 10 times it's their issue, not you at all. You can only control you. Most importantly, leave yourself open to being loved. Create a receptive soul, absorb the kindness and let people you care about know how you feel about them. I've noticed when I'm around impoverished people (where the word poor would be a step up) OR I'm exposed to the super rich, that in both cases it changes me. I start thinking deeper about life. What's it all for? Why are we on this planet? Seeing different levels of living conditions pushes your mind to reevaluate your own existence. The gap between the haves and the have-nots is nothing new in America. We are all living our own battle and we truly don't know what someone else is going through. Plato again, *"People are like dirt. They can either nourish you and help you grow as a person or they can stunt your growth and make you wilt and die."* When we meet people we can learn lessons from them all.

Since I'm on a philosophical run here - I'd thought I'd mention a conversation I had with Ric Payne the other day inside one of our bars. You haven't read about "our bars" yet but it's coming in a few chapters. He had taken his family to New York City. It's him, his wife Madonna, son Payton (27) and daughter Kennedy (25). They went into the American Museum of Natural History and it gave Ric a new perspective. He said, "The Big Bang pretty much maps out the origin of the cosmos. It's scientific proof." We were talking about his kids, our lives and what it all means.

"The earth was formed 13 billion years ago," Ric explained .

"Think about that, man. A billion is 1,000 millions, so take that times 13. It's crazy. We've had electricity in our homes for less than 150 years," I barked.

"It's mind-blowing. The earth was formed with the sun, what almost a 5B years ago and some sort of cells formed they say about 4B years ago," Ric said with passion.

"So dinosaurs were on earth, what - about 220 million years ago?" I say. Ric nodded. "So earth was cooking for 3.5 billion years before dinosaurs and man even didn't come around for another..."

"Dude, man and dinosaurs weren't even close to being together on this planet. They were 70 million years apart!" Ric proclaimed. "70 million! We can't even wrap our minds around how long ago that is."

This type of conversation went on and he said, "There's not a meaning to life. We are only here for a small blip," snapping his fingers. "The museum had a long chart, like a big 50' ruler along the wall and man was one sliver of hair on this timeline. That's all the time we've been on this planet since it formed."

I could tell this museum had Ric's mind wondering. Plus, we are both in the last quarter of our lives and that fact alone makes you think. "What's it all mean? What's it all for?" We are nothing on the scope of history. Abraham Lincoln will be a distant memory a couple hundred years from now, likely completely forgotten except for a few hardcore historians. Do you know who Boethius is? Younger people don't know who Doris Day was let alone Monte & Moose Payne. LIFE Magazine created a list of *100 People Who Changed the World*. What a joke! Nearly all of them were within the last 150 years. I could write another book on why that is so wrong. So what are we doing on this planet? My best answer is nothing. The best thing you can do is create freedom. Create happiness within your circle. Live life to not impede on someone else's path, be good to your fellow man and have fun. Enjoy yourself and do whatever it is that brings that to you. If possible,` find a way to *CLOCK OUT* and get off the generic, predestined train track of life that society pushes us all to follow. It's meaningless. Not spending your life selling widgets is a choice. Find a way to drive your own bus. If this book does anything, I hope it shows you it's possible to do your own thing. Chase a dream. TRY!

Putting myself out there and adding energy to my situation brought fascinating people in front of me. I took the path of nourishment and leapt at the chance to create something new. Once again, as my mom used to say, "Can't never did anything!"

The energy wheel was whipping us at a centrifugal force. Pieces of the puzzle were falling into place to make our movie. We were taking steps forward to create this into a reality. We had the crucial mansion scene location and Ric knew of another location that he thought might work as Dillinger's. That's the bar's name in the script that the

4 main leads end up opening at the end. Ric had been an extra in the 1988 movie Eight Men Out shot in Indianapolis using the old Bush Baseball Stadium. It starred the likes of Charlie Sheen and John Cusack. It was the true story of the 1919 Chicago White Sox fixing the World Series. One of the locations they used was an abandoned bar called J. Pierpont's Restaurant and Lounge. It sat vacant for 18 years and was the epitome of swank. It was located right off Monument Circle, which is Indianapolis' roundabout honoring the Hoosier soldiers & sailors who served in the Revolutionary War, the War of 1812, the Mexican War, the Civil War, the Frontier Wars and the Spanish-American War. It's only 15' shorter than the Statue of Liberty and has a real good look to it. Indiana's gray oolitic limestone is well known and this particular stone came from the Romona quarries of Owen County. Indiana proudly supplied many famous buildings with it's limestone. A short list includes: The Pentagon, Lincoln Memorial, Empire State Building, Tribune Tower in Chicago, Grand Central Station (NYC) and just about any federal or state building including schools, courthouses, capitols along with churches and libraries in the US. You can go to the top of Monument Circle too, like the Statue of Liberty or the St. Louis Arch. It is a bit weird and scary getting up to the top, but worth it.

We were slowly getting our locations and schedule down and now was it was time to "get this show on the road" as they say.

Same Movie, with Two Different
Titles and Artwork

Richard & Donna Deer
"The Jacket"

Monument Circle
Indianapolis, Indiana

Movie Making Ain't Easy

CHAPTER THIRTEEN

•

"The most honest form of filmmaking is to make a film for yourself."
—Peter Jackson

"We don't make movies to make money, we make money to make movies." *—Walt Disney*

"It's better not to know so much about what things mean or how they might be interpreted or you'll be too afraid to let things keep happening."
—David Lynch

"I try to live my life where I end up at a point where I have no regrets. So I try to choose the road that I have the most passion on because then you can never really blame yourself for making the wrong choices. You can always say you're following your passion."
—Darren Aronofsky

I JUST COULD NOT pick one quote from a filmmaker because there are too many that I respect so I chose four. The film Ric and I decided to make resonates with all the words spoken above. Lynch's thoughts nailed our experience, which was very limited. We did not know much and it made us bold. Being naive can be empowering. We weren't afraid of anything because we didn't even know what to be afraid of. We had both been in a few films, been around Hollywood, been on TV - but directing, casting, producing, financing, editing and distributing a film was a new experience for us and we didn't care. We were making *Back Home Again* for us, not to make money (although that wouldn't have been a bad thing), but it was not our motivation. Fame maybe... but not money. It was a passion project, a passionate dream and there you have it. Good, bad or ugly, we were "running to the woods" as Carl "Moose" Payne used to tell Ricky and we refused to listen to any naysayers. We were charging ahead full steam and making our own tracks along the way to get there. As Frank croons in his famous song, "I did it *My Way*" and that is exactly what we planned on doing. Doing it OUR way.

WE'RE GOING TO MAKE A MOVIE!

I was still living in Los Angeles (Santa Monica) and flew back home to Indy around early November to start pre-production. Ric and Kerry owned an old house in Eagledale (Westside) that we used as a production office and as a location for my character Decatur's childhood home growing up. We were recommended a guy named Josh Hurst who we heard had some experience as a line producer. He was young (late 20s) and eager. He had a bohemian vibe, tall & lanky, longish hair and was a hard worker. Looking back now, he reminds me of Matthew McConaughey if Matthew was a yoga instructor - if that makes any sense? Josh had gone to film school in Maine, graduated, went to Paris and then got a call from a film school buddy asking him to come work on Going All the Way starring Ben Affleck, Rachel Weisz, Rose McGowan and Jeremy Davis. It was a Dan Wakefield novel set in his hometown of Indianapolis. Josh knew quite a bit about setting up a production schedule. He created a production "shooting script" that broke down the days with color coordinated pages & post-its. It all looked very professional and although I was a skeptic at first, it ended up being very helpful. This time he returned the favor and brought in his buddy Dennis from film school. Dennis was older which surprised me. Josh said that Dennis was the oldest student in Maine at 40 and had just come out of the closet. He was on his own adventure and Josh befriended him when others wouldn't. That pretty much sums up Josh Hurst. In addition to being the Script Supervisor, Dennis helped by being the scheduler and he just knew the things that needed to be done without being told. These two were a big help behind the scenes. My sister Mary, who must have been about 38 at the time, became head of props and continuity. She took Polaroids of every scene including tables, costumes, hair, beer levels, cigarettes, wrinkles, watches, clocks, food - it was important because if we broke for lunch or a camera needed moved or reset we needed to know EXACTLY where everything was on the last shot. Continuity seems easy, but it's even easier to mess up. You'll look like amateur hour if you're not careful. A large chunk of our budget was spent on our experienced Director of Photography Jim Timperman (DP). Jim was a one-stop shop. If you've ever seen one of those musicians that have a drum, cymbal, horn chimes, kazoo and a guitar strapped to their body as a one-man band machine - this was our Cinematographer. He had a mini-trailer that looked like a U-Haul trucks you'd lug around when you are headed in a new direction. He had camera stuff, lighting, gels, gimbals, lenses, tripods, loads of reflectors and most importantly - lots of duct tape. Jim also had the elusive Super 16mm camera which meant we were going to make our film with real film, imagine that! Remember, in 1999 there was no acceptable digital format. If you were going to be a real filmmaker, then you needed to use celluloid. Super 16 had a sexy illusion of an artsy vision; seedy, grainy, David Lynch-ish, the texture's grittiness gave an absurd avant-garde look to the format. It serves the purpose of redirecting the eye to the otherwise perfectly clean visual of the scene and protagonist. One film roll of the Super 16 was 400ft long and 24fps, so a roll would last about 11 minutes. Each roll cost around $120 so anytime we yelled "ACTION" and heard the film clicking, it was like coins being dropped in a bucket. We were on a tight budget and if we flubbed our lines or goofed around it was literally hitting Ric in the pocketbook. We didn't want to stress the cast & crew out with how expensive each take was, but internally it was looming over our heads. Obviously, we could make this same movie now at about 1/4 of the cost because of updated technology.

Nowadays, you can shoot on digital and give it a film look and the outtakes & mistakes cost you nothing. Our drawback was that we had to get the perfect shot with the least amount of film used. Does that sound strange? I believe that we truly become creative under duress. Multiple takes, as many do-overs as you like, is not creative, it's repetitive elimination. Red Rover, Red Rover, send another flunky idea right over. Limitations in all forms make people become better and more innovative. In 1999 it was still expensive to buy celluloid. Plus the processing of real film was astronomical. If you add the cost of the film and processing you are easily at $250 every 11 minutes of "Action!". You always do a "master shot" of the overall scene. Basically a wide shot to capture the whole room. You may do that from several angles, but you need to be careful of the dreaded word of continuity. Then you do closeups (CU) of each person of significance in that scene and do a whole series of them. If you add up the multiple takes from the master, then several closeups, change angles, add a dolly or filters - then you've screwed the pooch on saving money. Movie goers mind's eye expects these quick cuts. Their visual pattern of how a "real movie" is made has been emblazoned in their memory banks and anything less will put you in the box as being an amateur. To avoid any shortcomings, we hired a professional sound engineer. Bad sound, bad movie. It's nearly impossible in post to save a movie with messed up sound. If you ever decide to make a movie DO NOT skimp on sound. If you do, you are dead in the water before you even leave the port. We also had a good gaffer (lighting) and a Best Boy that assisted the DP. Ric and I were co-directing as the *Moo Brothers* and were wearing every hat imaginable, plus as actors we were in nearly every scene. We had our hands full but the energy was amazing. I never heard Ric complain (well, except about money) and I was on cloud nine. We had a production team, locations, and all we needed now were the talking heads to make it all come to life.

The next step was casting. I had been in the paper several times in Indianapolis for this or that as an actor. We had gotten the word out on the street that Hollywood was coming to town and we had created a buzz. To be honest, I'm actually surprised how easy it was to whip up interest, or may I even say "frenzy" for us in town making *Back Home Again*. It probably helped that I was living in LA. The big dogs were in town! (HaHa) Suddenly Ric and I were on Fox 59 Morning

Show, WTTV 4 (CBS), WTHR 13 (NBC) and I think WRTV 6 (ABC) to get the word out. Our casting call at Eden Dance Club, which Ric and Kerry owned, had a line around the block. It was incredible. Having been an actor at so many castings I knew how to make it look professional. We had sides (lines) for each part and a sign-in sheet. I learned something new being on this other side of the process. Most of the time when a person walked in for their read, we knew instantly if they fit the image we had in our mind of what that character needed to be. It would take a very unique, talented person to overcome the director's predestined idea of what type of person they are looking for. Rarely, talent alone will not sway. We auditioned all day and saw a lot of good people and had cast quite a few of the parts, but were not satisfied with the talent pool just yet. Helen Wells was still the top talent agency in Indianapolis. They reached out to their actors and we were able to hold final auditions in their office. That was a game changer.

Ric had already worked with Jeremy Buck but my first meeting with this talented genius was in the HWA offices. Jeremy had instant charisma. Now he's evolved into *ROCKSTAR*! He followed his Pooh-stinks! We cast Jeremy as Jasper. Remember, all the cast have names of Indiana cities which helped in our local PR. We also had hidden Easter egg of famous Hoosiers peppered throughout the movie. A prop here, a line there, we were making our version of "Where's Waldo." One famous Hoosier was Ambrose Burnside, who was a Civil War General from Liberty, Indiana. He has an interesting story which lead to coining the term "Burnsides" that morphed into the facial hair that plants itself along the front of your ears we now call *sideburns*.

I'll get into that more later when I tell you about my bar building experience, but he is just one example of a famous personality, inventor, entrepreneur, astronaut, musician, actor - from the great state of Indiana. If you are embarking on a difficult task such as filmmaking, it NEVER hurts to throw some sentimental bones in the direction of the people you need help from. We are all saps to our history and if you're not, then sadly you are missing that gene that makes you feel empathy and pride. You may be a serial killer is what I'm saying. I knew if I plucked the heartstrings of my fellow "state-mates" that it could only help my cause. I wasn't doing this with greedy intent. I actually felt a connection and loved that we were planting little Hoosier eggs in our movie for people to find.

We finally had all the parts cast and had set a shooting date. We had Larry Crane from John Mellencamp's band playing a small part. I met with Jim Nabors and he agreed to let us film him singing "*Back Home Again in Indiana*" at the Indianapolis Motor Speedway. That was a BIG DEAL given his stature and the fact that he was basically singing the title of our movie at the location of the biggest race in the world! I let Jim know I was a serious fan of the Andy Griffith Show and Gomer Pyle. I grew-up with his catchphrases "Shazam!" "Go-lly", "Sur-prise, sur-prise, sur-prise!" and "shame, shame, shame!" Jim told me he had invested his money from the1960's in macadamia nut farms in Hawaii and was living a great life. He owned 500 acres and a mile of coastline in Maui at his death in 2017. We also had Heather Kozar - Playmate of the Year 1999, Bret Harrelson - yes Woody's brother but also a fine actor himself, Billy Keller - the great Indiana ABA Pacer's basketball player from the 1970's, Rik Smits - "The Dunking Dutchman" who was still playing in the NBA with the Pacers (1988-2000) and a very brief appearance by the Japanese star Eisaku Yoshida. The rest of us cast members were locals along with an appearance by my dad.

I won't go into great detail of the shoot, although there are always great stories behind the scenes. One of the surprising issues I was NOT expecting was morality. BHA is a comedy and of course it had some lowbrow moments. My character Decatur had the house that hosted all the freaks from the family that you'd see once a year for Christmas. I had invited Ric's character Gary to join. When he walks in and pans the room he sees all of Decatur's family in full bloom; uncles, aunts, brothers, sister, kids, and distant relatives. The same scene flashes and you see the same people dressed in outfits that fit their oddness: goth chick, golf nut, far right religious, hillbilly, overtly sexy and so on. During this flash of comedy I wanted a cuckoo clock to strike & a little bird to come out singing "cuckoo-cuckoo-cuckoo". As we'd pull back and see the clock surrounded by Jesus crosses. Also, I had put above the couch the famous picture of Jesus that was in my living room growing up. This scene caused our crew to refuse to shoot. We were implying Jesus freaks were cuckoo & they didn't like it. This scene was partly portraying my real family gathering at Christmas & Thanksgiving. My mom would invite all of our relatives over and many of them were cuckoo for Cocoa Puffs. They were strangers I saw once a year, had nothing in common with and we'd all mumble through the day. I pointed out to the crew that this was a comedy and that many great movies poked fun at religion. A compromise was met, hurting the scene, and part of it was shot with me running the camera with the crew standing out on the front lawn.

One other scene that caused a smaller rumbling was a nod to Bob Clark who directed A Christmas Story that was set in the fictional town of Hohman, Indiana. The classic clip when the boy gets his tongue stuck on the flag pole during a "Triple Dog Dare" always makes me laugh. In my story the three amigos Tipton (Brian Nahas), Decatur (Me) and Gary (Ric Payne) are all out partying one cold winter's night - like the good old days. They had met some girls and one of them suggested to go pick up her new friend who was on an exchange program from Sweden. The actress was Petra Areskough (Pippi). We knocked on her character Lafayette's bedroom window. It's super cold outside and her character does a "Swedish Mooning" and put her boobs up against the glass to get a rise out of us. They get stuck pressed up against the window just like in *A Christmas*

Story. Lafayette panics and Tipton stands on my back and begins feverishly rubbing the glass, blowing hot air on it, trying to thaw her orbs of power. They finally break free. I've rarely met anyone who didn't think this scene was funny. Once again, two people on the crew didn't feel it was appropriate and abstained from the shoot. We also had a strip club location at the Classy Chassis that didn't go over well along with some implied pot smoking. It was all very tame stuff but you have to juggle different people's ideology. The whole country is divided more than ever now, but there has always been a sliding scale on moral standards. I would have assumed that anyone working on the film might have read the script? Maybe not, but everything they were having issues with was right there in black & white.

You live and learn anytime you take on a new genre or try and tackle something you've never done before. Making Back Home Again (*69 the Highway*) was like going to film school for Ric and I. We definitely made some mistakes. I wrote it, Ric & I directed it as the *Moo Brothers,* Ric financed it and we both were heavily involved in the editing with Tim Dietz. If anything, we were just too damn close to it. It had all the elements to being a really good comedy. There were too many night scenes which we didn't realize until we were putting it all together. It ended up feeling more like a series of hilarious skits on SNL. Filmmaking is not an easy thing to pull off. The flow and how the puzzle goes together was more difficult than I thought. The pace and how the arch of story keeps people engaged is not a simple thing to balance.

We had the premiere at Richard & Donna Deer's mansion. They never do anything small and this was no exception. It was a beautiful summer Saturday afternoon. Richard had flown in Playmate Heather Kozar along with another girl featured in Playboy, but I can't remember her name. Heather had played Madison and had a great scene with Richard Deer as the producer. She did an amazing job. The short version, Tipton's character took his girlfriend Madison to a big Hollywood party of an important producer. Deer's character took one look at her and had to have her. He offered Tipton a part in his next movie but he'd need to put on 75lbs and shave his head. In the end, Tipton is fat, bald & bloated begging Madison not to leave him. We see her get into a red Rolls Royce with Richard and drive away. Once again, that was another funny skit in our movie.

The soirée was incredible. It was really a decadent pool party with a movie screening thrown in. An Elvis impersonator from Vegas was there, a sand volleyball court had been set up, a sweet rock-n-roll band played live 80's hits and there was plenty of booze flowing. You could tell that throwing a party was right up the Deer's alley. They knew what they were doing and didn't ask anything from us, it was all carte blanche. Richard had set up about 100 chairs and a big screen in his basement ballroom. He was very generous, but I do remember one particular guest made the mistake of being rude to him. We didn't have many investors in BHA but one guy named Pete did throw in $3,000. He didn't do it for an investment. He did it just to be a part of the party. Let's face it, the old joke "How do you make a million dollars in the movie business?" Answer, "Start with two million." Pete had partied a bit too much for sure. Seeing Richard walking by he stopped him.

Pete asked, "Man, how do you get all these beautiful women around you?"

"I don't know, they just like me I guess," Richard replied, smiling.

Pete retorted, "Yeah, but you're an ugly mother fucker!" Putting the emphasis on "Ugly" and you could instantly tell that Richard was seeing red. This rightly so pissed him off. He had opened his house to this amazing party, everything was free, there were beautiful people everywhere, live music - the hospitality was off the charts. Why this Pete guy felt the need to insult Richard is beyond me, but Richard washed the floor with him and Pete was dragged out of that house like a rag doll and tossed to the lawn. He messed with the wrong guy.

Back to the premiere of *Back Home Again*. It didn't go well. For one thing, the movie had problems and it was still a rough cut. Also, everyone left the beautiful pool party and Playmates playing volleyball to go inside a dark room and watch a movie. People were were polite and no-one said they didn't like it, but Ric and I knew that it had issues. No one was saying they liked it either, so the writing was on the wall. I do remember Heather Kozar telling Ric he was a "really good actor" so that raised his spirits I'm sure. After several more edits it got better but not great. We did get into several film festivals and had a few deals for distribution but it never really took off like we had hoped. It's hard to say why, because when I look at it I still see many elements of genius in it. It was close to being great, but fell short. It's like a recipe for a delicious batch of chocolate chip cookies. You've got the right pastry flour, sugar, fresh baking soda, the eggs & butter are at room temperature, amazing semi-sweet chocolate chips - it's all there, but somewhere along the way in the mixing of ingredients it went awry. Much like baking, little tweaks here and there in filmmaking can change the course of the final outcome.

Growing up so close to the Indianapolis Motor Speedway, I often use IndyCars as an analogy for life. If you tweak the wing of a race car just 1/16 of an inch one way you're on the last row, tweak it the other way and you're on the front row. Such minor adjustments can make huge changes in results. Any of us can be close to greatness and not even realize it. The key is to keep getting up to bat. The "never give up attitude" is usually in the spirit of successful people.

My "adjusting the wing" story above reminded me of another metaphor I toss around which I call *Trim-Tabbing*. I once pitched this as a title for an inspirational reality show, but the phrase trim-tabbing or trim-tab doesn't roll off the tongue easily. The example of a trim-tab I'm talking about are the ones you find on behemoth floating vessels like oil tankers, container and cruise ships. They need extra help turning their rudders without using a ton of force. For example, the rudder on the Titanic was 78ft 8in high and 15ft 3in long, weighing over 100 tons! That puts a LOT of stress on the steering engines to move it. A very simple solution is to put a little rudder that runs along the edge of the large rudder that can easily be moved. If the Captain wants to go left, the "Trim-Tab" will turn right and the force of the water will push the rudder left. This way very little energy is needed to move such a large object. This idea has always fascinated me because it could be used as a philosophy of life. Something so small can help move something so massive. I relate this to a smile at the store or a "How are you doing?" that makes a big impact on someone's life. The TV show I pitched was how helping people in small ways can send their lives in a much better direction. We can all impact each other with acts of kindness and generosity. It's not too much different than the term "Pay it Forward" we often hear. I think we can all look back on our lives and think of a situation when someone made a big difference in who we are with just one simple act of goodwill.

The movie might not have been the commercial success we had hoped for, but it ended up playing a big role in my life. I learned a lot and it sent me on a new journey I didn't see coming. *I was going Back Home Again and life began to imitate art.*

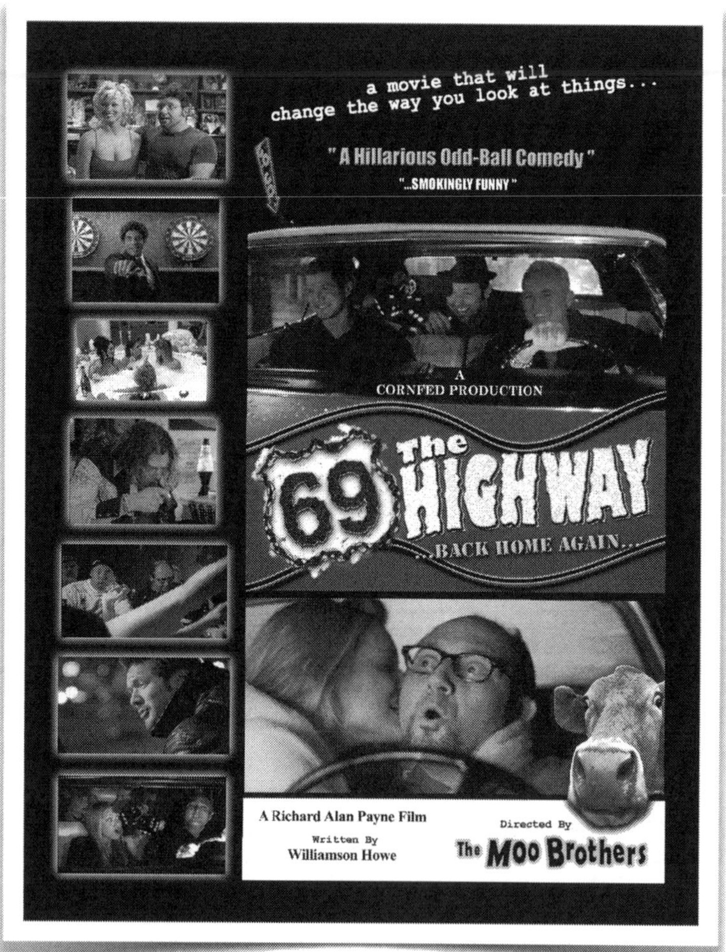

Our Movie Poster/One Sheet

Promotional Business Card

Bartender, Pour Me a Future

CHAPTER FOURTEEN

•

"Alcohol may be man's worst enemy,
but the Bible says love your enemy."
—Frank Sinatra

"LIFE IS JUST a cocktail party on the street," once uttered Mick Jagger. I wasn't in the bar business just yet, but the idea was intriguing. After BHA had it's "Martini Shot", which is a moviemaking term for wrapping up filming coined by a guy named Cody Whitehouse, I went back to LA. The *martini shot* was so named because "the next shot is out of a glass," Cody said referring to a post-wrap drink. The movie was in the can.

There were many lessons Ric and I learned while making our movie but perhaps the biggest was that the most difficult work happens after the filming stops. Editing is incredibly challenging and difficult. To make movie magic you need to put all the pieces together in just the right way. Editing takes a lot of patience and loads of compromise. Setting the pace, cutting but keeping the story alive, the timing of the jokes, the fixing of poorly shot scenes, bad acting, bad lighting, continuity mistakes, jump cuts, bad sound, boring long scenes that need to be in the film to keep the story straight- the headaches never stop. I know a brilliant editor named Marc Fusco that has been known to save a film or two. He's the Pulp Fiction fixer "The Wolf" that cleans up the mess. Saves the day, so to speak.

"While writing is a joyful release, editing is a prison where the bars are my former intentions and abusive warden my own neuroticism."
—Tiffany Madison

Unfortunately, we didn't use Fusco's wolf skills but I wish we had. Ric and I kept licking our wounds and trying new marketing. The film was close to being good, but we just never found the special sauce.

We changed the title to 69 the Highway and tried for about another year to get a deal worth getting excited about. I was back in LA and in constant communication with Ric.

I wasn't feeling too good about my future in acting. Playboy had released me because I was too clean-cut and my big break with NBC fell through because I was too dirty. The true me was somewhere in-between, but perception is 9/10th of the law and I didn't see a fast redemption of my unfairly soiled reputation. I mentioned earlier that when we were shooting our movie Ric took me to *J. Pierpont's* as a potential location for our grand finale. He had the keys to this bar in his pocket for 10 years and I don't just mean figuratively, but literally!! I think the broker had forgotten that he had lent them to Ric to view the space all those years ago. The building was at 120 East Market Street right off of Monument Circle. The area in 1926 was called "The Wall Street of Indianapolis" because so many banks had set up shop there. Indiana National Bank built this building in 1956. There wasn't FDIC insurance back then and to attract people to your bank you needed to look established, rich and reliable. Beneath the dust at J. Pierpont's was luxury. Marble floors, 35' ornate ceilings, thick marble partitions in the bathrooms, chandeliers - the place was a palace. J. Pierpont's had put in a large wooden bar that rumors say came over from Germany and was found in a barn somewhere in the US. It just added to the mystique of the room. Most people in Indy had no idea what was hiding behind the doors of that historical building. It was a forgotten era, a dinosaur of the powerful and rich. John D. Rockefeller's ghost could have walked around the corner with a gold pocket watch dangling from his pinstriped vest. Ric and I mused that first day that we should bring this beautiful space back to life.

Ric flew out to LA quite a bit the next year while we were trying to get a distribution deal. One of my favorite bars was on Main Street in

Santa Monica. It was called Circle Bar. I loved the sexy, dark vibe of this place. One night Ric and I were hanging out in there and we started talking about turning J. Pierpont's space into our version of Circle Bar. Indianapolis is nicked named The Circle City. The space was right off The Circle where Monument Circle is. We got excited. My acting was going nowhere fast but I had some money saved. I had been squirreling it away. If I didn't invest it I'd end up nipping at it while struggling to get my next gig and it would all be gone.

I wanted to label a chapter "***BLOWIN' CHUNKS***" because getting chunks of money is a theory I have on how to get ahead. We all tend to raise our spending habits to meet our current cash flow and that makes it hard to be an entrepreneur. To escape the "rat race" and to be your own man, you need capital. Money makes the world go around and without it you are stuck on the treadmill of workin' for the man. Let's say you get a promotion at work or are headhunted for a better paying job. You go from making $72,000 a year to $92,000, that's a whopping $20K raise. This is NOT a bad thing but it does keep you locked into corporate America - which you may or may not want to do for your life's work. This is a personal choice that only you can answer. It does feel safer to log in to a steady income, but don't be disillusioned because that safety is not guaranteed. Job security is a fickle thing and if I'm going to get sacked (Land in the Poor House) I'd prefer to do it trying to do something I love, something for myself. Practicality is not always practical. Life is not a series of boxes that all fit together nicely. It's all unpredictable and being practical becomes pragmatic. A steady income with the same hourly or monthly salary seems attractive. Week after week - month after month offers security, but this security comes with a price and that price is missing the chance to have wealth & freedom. When you get a raise and one's natural inclination is to take that extra money and buy a better car, a place to live in we like more, better vacations, maybe a new watch, better shoes - all great things, but you just raised your expenses to eat up the extra $20,000 raise. In a way, that bump keeps the mouse on the treadmill chasing the cheese. It's a vicious cycle.

My advice is to look for sudden CHUNKS of money. Stop blowin' chunks and think of what you could do with $20,000 that fell into your lap. I don't have a magic formula for you to get that "*chunk*" but it may come from a relative passing, an opportunity to do something extra on the weekends or a stock tip that actually is true (rare). Or you really get diligent and crack down on saving. I often got larger sums of money all at once from booking TV commercials. I didn't rush out and buy a new car or do something frivolous. Acting is such an up & down industry financially that it naturally stopped me from blowin chunks. I had no idea if I'd ever book anything again. I had put my theory into practice out of fear. When we finished the movie and my acting was slowing down I had a decent amount of money saved. My parents were both in their 70s and for the first time, in a very long time, I had the desire to move back home to Indianapolis. I had a great experience making the movie. The city was getting better and better every year. I had traveled the world, chased the acting dream in LA and was looking for a new challenge. A creative challenge that could let me continue to be my own boss.

Ric and I began talking more and more about creating Circle Bar. I told him I was all in and would move back to Indianapolis to become part owner with him and his brother Kerry. I would invest money to create all aspects of the bar and be the managing partner (GM) once it opened. I had already worked side by side with Ric making the movie and we both knew we were both hard workers. Our goal was to make Circle Bar the coolest place downtown Indy had ever seen. I had already learned if I got up at 6:45am, Ric would have gotten up at 6:30am. It was inspiring for us both to challenge each other's work ethic and creativity. I can't explain it well, but we both seem to have a creative flow that blends perfectly without pressing the other's buttons in a bad way. I guess you can call it a trust in making something together. Partnerships can be tricky. You need the right balance and conviction. We both always seem to have the same final vision of how we see the end product. Later, I'd learn his brother Kerry was an important part of the puzzle. We three all have roles & strengths that make us a successful partnership.

Leaving LA was hard. I remember one day I was walking near my place in Santa Monica and I saw a fellow actor I got to know over the years. He always seemed to be doing well and we both cheered each other on. I was never one of those competitive actors. I am competitive in most aspects of my life but with acting it never felt like apples to apples. It's a preconceived idea that the director, client, producer, writer, studio executive have imagined in their minds what they think the person for this part should be like, talk like and any other characteristic or personality that is impregnated in their thoughts. So when I see him sitting at a stop light at Main & Ocean Ave I wave and he pulls over at the next curb near Buffalo Exchange. I can't for the life of me remember his name so I'll call him Brad Pitt, just another actor who failed in LaLa Land!

"What are you up to?" I ask, seeing his car is completely packed full of clothing.

"I'm headed back to Missouri man. I'm throwing in the towel," Brad says, somewhat embarrassed.

"No way!" I say surprised. "You were booking stuff all the time, man."

"Ah yeah I guess, I just hate the ups and downs. I mean, am I ever going to be Tom Cruise? Let's be honest" Brad Pitt muses.

"You were close!" I say giving him one last boost of *'you were good'* as he literally turned left and headed to the 10E to the 605N to 210E briefly onto the 15 then 40E nearly all the way. Twenty-two hours later and he's out of the Hollywood Dream game, back in Springfield.

I really felt a sadness seeing him go. Do you have to get to Tom Cruise level to make it? Of course not. The highs & lows do grind on you when you're in a field where you are supposed to *pay your dues*. Growing up I used to watch the Beverly Hillbillies "So they loaded up the truck and moved to Beverly, Hills that is, swimming pools and movie stars" and that image stuck. Jed hit black gold, Texas tea, but I was trying to strike fame. A very difficult luck to acquire. You usually need to be talented (not always) but you always need a break. A hand from God to pluck you out of obscurity and give you that chance.

If you study to be a doctor, you become a doctor. Making it in the movie business as a writer, director or an actor reminds me of the 1849 California Gold Rush. Nearly 300,000 people (Forty-Niners) headed West to prospect for their fortune. How many people go to NYC or LA each year to be a star? In 1849 they headed in the direction of Sutter's Mill in Coloma, California. The spot where James W. Marshall saw specs of gold floating down the river. These days it's MGM, Warner Bros, Disney, Paramount and the likes that bring your wannabe stars out to pan for celluloid, screen time & fame. Back in late 1860s people left California beaten down and broke. Most never stuck gold. Now the shovels & pick ax are replaced by headshots and agents. When you go someplace specific for the purpose of "making it" then giving up feels like a failure. I was realistic enough to understand that in some ways I did *make it* in Hollywood. I mostly supported myself via acting. I was in people's homes all over the world and had signed my fair share of autographs. At this pivotal time in my life I knew I was making the right decision. I got out while I was still on top and more importantly, I had money. My *chunks* were not liquidated. I rented one of those "pull from behind" U-Hauls and packed everything I owned, just like my buddy Brad Pitt, and took the southern route back to Indiana. As I said, if drive non-stop it's 33 hours but I tried to only stay on the road about 8-10 hours a day, so it took me almost four days. My sister Jacque had a house in the northern suburb of Indianapolis called Fishers with an extra room. It had been 25 years since we were under the same roof - we became roommates. I agreed to pay her $300 a month which was 1/2 her mortgage and I settled in. I was back home with a new purpose which made leaving the excitement of LA easier.

The J. Pierpont space we were taking over to create *Circle Bar* was a deep clean, a significant remodel, equipment updates, plumbing issues, electrical obstacles and constant roadblocks trying to bring the building up to fire code. Remember, it had sat empty for 18 years. The plus side was that it had an amazing old world charm. The amount of marble in the space was mind-blowing. I was especially good at art, design, menus, drinks, promotion and construction. Ric and Kerry were the bar pros and understood setting up the mechanicals to make all the equipment function. They knew the rules for the Board of Health, Alcohol Beverage Commission (ABC), POS systems and all the liquor reps who would help us perform. Ric was also great at design and together we created a super sexy, one-of-a-kind bar. We put a black leather mechanical bull pit in the middle of the room with a picture of Bettie Page holding a whip in her hand. The place was edgy. The room was a complete surprise to anyone who entered it. Our starting palate was grand, old money elegance and that reeked ultra cool to me. The high fresco style ceiling was impressive. We added three (3) 30' leather pillars against the main wall that complimented the leather bull pit and added a decadence to the vibe. Kerry was and still is good at keeping our accounting straight, the POS and anything dealing with the money. He does the unromantic aspects of running a bar. It takes a team and everyone should have a a skill they bring to the table. Kerry showed me the system he and Ric used for liquor inventory and how they expected the back house of the bar to be run. I was completely green and soaked it all in. Whatever they told me to do, I did. Their simplicity was genius and still works well for us three.

Circle Bar was at 120 E. Market Street, which is right off Monument Circle in the heart of downtown Indianapolis. The drawback to the location was that no other bars were in the area. Downtown Indy is not that big, but people are creatures of habit and getting them to explore a new locale became a challenge in the beginning. When you first walked in, as I mentioned before, we had a leather blow-up air pad all in black that looked mean. Our mechanical bull was the famous El Toro. It's the same bull they used in the movie *Urban Cowboy* with John Travolta. The Micky Gilley's Saloon in Las Vegas (Treasure Island Hotel) has used this bull. Although we had a bull, we were not a country western place at all. When you entered the bull pit, a picture picture of Bettie Page with a whip in her hand greeted you. You really felt like you were in New York. It had two floors and the staircase to the 2nd floor was pure marble. Remember, we had that beautiful wooden bar we were told was from a German train station after WWII. It was never confirmed, but it was a spectacular show piece. The 2nd floor had a bar/lounge where you could sip your drink along a golden adorned railing overlooking the entire room. None of it made sense in Indianapolis and that put us on the map. Word got out about *Circle Bar* and we started to become really popular, especially on Saturday nights.

The nightclub hours were new to me. I was the GM so I opened and closed 7pm to 3:30am Thursday, Friday and Saturday, which meant I was there by 5:30pm and was getting home around 4:30-5am. We attempted opening on Wednesday and Sundays but you make all your money on the weekends, period. *Circle Bar* was a nightclub. No food, just booze, bull rides, lounge or dance. I usually placed the alcohol orders on Monday or Tuesday and accepted the deliveries every Wednesday afternoon from 11am-3pm. Plus, you are always planning events, drink promotions and exploring new ways to increase revenue. I eased into this lifestyle quickly. I liked it. I got a little bit of that same taste of recognition being the owner that I enjoyed as being an actor in LA. I was making steady, good money and dating was easier than ever. I bought a brand new Mini Cooper S, rented a 1,600sf swanky apartment downtown and was making a name for myself and really enjoying life. I also started seeing my parents a lot more. I made it a ritual to go to my dad's every Sunday for dinner and watch *American's Funniest Home Videos* with him. I had been away for so long that spending time with my mom & dad became important to me. I now look back on that and feel very thankful I got that time. They've both passed away now but I got 10+ years enjoying their company. If I had a little bit more luck in LA, or didn't see it was time to move on, I would not have had that amazing opportunity to appreciate them. I definitely feel that it all worked out for the best. It goes back to following my inner voice, my Pooh-stincts! That's funny, I just re-read that and it says "my poo stinks" which I may have to start saying a lot more often. The Tao of Pooh never stops giving!

Besides the countless bar stories, managing a nightclub added a good story and an interesting opportunity to my life. I always keep an eye open for new endeavors or look to create my own. I can feel satisfied but I always keep the drive alive to want more.

Here's *a good story*...once upon a time, *The Apprentice* with Donald Trump was hugely popular on NBC. I had gotten my real estate license at a very young age and was partly motivated by *The Art of the Deal* as well as seeing my mom, my hero, kicking butt as a R.E. Broker. I decided to submit a demo tape to *The Apprentice* outlining my story. I had owned 5 condos on Indiana University's campus, had my RE license, was inspired by Trump and now was part owner of a successful nightclub. I talked about my experience with US Steel and living in Japan. I left out my Hollywood years because I didn't want them to think I was applying for the TV show because I wanted to be in entertainment. The truth was that I wanted the adventure, possibly financial gains and I thought maybe the show could lead to both of these. You need to have many eggs in your basket of life because you never know which ones may end up being golden. I asked Ric to help me shoot a 10 minute promo and I mailed it off. A month later they invited me to Chicago to meet with producers. I put on my best suit, to this day putting on a suit feels like Halloween, and marched into that meeting with confidence. Dabbling in acting had erased my inhibitions and increased my confidence. Right off the bat they seemed to like me. When I was leaving, the casting director who organized my interview said I looked really familiar and asked, "Are you Williamson Howe?" Through all my submissions I was Will Howe. Ugh, I knew this was not a good sign. *The Apprentice* was immensely popular and every Apprentice would be scrutinized by the media. I was supposed to be there because I wanted to join the Trump Organization NOT to extend my acting dream, and let's face it, the PLAYBOY hosting gig would likely bite me in the butt AGAIN. Casting Guy was looking at some papers in a folder as I explained.

"I've always been involved in business. I got my real estate license, went to Japan and acting just fell in my lap," I tried to reason with the Casting Guy. "I'm done with acting!" I pleaded. "I'm here to be Trump's Apprentice!"

"Okay, but I've got to tell them your history," he explained.

I was sick to my stomach driving back to Indianapolis from Chicago. I didn't think I would hear from them again, but I did. A month later they called and said I would not be on Season 2 but they wanted me to come to New York and be one of the Apprentices for a complete mock-run-through. They bring in a full cast of Apprentices that go through all the challenges, including meeting with Donald Trump in the boardroom, getting fired and one of us would hear, "You're hired," from The Donald himself. I would get all the experiences from the show except it wouldn't be aired on TV. It's a dress rehearsal for them to see what works and what doesn't. They said I'd make great contacts and maybe something would come of it. I was disappointed but felt some level of pride that I was chosen as the guinea pig. The big hurdle was money. They were being cheap. They offered me $500 a week with no housing for 3-6 weeks. I called around New York City to see if I could find a reasonable place to rent for a month. It was Impossible. I'd lose money on housing alone and then add in travel, food and with the time I'd miss running Circle Bar I'd be short at least $5,000. Ric and Kerry would be excited for me to be ON *The Apprentice* but to be the "Run-Through-Guy" I doubted they'd be so forgiving to me to be gone that long. Plus, I'd likely not have my salary for over a month and be spending loads of money surviving in New York. I sadly, but smartly, said I would pass being on the *The Apprentice Season 2's* practice team.

Before I go into another "*Interesting Opportunity*" I want to talk about a philosophy I learned in Toyoda, Japan working with Toyota Motors that applies to my life.

Kaizen

This concept became famous in the Toyota factories. It has you strive for continuous improvement. If you have lofty goals then kaizen might be an avenue for you to get there. In Japanese this word means "good change" and the general term goes back to ancient Rome. The important concept is to start the change you want, no matter how small. If you want to start hiking but get winded just climbing a flight of stairs, the first step is buy hiking shoes. You can't cook but want to? Buy a nice knife. The point is to start with the babiest of all baby steps. Move forward no matter how small. You will stare at those shoes long enough and then you put them on. You may only walk around the block. You learn the perfect way to cut an onion and you cry with joy- or not! When I'm heading out on a long trip to someplace like Tokyo I always look at my wife as we step out into our garage, "This is the 1st step on an incredible journey!" I say smiling. Your amount of improvement or progress is up to you but at the very least, take a step or two. Think day to day, not long term. Small victories lead to conquering your goals. Don't bear all the weight at once!

The Opportunity - was keeping my eyes open or should I say "de-puffied"! Getting to bed at 5am was a new experience for me. The first thing I noticed was that I needed either my bedroom blacked out or a really good eye mask to block the light. My sleep chakras were way off. I've always been sensitive to light and I needed it really dark to get my REM (Rapid Eye Movement). Without good sleep I was feeling like I had permanent jet-lag. This led to my first true invention. I went to the mall and walked into a Brookstone to find an eye-mask. They had a few choices but the one that caught my eye, no pun intended, was the one that cost $38. It was expensive but it featured astronaut memory foam around the eyes that allowed you to open your eyes with the mask on. I liked that idea because in the past I had tried a few masks and the material laying on my eyelids bothered me. I splurged and bought the best one they had.

From the instant I started using my astronaut memory foam eye mask I loved it. Another ritual I often employed was a technique I read in *GQ Magazine* on how to reduce the puffiness under your eyes. They had several tips such as: limit your salty food intake, put two bricks under your headboard to let gravity keep water from pooling towards your head and in the shower wet your washcloth and put pressure on the bags under your eyes. This last bit of advice - pushing the fluid out from under the eyes like a compress caught my attention. I was doing this daily in the shower. One morning I'm laying in bed with my eye mask on and I started thinking 'Could I put pressure on the puffiness under my eyes while still in bed' using my Brookstone eye mask? I pushed the mask higher up on my forehead so the memory foam was right up under my eyes. It didn't feel uncomfortable and that constant pressure allowed me to pop out of bed with no bags. The foam was putting just the right pressure and not allowing liquid to pool. A lightbulb went off so I went to Google searching for this type of mask and it was not on the market.

Circle Bar had started out like gangbusters the first two (2) years, but the last 6 months our sales had started to dwindle. Another bar opened next door to us, trying to piggybacking on our success, in this uncharted quarter of downtown Indy. Their concept was not completely thought through and they were struggling. In an effort to boost their sales they re-marketed themselves has a hip-hop dance club and began to draw in a different clientele than Circle Bar attracted. Overnight there was violence which included shootings, stabbings and just an overall unsafe vibe right out in front of our place. Every weekend there would be 4+ police cars planted on our block. It looked like a war zone. Some of these undesired elements were seeping into *Circle Bar* and I was trying to figure out how to reinvent our space.

Some of you reading this will remember how cool it was to roam the malls and a must stop place to check out was *Hot Topic.* I bought a Gooring Brother's Hat with a Beaver on it. **M***TV* had a show called *The Real World,* in which one of the cast members had on this exact same hat. Like me, when he wore his beaver hat, he was always getting laughs and quite a few comments. I started thinking that people loved beaver! My hat was so popular I could not ignore it. Another hit show, was on *E! Entertainment,* hosted by Brooke Burke called *Wild On*! It was a new type of travel show that highlighted food, culture and nightlife of certain regions of the world. All of this had me thinking of transitioning *Circle Bar* away from a nightclub and into a saloon. That was the birth of the concept The *Wild Beaver Saloon.* I borrowed the "Wild" and "Beaver" names from the popular TV show and my hat. That was my marketing 101.

Back to *Thee Opportunity* first, The Wild Beaver comes later - I came into *Circle Bar* one night and tossed Ric my Brookstone eye mask. I pitched him the concept and he was all aboard. I bought 3 more masks and headed over to Ric's house to Frankenstein these masks into our new invention. His girlfriend Madonna is a wiz on a sewing machine and we got started creating an eye mask that would allow you to step out of bed without bags under your eyes. We decided this was an idea we had to run with and the nightclub was becoming more & more of a hassle.

We owed no money on the bar and Ric, Kerry and I decided it was time to sell. Ric and I were going to embark on a new lifestyle as inventors. On Saturday, our last night at Circle Bar we left Kerry alone to closed the bar one last time. Ric and I headed to New York City to TRY, TRY, TRY to be inventors. We drove all night and landed in New York on Sunday morning. A new chapter in life was beginning.

Block the Bags that Block Your Beauty

CHAPTER FIFTEEN

•

"Our greatest weakness lies in giving up. The most certain way to succeed is try just one more time"
—Thomas Edison

RIC AND I MOST definitely could never be accused of giving up. No matter what the project is we keep trying when most would likely throw in the towel. This attitude can make my wife crazy. If I'm looking for something that I've misplaced, I literally will be driven to the point of temporary insanity until I find it. Sure, this can be compulsive and considered unhealthy, but if your brain is wired like this and you have a goal it can be very beneficial.

Before our last night at *Circle Bar* we had done a lot of work on our eye mask concept. We added gel packs that you could put in the freezer to resemble a cold compress. We found a guy who could make our prototype and then a factory in China that would manufacture the mask for about $4.50 a piece. Before I go on, I'd like to give some simple advice on launching a product:

Making Your Own Product

1) Make it look like it's already on the market.
2) Get professional packaging.
3) Put a bogus barcode on it if it will sell in stores. The minds eye is used to seeing it on the box. Create the illusion.
4) Tags and branding have to be on the product when you pitch it.
5) All correspondence should have professional logos, mailing labels and I personally even type out my UPS or FedEx mailing labels.
6) Never let them see your smallness. Boutique is okay but creative and professional is a must. You will be judged before they test the product.
7) Research conventions & other avenues where you can be seen.

8) Work out of your home as long as you can.
9) Trademark your product's unique name. The name of your invention is very important. The names that convey what the product does are often the best ones.
10) Patents - the good, bad & ugly is discussed later. (P.293)

Starting Your Own Business

There are many choices when you begin your own business and that is part of the excitement. You're the boss. The buck stops with you. Succeed or fail, it's your decision; naming your concept, logos packaging, color, style and that's just the marketing. You set the price and the appeal. You need the honey to attract the bee.

Where will you sell this product? Online, brick & mortar, big box retailers, which platforms work for you? Do you create a website and sell directly to consumers?

I put myself on the outside looking in. Would I buy this product? What need does it touch in my life? You must live and die by the sword. If you feel strongly about how to market your concept then listen to your inner voice.

3 Things to Think About

ONE: *People have an expectation of what a good product will look like. Malcom Gladwell's book Blink applies here. The mind has millions of images of any given product or concept. They will make an instant judgement on your concept, a blink of an eye, and it tells their brain if they like or trust your product. Remember the "instaYOU" I spoke about in Chapter One? Well, that applies to knowing what you want the instant you see something. What made it capture your eye? If you are an entrepreneur worth a spit then your ideas will capture other people's eyes too. You need to create a concept that people want.*

TWO: *Find an avenue to reach your customers. That could mean licensing your idea to a larger company and letting them run with it. Go to a convention and set up a booth saying "Agent Wanted" and see if you get any bites. Is Amazon right for you? Shopify, Etsy, E-commerce website, Ebay? Once you decide the how & where, then you need to make your presentation the highest quality you can afford. Do not cut corners on images. Photos sell your concept. I recommend a minimum of 5 images, but the more the merrier. A good* *tag line and concise description is crucial too. It's competitive out in the marketplace and you need people to trust your company with their money. They want to know their credit card # is safe, that you're going to deliver in a timely manner and what they ordered lives up to the pitch that got them to pull out their wallet. If you over promise and under deliver you won't last long in today's marketplace. Reviews are the modern day word of mouth. Give people a reason to tell their friends about you.*

THREE: *This last bit of advice is to go big on your first run. I'm NOT saying to mortgage the farm, but it's going to take a significant push to get any kind of momentum started. Going viral or getting some lucky exposure is unlikely. Get everything ready to launch to the best of your pocketbook's ability. Along the way get advice, show your friends & family samples, do your own mini-version of a survey of likability. Once you feel confident, then spend a "Chunk" of money. Put ads on Facebook/Instagram if that's your venue, set up a drop ship vendor and place ads on TV, radio or other internet sites. You're going to have to spend money to test the waters. Maybe it's going to a convention? I recommend a two week trial of hitting the trail hard. There is no use beating around the bush. You need to find out if your concept resonates with consumers.*

∞∞

BagBlocker was my first true invention. We had asked advice from Richard Deer. He had made himself a millionaire with Mini-Thins and had been great to work with making our movie Back Home Again (69 the Highway). I remember Ric and I were at Richard's mansion pitching him the idea for our eye mask. We were standing in his garage between his Phantom Rolls Royce and Vanilla Ice's Porsche 911.

"What are you calling this mask?" Richard wondered. Now, of course we had been brainstorming names for months, but nothing tickled our fancy.

"BagBlocker," I blurted out. Where this came from I don't know?

"BagBlocker, BagBlocker, hmmm I like it," he smiled. Richard's smile was always more of like a smirk which made him seem devilish.

"Yeah, we thought it was good because it says what it does. It blocks the fluid from pooling and creating bags under your eyes," I said as if I'd said 'BagBlocker' a thousand times.

"You need a catchy slogan," he said.

"We've been thinking about that," Ric jumped in. "Block the bags!"

"That block your beauty," I suddenly said.

"Block the bags that block your beauty," Ric said in an ad pitch voice.

Richard seemed to really like the idea and suggested we go to a junk convention to try and get a distributor. We did some research and found that the Health & Beauty America (HBA) convention was happening in New York in April of 2004, which was about 5 months away. It was at the large Javits Center Convention Hall. All the big hitters in the cosmetics, health and wellness industries would be there. HBA was expecting more than 16,000 attendees and 575 exhibitors. It was a big deal. We called and there had a been a cancellation so we were able to secure a 10x10 booth for $4,600 with electricity. We didn't have a perfect prototype yet but we did have the logo designed and we were still working on the packaging. We pulled the trigger and went full tilt boogie. Once you know you have a deadline it is amazing what you can pull off. Richard Deer was an expert on conventions and had a beautiful 10x10 booth that he would lend us for free. Our graphic artist, Beth Weintraut, had her master's in packaging and her own company, Weintraut Kreativ. Finding her was a stroke of luck for us. Sending the designs for our packaging to China was a breeze with Beth. She made us look professional. Besides designing our box she also helped us deck-out our booth for New York. Presentation was very important. Ric and I were both designers at heart. Whether we were designing a bar, nightclub or booth space we wanted it to look cool. We had invested about $15,000 into BagBlocker and the HBA show would be our coming out party. This was *Rolling the Dice 101.*

We had easily found a buyer for *Circle Bar*. as stated, our last night as owners was on a Saturday and Kerry would lock up and be the last one of us out as owners. The timing was perfect. We had Ric's Suburban packed with our 10x10 booth and we were cutting it so close that our 25 samples, in their retail boxes, were to be delivered to our hotel the next day. We bid Kerry goodbye at about 11pm and headed to the Big Apple. You really can't roll into NYC with a dream and not sing in your head:

"If I can make it there I'll make it anywhere,
It's up to you New York, New York!"

The 2004 HBA show opened on Monday. We had planned it out so we could go directly to the Javits Convention Center to unload and setup our booth. New York is always chaotic and finding the loading dock and permission to be there was a tough hurdle but we figured it out. Ric and I muscled our way in with our booth, found our space and began setting up our dream. I've got to pat ourselves on the back - our booth was bad ass. We both got creative with our designs.

HBA Booth with Ric Payne

Me with our "*Brokers Wanted*" sign

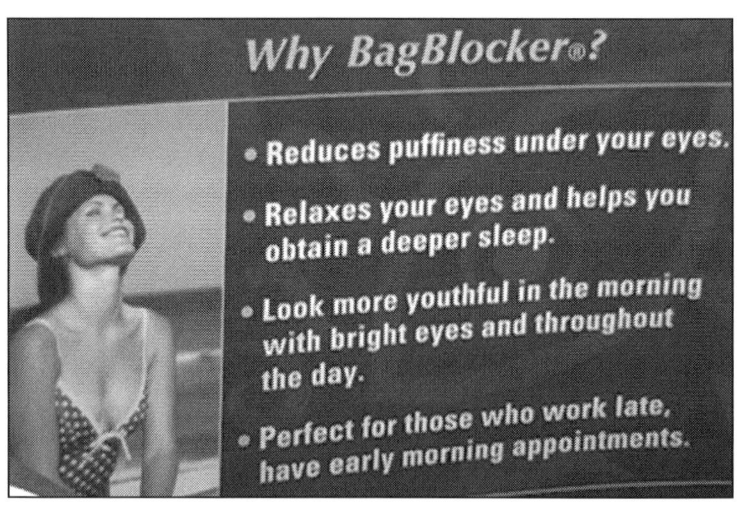

6' Banners like this helped SELL!

Long story short, BagBlocker was a huge hit. Everybody was interested in selling our product and we were overwhelmed and overjoyed. On the way "Back Home Again" to Indiana I have a video of Ric saying "Dino Ferrari" implying we are going to be rich. The competition for our product was fierce. QVC, Home Shopping Network, Ulta, Sephora, Beauty Brands were all telling us they wanted our product. We were the hit of the convention and people were giving us good advice. Getting a deal on QVC sounds like a dream come true, but the risk is big too. You'd have to supply them with product, pay to ship it to them, pay for warehouse rental space for BagBlocker and if it doesn't sell they charge you to return it to you. Many people have gone bankrupt, lost their homes, their life's saving by going to companies like that or even big box retail stores. There were about 5,000 Walgreens in 2005. Just to supply all their stores with 12 BagsBlockers would cost us nearly $200,000 AND they required us to pay for the coupon inserts they place in Sunday papers across the US. Once again, if our product didn't sell we would need to pay for stocking & storage and shipping it back to us. Just to get started Ric and I would have needed to put in $250,000. We believed in our product, but after hearing horror story after horror story at the HBA Convention we got understandably nervous. Success can also lead to your downfall if you don't have deep pockets.

On day 2 of HBA a couple of women from AVON Cosmetics stopped by our booth. They told us "DO NOT SIGN" with anyone else until you meet with our CEO tomorrow. We will bring her over to your booth. We also had a QVC broker practically shoving a contract under our fingers to sign. The warnings we heard from others about the possible pitfalls of that deal made us take a breath and see what AVON had to offer. Sure enough, on day 3, the CEO of AVON was standing in front of us. We had 4 powerful women telling us they wanted BagBlocker in their lineup ASAP. We told them we were getting it manufactured in China for $4.50 per item including shipping.

"We rule China," she said. "We can get this made for $1.20," she proclaimed.

"How would that work?" I asked her.

"We use Li & Fung, they are the biggest end-to-end supplier in the world," she explained. "You let us put BagBlocker in our catalog, which will be seen by 16 million people, and we will have your product selling in three months," she boasted.

This deal had Ric and I's heads spinning. We would have to take no money out of our pockets, they promised to introduce us to Li & Fung so we could set up a relationship with them. If BagBlocker did not sell, we would retain all the rights to the name & patent and could keep using Li & Fung as our distributor. They said they wanted to work with us and involve us in the process. We would be part of the AVON team. Everything we were hearing was exactly what we wanted.

True to their word, our product was in the catalog three months later. It was so surreal to see something we created in such a well established company's lineup. Our product had a full page too. We didn't like that it was being pitched with a girl putting mascara on. That's not how we saw the product being optimized. It looked a bit silly to us but the thrill of being recognized overshadowed this mistake in marketing. They are AVON, they know their market, right?

I can't say that Ric was able to buy his Dino Ferrari, but AVON did put some extra money in our pockets although it wasn't the huge financial windfall we had hoped for. The sales were good, which was hopeful, but our deal was confusing. This isn't exactly our numbers but it's what I remember. We would get 3.5% of the sales price per unit at $14.99, so roughly .50 cents per sale. When the true accounting came down the pipe we were getting our percentage based on the sale the "AVON Lady" was getting on her sale NOT the gross. That cut our profit down to only about .22 cents per BagBlocker sold! For example, if AVON sells 100,000 masks we would get $22,000. This calculation put us in the deep freeze along with Tupperware. BagBlocker was selling well but even if 200K people were using our product we'd hardly had a profit. We decided to pull out of AVON and try our luck where we could keystone our profits. This was a new word to us. "Keystone" is used in retail as a rule of thumb. Simply, it means that the retailer will double (2x) the wholesale cost they pay for BagBlocker to help them make a decent return. We had a suggestion for our mask to sell for $15 on the shelf which means we would sell it to a retail store for $7.50.

As they promised, AVON gave us a good relationship with Li & Fung. I had worked with one of their representatives daily trying to get BagBlocker just right. I did like that about AVON because they made us feel we were still a part of our own product. Once we decided to venture out on our own, Li & Fung stuck with us. After all the dust settled we were getting BagBlocker to Indiana via California from China for $1.45 per unit. They came in cases of 144 and we had a minimum order of 5,000 units. We would have 35 cases at a time delivered which cost us $7,308. In theory, each shipment once sold would make us $54,810. There was an additional shipping fee to whoever was the end seller. There would always be delays in getting paid, at least 90 days, and before we got one red cent, we were already putting another order in which could be as much as 70 cases. It was stressful, but working.

I remember the first shipment out of China came from Guangzhou which is also called Canton. I had been to this southern region of China as a tourist along the Pearl River. I had crossed over from Hong Kong. I highly recommend going to Hong Kong to experience this port city that was a British Colony from 1841-1997. It's rich history, the skyscrapers that intermingle Old World Asia and ultra modern is a site to behold. It by far is the most global community I have seen. I stayed at the infamous *Chung King Mansion*. Despite the regal name, this was the worst, scariest, sketchiest hotel I have and will ever stay at. My room was on the 9th floor along a dark narrow hallway. It was extremely small and dirty with no windows. It felt like a deathtrap. I could write a chapter on how disgusting and dangerous this place was in 1994. I have video of my stay there and it frightens me to watch it. My shower had an electric outlet inside of it! I'm proud I experienced the *Chung King Mansion* and anyone who knows about this place will want to give me a high-five for that feat of bravery. There is a movie called Chungking Express from 1994 that gives you glimpses of its stomach-turning vibe. Absolutely, there is no other building like it in the world. I later learned most Chinese are afraid to enter this building. Yet, I for some odd reason have fond memories of this hell-hole. A Badge of Honor!

After surviving the *Chung King Mansion* I took a boat to Macau (Mainland China) which is often referred to as the "Las Vegas of the East" but is actually much larger. Before COVID, Macau's revenue was 6x greater than Las Vegas which is mind-blowing. It has an interesting twist in architecture because the Portuguese leased the port in 1557 for trade, so many of the buildings look Spanish and street names are in Portuguese as well. Macau was the 1st European colonization in the

Far East. I was there in 1994 and it wasn't until 1999 that Portugal and China came to an agreement to release the area back to them. I had my guard up the entire time we were there. This was the second time I felt danger while in China. I stuck out like a sore thumb. The comforting rockstar vibe I got in Japan - being the cool foreigner was more of a bad curiosity in China. I was traveling with a Japanese friend of mine named Takuro. He was about my age and worked for Toyota Motors. He spoke Chinese fairly well, which you needed there. Almost no one spoke English and all the road signs were in Chinese except in Macau and then they were mostly in Portuguese. Either way, we needed his language abilities to get around. After hanging around Macau and doing a tiny bit of gambling, we decided to go see the Karst Mountains in Guilen. These hills have been an ancient attraction since the Tang Dynasty. They look like large stalagmites you'd see rising from the floor of a cave, yet these can reach 50 stories tall. The boat down the Yulong River was breathtaking.

The real story was getting to Guilen. Takuro picked a train that is normally only used by locals to get a true experience of China. That was a bad idea. We were packed in like animals with shirtless, hot sweaty workers for a long 6 hours ride. It was so crowded that people were hanging off the train for space. Train doors and windows were open as we clacked down the rails. I was the only non-Asian on this train and a constant flow of overly tan, dirty faced men wandered in front of me to get a look at the crazy round blue eye that dared to take this train. No one smiled. For the 3rd time on this trip I was feeling uneasy. Somewhere along the way we must have dozed off (although that seems impossible) because as we finally neared our station, Takuro had a 12" gash along his backpack. Someone had taken a knife just inches from his face and carefully cut open his pack in hopes of finding something of value. I know Napoleon is reported to have said, "There sleeps China! God pity us if she wakes. Let her sleep!" But from my experience once you step outside into the vast part of her land, it's very much 3rd world. People live a "Little House on the Prairie" existence. Oxen are pulling carts, Water buffalo roam the rivers and help with farming, Electricity can be scarce. Plumbing and clean water also were minimal. We took a long bus ride leaving Guilin. We only stopped once for a restroom break and the "facility" was a pond (cesspool). We were expected to poop & pee in a hole off the end of a rickety pier. A wooden wall you could easily see around was the men & women's divider. When it came to modern conveniences in 1994 most of China was still vastly behind. As far as beauty goes, China is more varied and spectacular than nearly any other country in the world. However, America is still running neck-and-neck with our own brand of wonders including the Grand Canyon, Yellowstone, Glacier National Park, the Rockies, rivers and the BEST farmland on earth.

So we are getting BagBlocker manufactured in Southern China in an area I was familiar with. When I spoke with Li & Fung's representatives I often tried to interject into the conversation that I had been to their neck of the woods. I'd write down the names of cities and rivers I had explored. I went straight through the heart of China's industrial epicenter. I knew how the people lived that I was working with. It gave me a good perspective and I could tell that it helped them to relate with me as well. This bond added to our experience in getting our dream manufactured halfway around the world.

I quickly learned that getting BagBlocker manufactured wasn't the hard part, getting it shipped to the USA was the true battle. I remember the first time our order was complete and my Li & Fung rep said in very broken English that it was being sent to Guangzhou Port.

Up until this point I thought they would arrange transportation to the US. They gave me some confusing numbers that I hoped would

Guilen Karst Mountains

Yulong River into the Karst Mountains

help the shipping company find our 35 cases of BagBlocker. I was in a panic after hitting several dead-ends. I needed a ginormous container ship to allow our tiny order to be in their cargo haul. I already knew it would take 30-40 days floating towards California, but how do we find it at The Port of Long Beach? If you've ever driven down the 405 in that area you've seen the sea of containers stacked to the sky. It always amazes me the needles in a haystack of products that find their way to their final destinations. Li & Fung reached out to me again to confirm that they had left our mother load at the dock. I envisioned our lonely pallet of eye masks sitting in some dark corner of a rickety warehouse near the water - never to be found again.

FedEx to the rescue! I called them and a woman named Dorothy answered the phone and she became by new business partner guru. I say guru because she calmly walked me through the whole process and assured me they could get BagBlocker to our doorstep in less than 6 weeks. Unbeknownst to me, FedEx had an international shipping division where they subleased space on giant container vessels. They would load in China, pick it up in Long Beach, CA and transport it to Indiana by truck. Dorothy understood the whack-a-doodle numbers I had for the Guangzhou Port and gave me a quote of $1,108. At first that seemed high but if I factored in we were shipping over 5,040 masks, that was only adding .40 cents to each unit. Now we were at $1.80 per unit. This first shipment was also more expensive because we needed packing slips and specific information to get through customs. A packing slip is given to the international freight forwarder, and ultimate consignee with information about the shipment, including how it's packed, the dimensions and weight of each package and the marks and numbers that are noted on the outside of the boxes. I was able to scribble this information together and get it to Dorothy. Coming through customs in Long Beach was going to cost us a registration fee and they needed information on all the materials that were used to make BagBlocker. There were port tariffs that we needed to register with and a company profile on Ric and I to make sure we weren't importing something we shouldn't be. The process of bringing goods into the US from China was a headache, but I was doing it myself instead of finding a "broker" or port authority expert to help me because I was trying to save us money. I let Dorothy (FedEx) know that we were green. This was our first time doing this. I also told her our HBA/ AVON story and got her on our side. We were the small potatoes trying to make the big meal. After jumping hurdle after hurdle, we finally had BagBlocker in our hands. It felt like a miracle to me. I'm not sure Ric knew all I went through? I felt like this was my baby!

We had orders for Beauty Brands in 10 states with about 30 stores total. We needed to create displays and changed our box design to a vertical profile to save shelf space. Merle Norman's picked us up along with several mom & pop stores. Our biggest success came in the catalogue business. At one point we were in 4 different ones. I was creating spreadsheets for inventory and sending out invoices. I became a regular face at our local FedEx and UPS store. It was a lot of work. The money from the invoices came in slowly but, unfortunately our sales were just marginally good. They were high enough that we weren't being dropped, but not high enough that we were making much of a profit. My sister Jacque had an idea for a 2-sided microdermabrasion wash cloth that could be used in the shower. We loved the idea and called it Celebrasion Wash Cloth. One side had a coarser texture than the other so you could choose which level of scrubbing you preferred for different parts of your body. I reached out to Li & Fung and sent them our prototype. I designed the logo and packaging and soon enough we had Celebrasion added to our cosmetic lineup. We started questioning the name *BagBlocker* as possibly too masculine. Sales were happening but we weren't getting the same reaction we had in New York. I visited the Beauty Brands in Indianapolis and talked with the floor staff. There seemed to be a consensus that a name change might help soften our pitch. We redirected all our packaging to EyeLOVELY.

BagBlocker Eye Mask
"Original Retail Box"

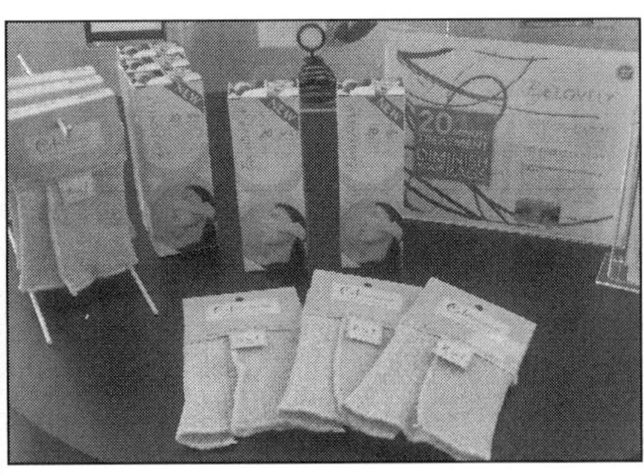

Beauty Brands Display: This is our full line-up with the new EyeLOVELY and Celebrasion Wash Cloth

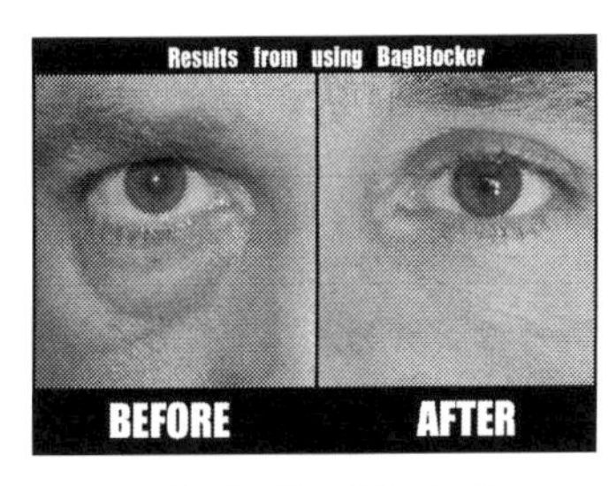

Ric is the Model!

EyeLovely One-Sheet Sales Pitch

We continued down this road for three years. It was not easy. Beauty Brands asked us if we had other products to add to our sku (stock keeping unit) because having too many smaller supply companies makes their accounting more tedious. They ultimately dropped us and added a company that makes normal eye masks and shower scrub gloves along with 20 other junk items. I use the term "junk" not as an actual slam but meaning little, non-expensive fringe cosmetic items that China churns out by the millions. At Invoke Beauty we were trying to create unique items that improve your quality of life. We believed in our products. The ads in the catalogs were still selling well, but we were basically just staying afloat. What money we were making we had to put back into the next order from China. It was a vicious cycle. Hamsters on a treadmill!

We had several more trips to New York City while working on launching our cosmetic company Invoke Beauty (***ib***+). Ric and I were exploring the Meat Packing District. We fell in love with a restaurant called Pastis. The white tiled walls, large mirrors and spherical light fixtures hanging around gave it a quintessential New York vibe and the amount of celebrities that frequented this place felt like Beverly Hills. Their crisp fries in duck fat were to die for and if you are looking for an exceptional meal, the steak sandwich with onions and Gruyére cheese will not disappoint. I remember the first time we went in this French joint the cast of the Soprano's was hanging out there. It was the perfect cliché, "Yo, Ricky we'd be hangin' at the Meat Packin' District, bada-bing-bada-boom, you know what I'm sayin!" I bring up this area of NYC because two bars within a 100 yards of Pastis helped guide our future in the libation profession. AGAIN! *First* we went into Hogs & Heifers. This was the original hole-n-the-wall bar they modeled *Coyote Ugly* after, which seems like a kick in the utters to Hogs & Heifers. I walked up to the bar and ordered two Coronas and the bartender grabbed a megaphone, turned the music off from a hidden dial under the bar and hollered, "Hey everyone, I've got a big pussy here trying to order a couple of sissy beers!" The room roared into "Boooooo!" and she continued "Who thinks this guy needs a couple shots of tequila?" The room erupted into cheers of "Yes" and I smiled and added the two shots to my order for a total of $42. The tequila was Patron, which was hot back then, but this bartender had just squeezed an extra $28 out of me. Genius! I learned something that day, that we incorporated into our future bars.

I took my handful of drinks back to Ric and he laughed, "What the hell was that all about?" We liked the vibe in this place. They had female bartenders stomping on top of the bar, bras hanging from the ceiling and the whole place just seemed like fun.

"You know that idea you have for the Wild Beaver Saloon you keep talking about?" Ric said. "You're right, we could make it just like this. The space on Delaware Street where the Indy News Room used to be is vacant," he said, with a look of 'Ta-Da' on his face.

"Yeah, I've been in there. It's tiny though. Do you think it's big enough?" I asked suspiciously.

"It's the perfect space to try out the Wild Beaver Saloon," he declared. "It's small and cheap!"

After leaving *Hogs & Heifers* we heard of a hidden gem called *APT* which we realized stood for apartment. We passed this bar two times and then saw a large man just standing along the sidewalk with a suit on. We asked him where APT was. He turned and opened a door. When we entered we were in front of a three-story Brownstone home. This was the bar? They took a house, or I guess it could be rented as an apartment, and turned it into the ultimate house bar. Walking in you felt like you were invited into someone's home for a party. The kitchen still looked like a kitchen but two bartenders were scrambling to serve you over the butcher block island. We were blown away by this concept. This little nugget of creativity stuck with us because years later we created our own version in Indianapolis called The Burnside Inn. I'll get more into that project later in this book. Remember to always keep your eyes open. Absorb the things you like and store it away in your memory.

Wild Beaver Saloon 101

CHAPTER SIXTEEN

•

"Nothing is impossible, the word itself says I'm Possible"
—Audrey Hepburn

A DIFFICULT DILEMMA in opening a bar or restaurant is that it is nearly impossible to own the building you're creating your concept in. We all know Location Location Location are the three most important things to consider in building a business that relies on customers to walk in to make you money. All the good locations are taken in most thriving cities. You are going to have to accept that your space is not owned by you. The issue is dealing with a landlord. You're at their mercy every 5 years or possibly 10 with a strong option put in your lease. If you become successful in their location they can decide to raise your rent when it comes time to sign a new lease extension.

In 2015 Hogs & Heifers founder Michelle Dell closed her original location in the Meat Packing District after 23 years. She said, "My monthly rent jumped to $60,000 a month from $14,000 and I'm unwilling to start charging customers $17 for a can of Pabst that currently costs $3 at the bar." This is always a fear that comes with success. You may take over a stinker location, but once you turn it around and make it successful the landlord starts licking their chops. It comes with the territory.

Ric and I talked about launching the *Wild Beaver Saloon* when we were in NYC meeting with AVON. We didn't pull the trigger on opening another bar right away because we were busy trying to make BagBlocker / EyeLOVELY / Celebrasion a success. I remember I was on the Canadian side of Niagara Falls in 2005 and wandered into a bar that looked like a beaver den. The beaver is on the Canadian 5 cent piece and has a special place in every Canadian's heart. I called Ric as I was sitting there and said I thought I had found the buildout of what our Beavers could look like. Ric found an artist and had a beaver logo designed that we really liked. We now had a logo, a buildout concept and the Indy News space was still available. The cosmetic sales were steady with EyeLOVELY & Celebrasion but not cutting the mustard as far as making us enough income to live off of that alone. It was time to pull the trigger on the *Wild Beaver Saloon.*

We opened our first *Wild Beaver Saloon* in 2006, the same week that Indianapolis was hosting the NCAA Men's Final Four Basketball Tournament. It couldn't have been a better start. The energy in the city was off the charts. We were packed from open to close. Zink Distributing is the Budweiser distributor in Indianapolis and we quickly developed a great working relationship with Jim Zink Jr and our rep Grant Beaumont. Grant still works with us today. They brought in *Ted Ferguson,* Bud Light's 'Daredevil' who had some hilarious commercials poking fun of him listening to his girlfriend. We had a plethora of Bud Beauties coming through that opening weekend for the Final Four as well. From the very start we knew we had a *winner-winner-beaver-dinner* with the Wild Beaver Saloon concept.

The little Beaver experiment in downtown Indy is only 1,500sf. It's success let us know we had lighting in a bottle. Our Wild Beaver Saloon sign still is the #1 photographed sign in Indianapolis 17 years later. We opened our next Beaver in a suburb of Indy called Broad Ripple and it took off like gangbusters too. Our 3rd location was the country music capital of the world - Nashville, Tennessee. It was December of 2008, which means in 2 years and 10 months we had launched three bars. This was the first time we didn't take-off right out of the gate. A valuable lesson hit us hard...

People are Creatures of Habit and Getting Them to Try Something New is Never Easy

Nashville, TN was our first true tourist town location and it was hard to get people to not want to return to their favorite spots from the last time they were in NashVegas. People want to go back to Tootsies and The Stage. It feels like home to them. Trying to get them to venture out of their *nostalgic comfort zone* is a tough safe to crack. We opened the Wild Beaver Saloon in Nashville trying to be like everyone else. We had live music from open to close. We weren't on the main strip of Broadway and in 2008 we were definitely considered off the beaten path.

What did we do? We reinvented ourselves. We quickly realized we could not compete with the honky-tonks mano-a-mano which in Spanish comes from bullfighting, describing a type of duel between two matadors. It didn't happen overnight but two big changes launched us to the highest numbers in sales that we had ever seen. We became the *"Best Dam Karaoke Bar"* playing up the "Dam" being a Beaver Bar. We made our customers the star. We also added a mechanical bull right in the middle of the room. It had two effects; 1) it ate up a lot of space so we looked crowded with less people in the room and 2) it gave us something none of the bars on Broadway had. Plus it kept people in the bar longer to watch people ride.

Over the last 16 years the Wild Beaver Saloon has continued to thrive in Nashville. As we got better as a bar, Nashville became NashVegas - meaning it became a major tourist attraction. It had always been popular but over the past 10 years it has boomed.

In early summer 2010 we did our first licensing agreement with Jerome Abood in Lansing, Michigan near the MSU campus on Main Street. We would guide him through construction and basically set up the entire Wild Beaver Saloon for him. One positive in this scenario was that Jerome was willing to splurge on decor that Ric and I might not have. For example, he bought a huge $3,000 antler chandelier that made the room special. On one hand it was great to build our dream Beaver with someone else's money but looking back, that designer joy was highly overrated. It's hard to have someone else run the concept the way you want them to. Plus, the money we would receive in the agreement was nowhere close to the returns we would have reaped if we owned it ourselves. Jerome had a big hit on his hands. The Lansing Wild Beaver Saloon was printing money but he didn't know how to keep the ship on course. We blame ourselves for not having a stronger "Licensing Agreement" in place. This was a lesson we learned the hard way. You live and learn. You can't let mistakes like this eat you up or you'll paralyze yourself to the point of missing other opportunities.

Life Lesson

I see my bartenders getting a lousy tip early in the night and it puts them in a negative mood. I tell them to shake it off. Don't let that poor tipper cause you to miss an opportunity to impress a good tipper. Sure, you got $2 on a $40 tab, but if you stay positive you may get a $20 tip on a $10 tab. This can be true in all aspects of life. We have our ups and downs. It's all about mojo, it's the energy you are putting off. Haven't we all worn a certain shirt or outfit and we seem to be on fire. You're the most popular person in the room. Your jokes are funnier, the opposite sex seems to love your every move, you're oozing aura. You think, "This must be my lucky shirt" but the next time you wear it, the luster is gone. The magic spell has disappeared and you're wondering what happened? What happened is YOU! You were giving off the vibe of confidence the last time you wore that article of clothing that you think was your lucky charm. In truth, all of us have a lucky charm and it's eye contact, smiles, positive energy, confidence, playfulness and a spark to make the people you are in front of happier, or at the bare minimum at ease and comfortable. Remember, when something bothers you, let it go. I love the expression "Don't sweat the small stuff" and usually most of it is!

ooooo

At our peak we had five bars: (4) Wild Beaver Saloons and one (1) Wild Cat Saloon. In December 2017 we added another concept that's flourishing in Indianapolis called the Burnside Inn. So what's the reason we slammed the brakes on expanding our entertainment concepts?

The bars were causing some headaches. We were spending more & more time in Nashville TN, Lansing MI, & Lexington KY along with our two in Indy. I felt like a trucker who was constantly on the road. We all felt like we needed a break. Financially we were all doing well. The best raise is not always money, but time. Freedom is priceless!

At this time, I had my 2nd invention idea that was about to change everything. BagBlocker showed Ric and I that anything was possible but now we had a golden ticket (idea), or should I say *green ball of steam*? *Mister Steamy the Dryer Ball was about to change everything!*

Ric and I were going to **TRY** to launch another product. Kerry does the lion share of the work, as our certified bean counter, payroll provider and tech guru, after the bars are up & running. Plus, opening bars out-of-state was adding to his headaches. We were all ready to take a break from expanding. The bars still continue to do well. To this day, they continue to feed the monster for our other dreams.

Ric (R) and I outside the original Wild Beaver Saloon in Indy

Wild Beaver Saloon Calendar

Promotional Poster for our 2 Indy WBS locations.

Come Sing-Along, Drink-Along & Rock-Along

Wild Cat Saloon 2010 in Lexington, KY

Wild Cat Saloon Entrance at Christmas

Wild Beaver Menu in Lansing, MI

Wild Cat Saloon Logo
Lexington, KY

Wild Beaver Promo for
Best Dam Karaoke

Wild Beaver Lansing Exterior

Wild Beaver & a Cat

Wild Beaver Saloon Bartenders in Lansing, MI

Mister Steamy

CHAPTER SEVENTEEN

•

"Do not look back in anger, or forward
in fear, but around in awareness."
—James Thurber

WE HAD OPENED three bars and were licking our wounds that *BagBlocker* and/or *EyeLOVELY* and *Celebrasion Wash Cloth* were not going to make us rich. Better off, yes, but we still needed to grind away at doing what we know. During that brief window, after launching BagBlocker at HBA and getting the AVON deal, Ric and I got an office in an industrial building in downtown Indianapolis called The Stutz. We were using this space to work on the logistics of our newly formed ***ib***+ (Invoke Beauty). During this period I was out at Ric's house for one reason or another. As I was leaving, I walked through his laundry room to get to his garage. It looked like a bomb had gone off. He had two young kids in 2006 under the age of 10 years old. I looked in his dryer and there was a clump of half dried clothes that were all rolled and wrinkled up. This was September of 2006.

"You should throw in a tennis ball and a wet wash cloth or grab something out of there and get it really wet," I explained as I pointed to the dryer. "My mom used to always do that when we left clothes in the dryer too long. They're all wrinkled now."

"Yeah man, kids. You have no idea how hard it is to keep up with it," he laughed. On the way home I started thinking about the tennis ball/ wet wash combo and wondered if there was a dryer ball out there that had a sponge inside or a way to add moisture to the load? The tennis ball theory works by bumping into the clothes and separating them, allowing air to fluff them up. The water would add a mist or light steam that would release the wrinkles. I got home and went straight to my computer and Googled everything I could to try and see if this simple idea was out there. To my surprise no one else had thought of adding moisture to their dryer in 2006.

I called Ric right away and I'm sure he could tell by my voice I thought I had stumbled upon a genius idea. Later that night he took his family to McDonald's and they had a Mario campaign with him as a little ball (see photo). Ric called me the next day and said he was going to cut a hole in his Mario ball, add a sponge and see if my idea worked. Ric's experiment left him with only a "maybe" as to how effective it was at helping to removing the wrinkles. He wasn't completely sold. This trial helped because we realized the dryer ball needed to be bigger & heavier to not get caught or wrapped up in an article of clothing. There also needed to be more holes to allow the moisture to escape more easily. Trial and error was our friend.

That December I bought a colorful round dog toy with multiple protrusions like a spiny Sea Urchin. I took an x-acto knife and cut a 1" top hole where the squeaker was, took a drill and placed holes all over the ball. I then placed a sponge inside and began experimenting with it. I quickly realized we didn't want holes directly below the opening where you poured in the water to wet the sponge. The water ran down and leaked on the floor from the sink to the dryer. I chose an area 2.5" x 2.5" and left it solid on the bottom. I experimented with this "dog toy" dryer ball and felt like I was onto something. Our first name was "*Dapper the Dryer Ball*" because it rolled off the tongue well and if your clothes look well groomed you'd be a stylin' dapper man. We remembered the sting of the masculine BagBlocker name and "Dapper" is a term many younger people thought was an old fashioned term or didn't even know what it meant at all, so we kept brainstorming for a better name.

We still had a relationship with Li & Fung and I sent our prototype off to China. On January 19, 2007 they sent back our first manufactured model. They had put a slit on top - like an old coin holder. We didn't like the looks of that and told them we'd prefer a well constructed hole as the opening. They then told us that mass production of our current design wouldn't be possible because our spines, I'll call them pistons, were too narrow and the mold could collapse and the holes would be blocked. Basically, our pistons needed to be bigger to help manufacturing. I remember seeing a steam roller with teeth on it along the highway and it got me thinking. I pulled out a tape measure and thought 3/4" diameter would be large enough and 1/3" tall. I emailed Li & Fung back and forth and sent them a drawing of what I was thinking. By March 2007 they sent me a photo of a wax mold that looked perfect. They charged us $2,000 for the mold and by June we had five (5) complete dryer balls delivered to my doorstep. These prototypes got me excited!

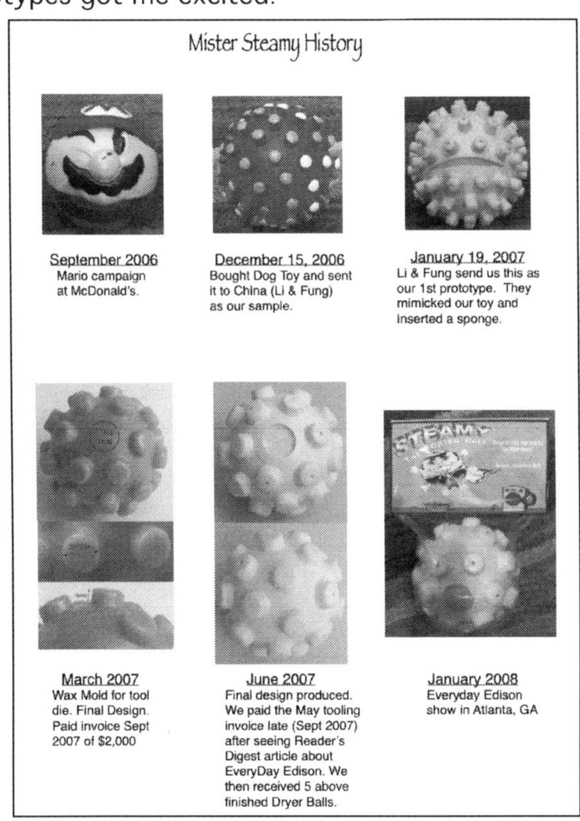

Mister Steamy History

September 2006
Mario campaign at McDonald's.

December 15, 2006
Bought Dog Toy and sent it to China (Li & Fung) as our sample.

January 19, 2007
Li & Fung send us this as our 1st prototype. They mimicked our toy and inserted a sponge.

March 2007
Wax Mold for tool die. Final Design. Paid invoice Sept 2007 of $2,000

June 2007
Final design produced. We paid the May tooling invoice late (Sept 2007) after seeing Reader's Digest article about EveryDay Edison. We then received 5 above finished Dryer Balls.

January 2008
Everyday Edison show in Atlanta, GA

Did we run out and start trying to get a deal right away? No, and the reason why is because we now knew too much. The sting of BagBlocker was still ringing in our ears. How should we market our new dryer ball with the power of steam? That's it!!!! We decided to call our invention *MISTER STEAMY the Dryer Ball.* Mist was playing up on the fact that we wanted our dryer ball to release misty moisture into the dryer. Steamy also had an element of playfulness because *McSteamy* was all the rage on *Grey's Anatomy*. Mister Steamy would be a Superhero to the laundry rescue.

Our complete prototype sat on my desk at the office of **ib+** in the Stutz Building in Indy for 6 months. It had been well over a year since we decided to move forward with *Mister Steamy the Dryer Ball* and now we were sitting on our hands. We practically stopped talking about it. We knew the uphill battle. BagBlocker had been a big success but to make it to the big leagues we needed big capital. To get *Mister Steamy* off the launching pad we'd need to go to a convention again that specializes in home products and hope to get an agent or figure out a way to do it ourselves, but that would take a big gamble with our money. The expression "Put your money where your mouth is" is never more true than when you are the one who is in the driver's seat. The truth is - it's scary! We had three bars at this point. Nashville was struggling. We were in talks to possibly build a Wild Beaver Saloon, as a licensing agreement in Lansing, and EyeLOVELY and Celebrasion were making money, but to push all our chips forward (which is what it would take) seemed like too big of a risk. Hindsight is 20/20, YES, WE SHOULD HAVE, but that was then and this is now. We were in a holding pattern with *Mister Steamy* and hadn't even patented it yet. A *deer in headlights* might describe us at this point.

In October 2007 I was at my parent's house and I grabbed a couple of *Reader's Digests*. I love the *Humor and Word Power* sections and it always has good articles. I got back to my place and like any sane American I'm flipping through RD while on the can. The "can" is what my grandpa usually called it, but for fun he entertained me by occasionally calling out, "I'm going to — the John, the loo, water closet, crapper, the throne, my office" and my favorite "I'm going to drop the kids off at the pool" which he was always proud to say.

People sometimes comment they'd like to go back to "simpler times" but as far as hygiene we are living in the sweet spot of sanitation. The history of human waste is disgusting and living within modern day infrastructures is a blessing. No idea why I added that?

So anyway, I see an article about a PBS show called *Everyday Edisons*. It was an early version of *Shark Tank*. The article was highlighting some products they had launched. Like *Shark Tank*, they would help get the product right, manufacture it and setup distribution. The inventors would not have to pay any money out of pocket. The inventors of Gyro Bowl, Emery Cat Scratcher and Eggies all gave testimonials of how happy they were with Everyday Edisons. Since Ric and I had already had a few products out in the marketplace I thought we could bypass the protocols. I didn't really want to go on the show. The Reader's Digest article named two guys who seemed to be in charge of Everyday Edisons; Todd Stancombe, president of Edison Nation and Louis Foreman the CEO of Enventys, Edison Nation and Everyday Edisons. All these divisions are connected under the same roof in Charlotte, North Carolina. I tried calling and bypassing the dog & pony show but the RD article forced these two guys to put up defense walls. I'm sure I was NOT the only inventor trying to get the inside pick & roll. Inventors have a "break the rules" mentality but I finally realized the only way I was going to get in front of them was to go to one of their open calls.

Season 3 of *Everyday Edisons* was going to 5 cities. The one that made the most sense was Atlanta. It was their first stop on January 12, 2008. It's always is good to be seen early. They would be rested and full of enthusiasm. I walked into our **ib**+ office and pitched the idea to Ric.

"Check this out," handing Ric the Reader's Digest. "This could be a way to get a Mister Steamy deal with no money out of our pockets," I enthusiastically explained.

"I don't know, you think it's worth it?" he questioned. "It's a dog toy with a sponge inside," he barked half laughing.

"I think we should try, man," I said pacing around. "The first city they're doing a casting call in, you know what I mean, inventions, is Atlanta in January!"

"That's a long way down there to pitch at a cattle call," Ric said resisting.

"Fuck it, we can go down to Nashville and baby-sit the Beav and then it's only about three hours from there," I explained. Ric did not bite or fully commit at this point. I understood why. We had been up to bat with BagBlocker/EyeLOVELY and Celebrasion. They all had been in multiple states, tons of catalogs and it was grinding. Launching a product is not for the faint of heart.

We have a guy named Bob East who is a cartoonist by trade and he helps us with a lot of our Wild Beaver Saloon designs. I asked him to create *Mister Steamy* as a superhero flying out of a dryer to the rescue. As always, he delivered an amazing mockup. I ordered some plastic bags, took Bob's drawing and made a header complete with a fake barcode. It gave it the appearance that it might already be selling someplace.

The Original Pitch Packaging in Atlanta
in Front of *Everyday Edison's* Judges.

Yahoo "Make it Green" in S.F. (Maker Faire)

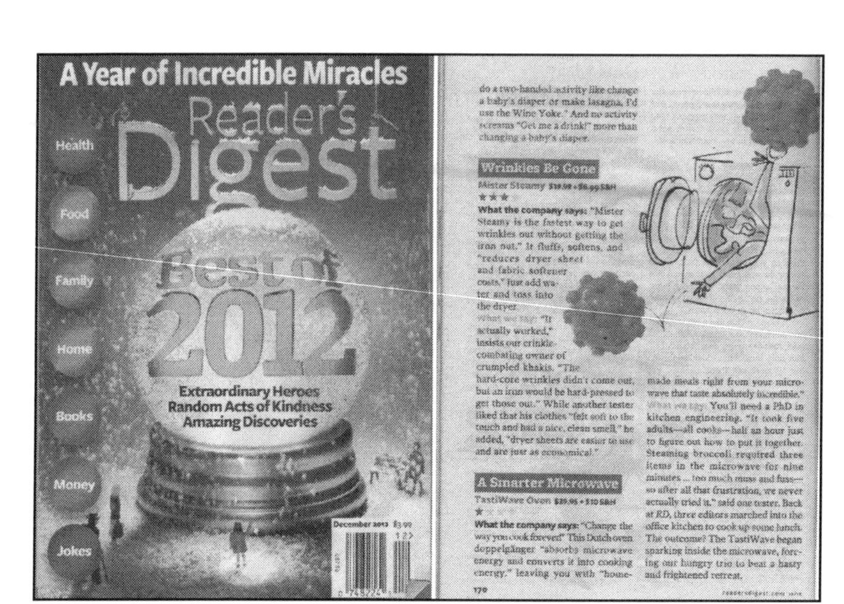

do a two-handed activity like change a baby's diaper or make lasagna, I'd use the Wine Yoke." And no activity screams "Get me a drink!" more than changing a baby's diaper.

Wrinkles Be Gone

Mister Steamy $19.99 + $6.99 S&H

★★★

What the company says: "Mister Steamy is the fastest way to get wrinkles out without getting the iron out." It fluffs, softens, and "reduces dryer sheet and fabric softener costs." Just add water and toss into the dryer.

What we say: "It actually worked," insists our crinkle-combating owner of crumpled khakis. "The hard-core wrinkles didn't come out, but an iron would be hard-pressed to get those out." While another tester liked that his clothes "felt soft to the touch and had a nice, clean smell," he added, "dryer sheets are easier to use and are just as economical."

A Smarter Microwave

TastiWave Oven $29.95 + $10 S&H

★

What the company says: "Change the way you cook forever!" This Dutch oven doppelgänger "absorbs microwave energy and converts it into cooking energy," leaving you with "home-made meals right from your microwave that taste absolutely incredible."

What we say: You'll need a PhD in kitchen engineering. "It took five adults—all cooks—half an hour just to figure out how to put it together. Steaming broccoli required three items in the microwave for nine minutes ... too much muss and fuss—so after all that frustration, we never actually tried it," said one tester. Back at *RD*, three editors marched into the office kitchen to cook up some lunch. The outcome? The TastiWave began sparking inside the microwave, forcing our hungry trio to beat a hasty and frightened retreat.

170

This was huge for us!!!

We were told about 16,000 people would pitch their product ideas in all 5 cities and they would narrow it down to 40 and then a final 9 would be flown to Charlotte, NC for a week of brainstorming and pitches. It had an air of competition but mostly everyone was cheering each other on. We would all be winners if our idea made it into stores. As January was approaching I was gearing up to head down to ATL. I had five extra *Mister Steamy* placards made that would fold and standup in front of each judge. They didn't give out much protocol so I decided to do what I'd like to see if I were in their shoes.

"You really should go with me Ric!" I said with conviction. "Fuck it man, what do we have to lose?" Ric conceded and said he'd go. Thank god he did because it might have put a little rift in our more than copacetic relationship.

We checked into a hotel Friday January 12, 2008 in Atlanta and headed over to the convention center at 7am the next morning. There were already a line of inventor hopefuls outside wrapped around the building. As we pulled up I made a "Moo Moo" sound mimicking the sound of a cattle call. Ric laughed, "I told you it'd be like this!" There were probably about 3,000 people but Everyday Edison was very organized. You basically sign over your product to them before you even present anything. Obviously, if they pass on your product you walk out with your full rights, but if they like you then you're locked in. This is really the only way they could operate if you were on their side of the fence. The Reader's Digest article said they gave 10% to the inventors minus development and expenses, which we all know can be a slippery slope, that allows them to control this number. It did give the rights to auditing, but once again how deep can you probe if they hold the "accounting cards" so to speak?

The real shocker was, as we walked up to the document booth, since we had no patent we would only qualify for 5% of the profit! In Season 1 & 2 this stipulation was not in place. This might have been a deal breaker had we known this heading down to Atlanta. In the tight retail margins the difference between 5% & 10% is astronomical. We also knew *Mister Steamy* had been sitting on my desk for a year, and with the uphill battles our other products had presented to us, we decided to march forward and sign up & sign away the rights to our dryer ball with the power of steam for 5%. Sure, hindsight is 20/20, but we were there, as Ric always said, "With a dog toy with a sponge stuck inside" and we only had $2,500 invested. That loss of 5% ended up costing us a pretty penny, c'est la vie!

TO PATENT OR NOT TO PATENT
(that is the question)

Patents are a double edged sword that are only as good as the depth of your pocket book to protect them. Let's face it, Saks Fifth Ave was duped into selling fake Louis Vuitton. If giants of industry cannot stop knock-offs how can you? The Catch 22 is that a patent does help you when you are pitching to a legitimate company. For example, we did patent BagBlocker before we went to NYC to launch it. AVON likely would not have picked up our product if it had not been patented.

The troubling truth is that idea thieves roam these shows looking to steal innovative concepts. They can often get them "knocked-off" before you even get to market. We had this experience with *Mister Steamy the Dryer Ball* but I'll explain that later.

We've paid as little as $5,000 for a utility & design patent and as much as $15,000. It depends on the intricacy of the concept. A dog toy with a sponge inside would be on the low side. You can pay $500-1,000 for a patent search prior to applying for a patent to see if your idea has already been filed. You risk paying an attorney and have your patent rejected and for that reason I recommend paying for the search. A *utility patent* is to protect the function, composition, machine or process for 20 years. The *design patent* does what it says: it protects the new, original, and decorative appearance that lasts 15 years. I recommend doing both. A design patent alone will not stop someone from creating a product that does what your invention does - they have just made it look different in appearance. The utility can include multiple claims of use and stop variations of your invention. That being said, the *utility patent* is more complicated and is on the upper echelon of the cost on the sliding scale.

Since we are on the "Meat & Potatoes" of starting an invention, I want to discuss naming your product. Not everybody may agree with me on this but from my experience the name you give your product is very important. Naming a book like, this one, is crucial for sales. Questions to ask yourself:

1) Is this name being used currently? Go to the U.S. Patent and Trademark Office (USPTO) and do a SIMPLE search. Is the name active or alive?
2) Do a website search of your name. Try variations of your product name.
3) Search Facebook, Instagram and other social media platforms and register your name with them.
4) Think of a name that reflects your concept or what it does. When

people see your name do they have a sense of what it does, or invoke a reaction?

5) Your end user's age, income, sex - know your market.
6) The brand and logo are important. Get professional help. I like Fiverr.com to create logos, unique branding.

I always trademark my name myself at the USPTO. I do a quick search and then go on the government's website. It costs $275. Unless you are afraid of losing the name, I recommend having your logo already designed so you can download it during the application fee. I've done it several times without a completed logo, so the choice is up to you, but as a general rule I would have it ready at registration.

Back to Atlanta... in our situation I wish we had patented Mister Steamy. That would have been the best $5,000 we ever spent. Once checked-in and registered we were given a number. There was a large digital screen in an open room set up with chairs. Once you saw your number you were directed to a table to give your first pitch. Then you waited for the first round of cuts. They posted about 100 numbers (inventors) so they cut nearly 3,000 ideas. We had our two (2) Mister Steamy prototypes in a little box which was a blessing. I mention this because I felt sorry for many of the inventors which had ideas that were bulky, large and/or heavy. Ric and I looked like we had nothing at all to pitch. Then seeing nearly all of them haul (lug) their dreams back to their car was sad. We had been there four hours already and were told the 2nd round would start up right after lunch. We had an hour break - back at 1pm. Ric and I were getting a sense that our idea was strong. Our number popped up on the screen and we headed over to a table to meet a patent attorney and researcher. They saw our product wasn't patented so they were trying to do a quick search to see if someone had already beat us to the punch. I had done some of my own research and felt confident we had a unique concept. It was such a logical idea, so commonsensical, that you'd assume someone in the billion dollar laundry business had thought of it. There were plenty of dryer balls out there, didn't one of them think, "Hey, let's add some water, a scented liquid!" Up until this point, dryer balls were used with wet clothes to separate them and fluff them up. Mister Steamy was thrown in with dry clothes, GROUND BREAKING! I say that facetiously because it seemed so obvious. "Everything should be made as simple as possible, but not simpler," Einstein quipped, or my favorite by Forrest Gump's mama, "Stupid is as stupid does" but I'd like to make my own phrase, "Simple is as stupid as simply doing!" Keeping your eyes open for the simple solutions is not stupid, it's fortuitous awareness. Hillbilly engineering or rigging a fast fix on the fly is the Mother of Invention. The key is to step back, analyze what you just came up with and think, "Would someone else like to benefit from this idea?" And if so, DO SOMETHING ABOUT IT! People often have great ideas over the weekend, but come Monday they either can't remember the genius idea they had or don't have the drive to follow through.

After the interrogation by the suits we once again had to wait and wait to see if they felt our idea was genuinely not on the market or had not been patented. This was the ONLY time I felt a little nervous pitching to *Everyday Edisons.* Finally, about 5pm our number came up again and we were called over and told we had passed the background test. They asked us to come back at 7pm. Holy cow, this is an all day adventure. It was like acting, you wait for hours, spew a few lines from your brain and you're back to waiting again.

Back at 7pm and there were only about 15 of us left standing. It was survival of the fittest. Our fellow inventors were dwindling by the hour. We saw our number again, I think it was 917, and as we are walking over to the table I saw Todd Stancomb. I recognized him from

Reader's Digest. I gave him a big smile like we were long lost friends. I had stalked him so thoroughly I felt like I knew him.

"Hey, you're Todd Stancomb!" I smiled, reaching out to shake his hand.

"Yes I am," he said.

"I recognize you from Reader's Digest. I tried to track you down but I couldn't get past Linda," I laughed. Linda was his gatekeeper. I had spoken with her 3 times.

"Good to hear she's doing what I pay her to do," he smized.

"I gave her my 'I'm an established inventor' story but she still shut me down," I said.

Todd seemed to like Ric and I from the start. His approach with us was more of a meet and greet. We told him who we were, what we did, how we had other products on the market. I could tell he was VERY interested in Mister Steamy. Although we had already confirmed several times, he wanted to make sure himself, that this was truly *Steamy's Coming Out Party*.

"You've never shown anyone this product before?" he asked earnestly.

"No, no-one had seen it," Ric promised.

"Where did you get this made?" he asked rolling Mister Steamy around in his hand. I explained a bit about BagBlocker, Celebrasion and our AVON deal. I had pictures queued up on my phone of our other products on the market. I was trying to impress him with our success. I didn't say it, but I was nonverbally saying, "This isn't our first rodeo!" and I figured he knew what I was doing. Dare I say, "Swinging our you-know-what around"?

"Li & Fung made this prototype for us. I'm not sure if you are familiar with them but they run China. AVON introduced us to them. They work with Levi's, Canon Cameras, I mean they are a huge manufacturer," I explained. Todd said the show would choose a max of 40 inventors from five (5) cities depending on what they find and then a final 9 would be invited to Charlotte, NC. Two (2) hours later Ric and I would be taken to another part of the convention center we had not been to yet. We would pitch our product to three judges who held our fate in their hands. For this part of our pitch, we would be filmed! It had been a very long day. At 11:45pm we were escorted into a mock studio, mic'd up and shuffled towards a staging area where we would give our pitch. There was a small table in front of us and a backdrop showcasing the Everyday Edison's logo. I walked straight over to the judges and put our cardboard promo pitch in front of each one of them and handed over one of our complete *Mister Steamy* prototypes in it's packaging. I recognized one of the judges from Reader's Digest - Louis Foreman (CEO). I also noticed Louis was a snazzy dresser, his jeans looked perfectly pressed, so that was a good sign. I was surprised Todd Stancomb wasn't one of the judges but we learned he was more like the Wizard behind the curtain. I lead off with this pitch. You can find it on the internet:

> "This is Mister Steamy the Dryer Ball (I had one in my hand). This is a problem we've all had. You put your clothes in the dryer, you forget about it for an hour, 2 hours sometimes for 3 days, if you have kids you know what I'm talking about. So what happens? The laundry ends up clumped, it's in there for a while, it's all wrinkled. What do most people do? They turn the dryer back on for 20 minutes, it heats up a little and it does get some of the wrinkles out. So my mom for years would grab a wash cloth, wet it, ring it out and throw it in the dryer with a tennis ball. She said a little bit of moisture helps get the wrinkles out. I was at Ric's house, he's has 2 kids and his laundry room it looked like a bomb went off..."

They cut me off and peppered us with questions. They knew we had spent money on the tooling and seemed surprised we had not tried to get it to market. ALL THREE JUDGES VOTED YES! That Spring (about 3 months later) we were invited up to Chicago to the Science and Industry Museum along Lake Shore Drive overlooking Lake Michigan. Everyday Edisons had toured all five cities and were inviting 9 finalists to Charolette, NC to brainstorm and launch products. I remember on the 3 hour drive from Indianapolis I got stopped going 86mph in a 70mph zone. I pulled way over, nearly off the road. The State Trooper was an impeccably dressed black man.

"Why did you pull so far over off the road?" the State Trooper asked.

"I saw on the news that an officer had been hit by a car while writing someone a ticket," I explained.

"Are you in a hurry?" he asked.

I had miscalculated the time difference in Chicago and I had realized shortly after leaving Indy that we had an extra hour, "Well, we are coming from Indianapolis for a meeting and honestly, I messed up, we're actually an hour early," I half laughed. I gave him my license and registration. I see him coming back to my car in the rearview mirror.

"Young man, I'm just going to give you a warning," he kindly said. "Slow down, it's dangerous out on this highway," or something like that. I was set free. I was like the gazelle sipping water along the savanna and suddenly a crocodile springs up out of the water but it barely scampers free. I was randomly chosen by this Trooper, the unlucky prey, hundreds hourly are speeding up & down Interstate 65, but miraculously I was caught only to be let go. I escaped because I showed compassion for his safety? Because I was honest? I often wonder why?

"I can't believe you got out of that ticket," Ric said astonished. "I look at a cop wrong and I get ticket!"

"This is gonna be our lucky day," I said with a smile.

We park at the Science and Industry Museum and we see a sign for *Everyday Edisons* where we are greeted by one of the production assistants. It's eerily quiet. The museum was dead, no pun intended, and there were very few crew members with the show. They mic'd us up and we were taken into a room with a round table and some car invention stuff placed around us. I think the idea of meeting at the Science and Industry Museum was to be creative, but this reveal could have been anywhere. The camera was tight on us and mostly all you see are three (3) guys sitting at a table. Louis Foreman was the third person at that table. His blue dress shirt and cream jacket were perfectly pressed. There were two round coasters on the table - one red, one green. Yes, it felt like we were at a Fogo de Chao and were hoping to signal the gauchos for more meat on a sword. "We want green, we want green" I was saying in my head. Sure enough, Louis teased us but then turned over the green card and gave us the ticket to Charlotte, we were moving on to development and the launching of *Mister Steamy the Dryer Ball* worldwide!

Just to be clear, police officers aren't always so nice to me. I was driving my grandma's Oldsmobile Omega in 1997 near the Beverly Center Mall on La Cienega Blvd and I saw the gumballs light up behind me. I knew I hadn't done anything wrong. Two police officers approached my car very carefully. From the passenger side one guy swooped around with his gun out, pointed along the ground. I had seen enough COPS TV shows to know what "Bad Boys, Bad Boys" whatcha shouldn't do and I put both my hands in the air and stayed very still. Apparently, I resembled Andrew Cunanan who was in the middle of a killing spree that ended in Miami after he murdered Gianni Versace on the steps of his mansion. I attribute that mixup in identity to driving a crappy car. Although I did have a full head of dark robust hair like Cunanan. If I was driving a new BMW would I have been stopped? I'm no Malcolm Gladwell and this social economical question is a tough riddle to resolve, but this white, privileged male has seen glimpses of both sides of the track. I can only imagine it is harder for those less affluent and non-white. I will say straightly, being kind, polite and respectful can go a long way in fading color lines. I was let off the hook by a black State Trooper not because I was white. I was "caught & released" because I was being human. We are humankind, be both - human & kind. It can go a long way in helping humanity get along. I always liked the expression "*You attract more bees with honey than vinegar*" and try to live my life with that in mind. Speaking of class & wealth, this is an observation I always found interesting:

The poor are poor because they spend most of their money
The middle class are middle class because they save most of their money
The rich are rich because they invest most of their money

Of course, this brings up all kinds of reasons for imbalances in dealing with money. It's never straight forward. Poor is a relative term, but poor are in this predicament because their income doesn't meet their consumption needs, but we all have different spending needs or what we feel we need. The word "poor" also seems harsh. I prefer to say, "Broke" because it gives an air of hope. Poor sounds like long term agony, but I can be broke on Thursday and eating steak on Friday. You're broke until your ship comes in, you pick up your paycheck, your bid is accepted, people can be broke-ass, but not poor. I can imagine being broke and happy. Poor is just a downer of a word. I know there are people it applies to sadly, but far too often it's a bad label. Past the broke, you move onto the ordinary people, the middle class. The *Ordinary* used to make up 61% of the US population, now it's barely 50%. Where did that 11% go? Did they go broke (lower class) or slide up to the elite (upper class)? 7% chose the George Jefferson route, they moved on up to a deluxe apartment in the sky with the other 4% on the struggling slide to less income.

The middle class (ordinary) meet their consumption needs and squirrel away savings to feel secure. The reality is the middle class do own a home, but with a mortgage, they own a nice car, but with loan/ lease, their kids go to college and create debt. They *"owe owe owe owe off to work they go"* so they can afford these things along with money to save, go on vacations and procure luxuries. Rich is a relative term too. I've met plenty of people I'd call "rich" but they tend to say they are secure. The word "rich" is a dirty word for some. They are the elite, the top of the heap because they can risk capital. Their income surpasses consumption and allows them to pad their savings. They have so much overflow income leftover to invest in long term funding to help them build wealth in real estate, stocks, mutual funds and side businesses. They fly first class and can eat at a Michelin Star restaurant at $400 a plate. It's decadent and carefree.

"If Poor People Knew How Rich Rich People Are, There Would Be Riots"

This quote came from Chris Rock and I think about it all the time. I was in the Delta Sky Lounge in LAX recently and the amount of luxury made me happy and sad. I made sure I stepped back and thanked my lucky stars. It is a blessing to be able to be in a place like that. As a cross-section, petri-dish of society, this place actually cut the mustard. It was Grey Poupon but still made with the hard working mustard seed. When I looked around the color of the human skin was a shining rainbow. It was bright. If an Alien had landed in that Delta Sky Lounge it would have not have noticed race. It was a blend, a stew of Americans of all types. Unfortunately, I don't believe this microcosm of frequent fliers represents the US population but I wish it did. It felt right.

The broke, ordinary and elite are more alike than different. I'm not sure exactly what makes some people reach a higher standard of living. Obviously, where you're raised, what part of the world, what part of that part, of the world. Many factors lead us in the direction we go, the level we feel we want and can reach. I did not grow up in a wealthy family. As I stated, my father left my mom with three small children. I was the youngest at 4 years old. My dad disappeared for a while. He never paid child support. My mom was driven, she was a natural born entrepreneur. By the time I was 12 some of my relatives thought we had money. I give all the credit AGAIN to my mom. She planted a seed in me to be DRIVEN. When I talk about class and the broke, ordinary and elite I often think part of the separation is drive.

Where that drive comes from, to be driven, is something I cannot pull out of a magic hat, but I do believe DNA plays a role along with opportunity. Some people are driven to try, try and try; one more time when striving to make a better way in this world. Trying and allowing that drive to flourish is not a fair playing ground. Who gets these opportunities and how they come about is a whole other book.

I have always been driven. I never see walls. I don't see obstacles. I just see opportunities. We had just been chosen by Everyday Edison to launch an idea that I created from thin air. Ric and I were getting ready to go on a journey that would change our lives. I felt positive it was going to be a game changer. I cleared my mind of negativity. Bring on the joy.

Steam Roller Inspiration

Dapper the Dryer Ball Artwork

Negative Thinking -vs- Positive Thinking

Which is worse? I wanted to give my 2¢ worth on this subject. I think there is a clear winner. It is much more detrimental to be negative. Positive thinking does not overcome the dark, villain of gloom-ridden cynical obstruction. It's like when you meet someone of the opposite sex and you want to don a cape and show them the happy side of life. Well, guess what? They usually drag you down to their misery. It's the same for dreams, ambitions & creativity - the negative will paralyze you. The positive cannot overcome this motivation killer. You can look at (-) vs (+) as pessimist vs optimist, 1/2 full or 1/2 empty. The moment negative thoughts come into your head you need to try and squash them. Positive numbers are greater than zero. Negative numbers are less than zero. At the very least you want to be starting out at ground zero. Get rid of below zero, it's cold & harsh.

Positive people are proven to be empowered to act while negative attitudes stop us to even TRY to achieve our goals. 70% of being negative is the not knowing. You are stopping yourself from trying based on what you "think" will happen, yet that is the fear talking, the negative winning. Don't expect the worst. Be positive, shoot for the stars. Look to me as an example of how to ***Try*** *to conquer the unknown. The only way is to move forward. My advice is to stay away from negative people. Avoid their toxic ways of destroying good. Bobby McFarrin "Don't Worry, Be Happy" is a song to hang your hat on. Live that mantra instead of the derailment of being too worried to try at something.*

STOP DOUBTING! STOP WORRYING! BE POSITIVE!

I can't leave this subject just yet, it's GOT A POSITIVE HOLD OF ME! It should not surprise you to learn that pessimists experience far more disappointments than optimists. Why? It's simple, they are looking for failure. They search out verification that they are correct in their negative assumptions. Optimists, however, understand that no one has a crystal ball and that you can't predict the future. Optimists have the belief you don't know what's going to happen. It's far more pleasant and joyful to expect the best. The power of positive thinking, according to statistics works. If you are optimistic you look good in your little black skirt you will convey confidence and will more likely find someone that agrees with you, you look hot! When I've spoken with elderly people their common theme is always the same.

life is short, don't sweat the small stuff &
don't worry about things that may never happen

The last one, *don't worry about things that may never happen,* grabs my attention. You're not Voltar, your future, your fortune is in your hands. "Can't never did anything" my mom liked to say. Start with the belief you can. One of the most basic laws of life is energy flow. If your energy is primarily negative; looking for flaws, problems, and verification that life is essentially bad, that's where the bulk of your energy will lie. Your ability to manifest abundance will be severely limited because your energy will be directed, focused and grounded in negativity. You're setting your limitations before you even begin your challenge.

Ric and I were prepared to fuel our positive energy forward with Mister Steamy. We had a hit product again, but this one was even bigger than BagBlocker. Everyday Edisons flew us to Charlotte, NC to meet with their product development and marketing team. Season 2 of Everyday Edisons aired on PBS and I imagine you can still find the episodes somewhere on the internet. They were Shark Tank before Shark Tank. We knew executives at Everyday Edisons were excited about Mister Steamy the Dryer Ball. It was evident the way they treated us compared to the other inventors. We had handed them the Golden Ticket to big revenue.

They approached us saying they wanted to bring in *AllStar Marketing* (Innovations) to become a partner and launch Mister Steamy via DRTV. *AllStar* is one of the biggest players in the infomercial arena. They are known for Snuggies (blanket with sleeves),

ShamWow and soon to be well known Mister Steamy. They've had a plethora of other successful AsSeenOnTV products. DRTV means Direct Response Television which is the fastest way to build a brand and setup a marketing campaign to get products in big box retailers with some name brand recognition. You hope to make some money off the 800# TV ads you're hocking on late night, but if you can break a bit more than even, the big money comes when your product hits CVS, Walgreens, Walmart, Bed Bath & Beyond, Target and every other consumer retail store you can think of. Mister Steamy followed this path to a T. We also sold-out consistently on QVC. It was a very exciting time to see our product on TV and in so many stores. It became a phenomenon.

Me Holding Steamy Gold Inside a Store

End Cap Display w/Video, Amazing!

Ric and I for a Promo

Featured on Walgreens' Sign

Yahoo! invited Ric and I to the Maker's Faire in San Francisco for their "Make it Green" campaign. We were thrilled because from the very beginning we felt Mister Steamy was an environmental plus for the planet. We had been on the Dennis Miller Show touting the water you save using our dryer ball and someone heard us. The average family uses 150 gallons of water a day. They say machine washers (top loaders) account for 20% of your indoor water use. A standard top loading washing machine uses a total of 40 gallons of water in the clean and rinse cycle. The average household does 300 loads a year. That's 12,000 gallons of water to just clean your clothes. If you heat up that water, your washing machine becomes the biggest energy sucking appliance in your home. If you could just cut down on washing your clothes 50 times a year you'd save 2,000 gallons of water. Mister Steamy can help you achieve that goal and that's why Yahoo! invited us as one of only three elite products they felt could make a "Green" impact. There are so many times you don't need to wash your clothes, you only need to refresh them. Get the wrinkles out, add a fresh smell. When you travel you may only wear a skirt or blouse/ shirt one time. It gets crinkled up in your suitcase so you throw it in the wash. Bad news for water usage and bad news for wear & tear on one of your favorite garments of clothes. We don't always need to wash our clothes to make them look good.

As you can see in the above promo we were told *Mister Steamy* had reached $50 million gross sales. Our product is the highest grossing sales of any product that has been promoted via Everyday Edisons. 50,000,000 is a hell of a big number. The success of our product is not negotiable. Winner-winner-chicken-dinner, consumers worldwide gravitated to our invention. It feels good to create something and see it thrive. My sales calculations are more along the $35,000,000 range given our dividend checks. We weren't complaining because Everyday Edisons took our product and launched it to the stratosphere and at the end of the day we were getting large dividend checks, but neither of us was running out to buy Cigarette Boats in Miami or book a submarine dive to go see the Titanic (*thank god I didn't do that!*). Yes, we were making good money for hardly doing anything, BUT we did invent the product. We aren't in any kind of litigation or contemplating legal retaliation with Everyday Edisons. We had signed the contract giving us only 5% of the sales minus expenses. I don't think that aspect of our deal was murky or shady. Ric and I both feel when they brought in AllStar Marketing that the clause in our contract that stated if Everyday Edisons got into a license agreement that we got "(50%) of any royalties" gives us pause to think maybe we should have gotten a lot more?

2 ANNUITIES

2.1 During the term of this AGREEMENT, ASSIGNEE shall make annual payments (hereinafter "ANNUITIES") to ASSIGNOR, subject to the terms and conditions herein provided, in an amount equal to:

(a) Five percent (5%) of the NET RECEIPTS of ASSIGNEE that arise from ASSIGNEE'S sale of any products that incorporate any of the INVENTIONS ("INVENTIVE PRODUCT"); plus

(b) Five percent (5%) of the NET RECEIPTS of ASSIGNEE that arise from ASSIGNEE'S sale of any products that are covered by one or more claims of an active patent of the PATENT PROPERTIES ("PATENTED PRODUCT"); plus

(c) Fifty percent (50%) of any royalties that are paid to ASSIGNEE under a license agreement pertaining to any of the PATENT PROPERTIES.

2.1 (c) Fifty percent (50%) of any royalties that are paid to ASSIGNEE under a license agreement pertaining to any of the PATENT PROPERTIES.

This isn't a sour grapes book. I rarely have a platform to air a grievance so I just wanted to point out that these contracts are tricky. Everyday Edison (ASSIGNEE), said it wasn't a partnership with AllStar Marketing and that no "royalties" were paid, but the obvious fact is they went into some sort of agreement with them to market our product. They seem to have manipulated the jargon, not calling the money AllStar gave to Everyday Edisons royalties. If Edison Nation (Everyday Edisons) were producing the infomercials, paying for the air-time, manufacturing all the product and putting their nuts on the line, then I can understand them taking 95% of the profit. But once they pass those expenses onto a 3rd party their risk is marginalized. I believe we should have gotten 50% of what Everyday Edison got from AllStar Marketing. What that number would have been is a mystery, but it would have definitely added several millions of dollars to our portion of the steamy pie.

Live and learn is all I can say. It's a Catch 22 because if we had not put in an effort to **TRY** and trusted the article I read in Reader's Digest about Everyday Edisons on PBS, we would not have made the money we made. It was an exciting, wild ride that I look back on fondly and if given a choice I would still do it all over again. Do I feel some money was conveniently washed away? Were we taken to the cleaners? Yes & no, because we had absolutely NO MONEY out of pocket. We literally sat back and collected checks. One disappointment was the exit of sales with Mister Steamy. It's baffling. The Reader's Digest December issue had us listed as one of the Best Gadgets of 2012 with a 3 out of 4 stars rating, yet it was getting harder and harder to find Mister Steamy out in the retail market. Todd Stancomb had told us we could likely expect a consistent $100,000 a quarter for the next 5 years. That was less than what we had been making but who's going to look a gift horse in the mouth? It was WORK FREE money. That Christmas of 2012 I had a good relationship with the managers of my local CVS & Walgreens. I had introduced myself to them as the inventor of Mister Steamy the Dryer Ball. Ric and I had been in the local paper quite a bit and even cracked nationwide coverage a few times. A week before Christmas both managers told me they couldn't get Mister Steamy on the shelves. This drove me crazy. I'm used to driving the bus. They told me it was a popular product and would be a perfect stocking stuffer. Christmas came and went and slowly our 5 minutes of fame as the "Inventors of Mister Steamy" came to a wrinkly halt. We tried to get answers to why but whatever the true reason was, we were not having any luck finding out. After pleading with Todd Stancomb for answers he got us a personal phone call with Scott Boilen (CEO/Owner) of AllStar Marketing. He's worth $200M, according to Google, a very successful guy. I had met him twice and liked him, but his explanation as to why they were pulling Steamy just didn't cut the mustard. It felt like the runaround. The most baffling thing is why would they want to stop making money? I'm not sure if there was some internal conflict we weren't privy to, but our sales plummeted, then basically stopped. We got tiny trickles of money over the next few years but we had lost our steam, so to speak.

Dry-n-Steam in Walmart. We tried to make another run at the Steamy magic!

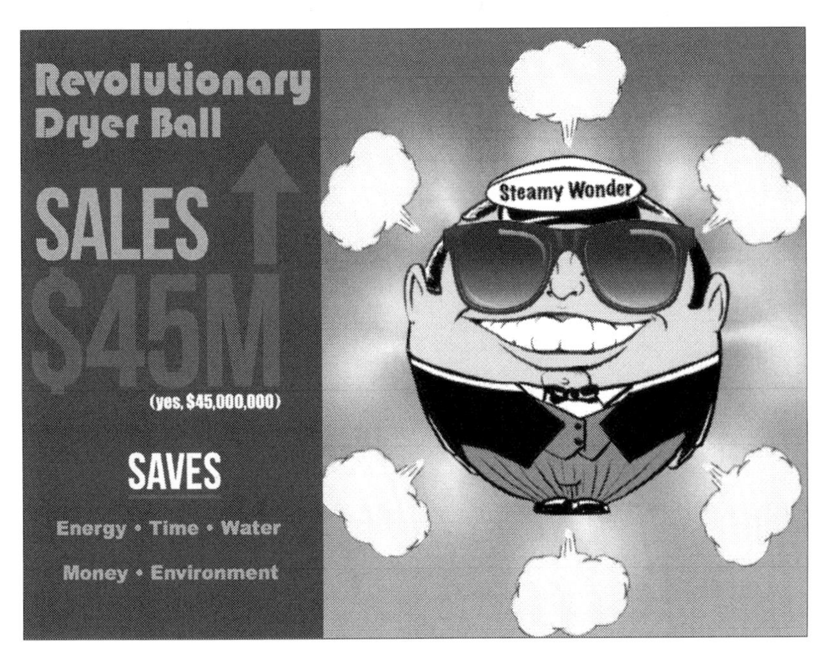

STEAMY WONDER a concept we almost launched

The DISH

Cheers

General Merriment

A Civil War–era Hoosier general seems like a peculiar association for a new hipster bar on Mass Ave. But the hirsute Ambrose Burnside—immortalized through the term "sideburns"—inspired the quirky **Burnside Inn**, a three-level drinking hole. Its sense of humor is reflected in an eclectic mix of old and new, from baroque velvet wallpaper to a mustachioed Mona Lisa. Wednesday through Saturday, the upstairs hosts acts like poetry readings and vintage rock shows while patrons sip twists on the gingery Moscow Mule, such as one with housemade lavender syrup and local Starlight vodka. Burnside's other signature item: old-school ice-cream sandwiches. Pretty cool. 314 Massachusetts Ave., 317-991-4150
—PAIGE PEARSON

TONY VALAINIS

APRIL 2016 | IM 43

Got a deal on a reasonable model, my wife, Jill Kelly! We are promoting our newest bar in Indy called the Burnside Inn. The magazine is The Indianapolis Monthly, Jill's a big deal!

Wabi-Sabi

CHAPTER EIGHTEEN

•

"Most people are about as happy as they make up their minds to be."

—Abraham Lincoln

I WAS DOING a word search on my writing for this book and realized I've used the word "Freedom" 22 times. That doesn't surprise me because I use that word quite a bit to describe my life. People ask me if I'm a millionaire from time to time. I always respond with, *"If your idea of a millionaire is having total freedom to wake up whenever I want, not having to answer to anyone and basically doing what I enjoy everyday, then yes, I'm a millionaire. Freedom is priceless, worth more than all the tea in China."*

We all need to learn to have a balance. Would more money motivate me enough to work an extra 15hrs a week? That answer may be "Yes" depending on your situation, your goals in life, but I recommend weighing your life's balance sheet carefully. Knowing when to be satisfied is not always simple. Stopping to enjoy your spoils is not easy for driven people. When is enough, enough? Free Time is a glorious thing that you should file as a deduction on your income tax. You're saving the government money by reducing stress via less healthcare, crime, domestic abuse, mental disorders and so on.

Less stress is not quantified like your bank balance, but it should be. You work harder so you earn more money. It's easy to see the correlation, but reducing stress, the leading cause of death, is hard to pinpoint. Yet we know it causes weight gain, cancer, fatigue, headaches, high blood pressure which leads to heart attacks - stress' negative impact is endless. Before giving away more of your time, be sure you have enough. There's a value on family time, hobbies, health, less stress, and relaxation that's immeasurable.

I can't write a book and not draw from a Nietzsche's philosophy. He talks about "freedom of the spirit" as a good thing and asks, "freedom *from* what?" and "freedom *to* what?" We have psychological needs and concrete physical needs. Freedom can be positive and negative. Remember, negative freedom must come before positive freedom unless you are an heir to a fortune. Negative, in this sense, means you have to follow some realm of order, march to society's rules, get your hands dirty and put forth time & energy to hopefully get the reward of positive freedom - independence. Self-mastery in whatever you do is the key to releasing constraints. Become really good at what you do. The power of freedom is intoxicating and is a bigger drive than money for me. It's a delicate balance, but as I get older I realize how short life is. "*Working for the man*" as they say, is not the path I felt destined to take. I have been *Winnie the Pooh* meandering and following my soul's presence. You truly begin to understand or yearn for freedom when you don't have it. Remember, my 1st job out of college was with United States Steel (USX) up in Detroit? My jaw dropped when I learned I would get only 1 week vacation per year until I was with them for 3 years! It was like being placed in prison. I went from footloose & fancy free in college to lockdown. It was an episode of *Scared Straight*, but instead of prison it was white collar incarceration. The people scaring me weren't ex-convicts, they were my older fellow workers. They began plotting my escape before I did - "This company doesn't give two squats about you" - "You're too young to waste away here" - "Get out of here why you still can" - "If I had to do it all over again I'd live a totally different life" and so on. They'd rally around the water cooler in shifts telling me their stories of misery. My floor looked like the TV show *The Office* with cubicles and florescent tubes, but this was NO comedy. I recently watched a heart-wrenching episode on *Our Planet* where walruses were climbing up a very steep rocky cliff and then seemingly leaping to their death on purpose. They seemed tired, hopeless and plunge down by the hundreds to their demise. This is what it felt like in that office. I'm thankful for their candor. It convinced me to go in a different direction. *Remember, you can profoundly impact someone by saying the right thing, at the right time*. You can also get punched in the nose, but hey it takes a village, right?

Freedom From What?: The constraints of life. The grind of living varies from person to person. There's an inner voice that compels you to go in a certain direction. The "What?" you want freedom from can be whatever you feel is holding you back from living the life you want to live. It could be a job, spouse, parents, addictions, pressures, the list of what you need to escape from is something you need to look deep inside yourself to find. Then do something about it is my best advice. Simple but true. Get away from what is holding you back. Follow your natural inclination, your unique chi.

Freedom To What?: This is the BETTER QUESTION. It's easy to pinpoint the "Freedom From What?" answer. People ask me, "What did you dislike about the 9 to 5?" and my knee jerk answer is, "THE NINE!" I wanted freedom from my alarm clock. I wanted to make my own time. I haven't had an alarm clock in my room for 20 years. *Freedom To What* is the true mystery of a happy life. Let's really look at these 3 words and think about what that means.

FREEDOM TO WHAT?

This is what we are all looking for. It's your career. It's your dream. Sure, you know what you want to leave, but you MUST know where you want to go to. There are predictors to success: Zeal *(strong desire)*, Resilience *(beat hardship/adversity)* and Perseverance *(not giving up)* ***ZRP***. In my high school yearbook my mom surprised me by putting a quote under my picture "Life...look forward to it with zeal". I had never heard her use the word "zeal" before and I liked it. I grabbed my little red pocket Webster and it defines zeal as: *dedicated or enthusiasm for something. If you have zeal you're willing, energized and motivated. Eagerness and ardent in pursuit of something*. Zeal is what you need to find your 'Freedom To What.' You need to find your niche and go after it with fiery courage. My grandmother grew up on a farm, dropped out of school in the 6th grade and started smoking cigarettes at age 9. She was a tough cookie and a lot smarter than her education would lead you to believe. She told me, "It takes a lot of pluck to try and do what you want in life!" You rarely hear someone use the word "pluck" but it packs a helluv a wallop. Pluck tells you to go after something with spirited *resilience.* Be tough. Recover from difficulties quickly is resilience. Being a woman, poor and born at the beginning of the 20th century, I think she thought it was quite impossible for her to do what she wanted in life. Typical story, I know, but she grew up with a wood burning stove to heat the whole house, no indoor plumbing (outhouse), a well pump to collect water and of course air-conditioning wasn't even invented yet, but they couldn't have afforded it anyway. My mother grew up on that same farm, but with a few upgrades. She was born in 1934 on Christmas Day. In honor of that, her middle name was Carol, as in Christmas Carol. I mention my mom several times and in Chapter Two you see she had the "Pluck" my grandmother envied so much. This pluckish drive, the Zeal, Resilience and Perseverance ***(ZRP)*** are what set people apart. Long-term goals and always striving to reach them is a strong indication to who will succeed and who will not. You must be driven. Perseverance is the last piece of the puzzle that separate the men from the boys. It's not easy to not give up. You sometimes need to step down a rung in life to set yourself up to spring forward. Even after some good successes I was a waiter in Los Angeles and a factory receptionist in Indianapolis. I set my pride aside because I knew I had a goal. Who cares what other people may think during that bump in my road, screw it, I knew I was working towards a bigger reward, I knew I had the ZRP!

Two childhood stories pop into my head that I feel fit this chapter nicely. The advancement of mankind over 100 years is a testament to man's endless imagination & ZRP. My grandmother, named Dorthy Hamill (smoker from 9 to 81), before the skater was born, used to give my mom a nickel (5¢) to go to the picture show once a month and my mom was to pay particular attention to the News Reel before the movie started. Grandma wanted a full report on what was going on in the world. WWII was brewing but the Japanese had not yet bombed Pearl Harbor in August of 1941. Mom came tearing into the kitchen like a bat out of hell. She was nearly 7 and could barely get the words out with all of her excitement:

"Mom, mom you aren't going to believe this," little Beverly (my mom) shouted.

"Calm down! What's going on?" grandma demanded.

"There's going to be a box you put in the house that will show movies,"

Grandma shook her head, "What are you talking about?"

"The movie comes from the air!" little Beverly tried to explain.

"That's impossible," Grandma told her straightly, "You must have gotten that wrong!"

I loved this story because even today it seems magical. In 1976 I was 11 years old. My mom gathered me and my two older sisters and we piled in the car. We headed to grandma's house to witness something special. We stood in her kitchen and there was a huge heavy metal box on her countertop. It must have weighed 175lbs. Grandma called it a RadarRange which sounded scientific. Even at that young age I knew radar had helped us win WWII. She walked over to the sink, filled a glass with water, opened the "microwave" oven, placed it inside and turned the dial to 1 minute. It dinged. We each took turns dipping our finger into the very hot water. There was no fire. No heat. This was incredible. Now we have satellites circling the globe and the world at our fingertips. These stories are the backbone of limitless possibilities.

To live the impossible dream is what we are striving for. When I contemplate trying to invent something or open a bar, I always laugh when I think how minute that is compared to some of the incredible things man has accomplished in modern day. It actually motivates me. If you don't make a big deal out of whatever you're doing you won't scare yourself out of doing it. The book, "*Don't Sweat the Small Stuff & It's All Small Stuff*" by Richard Carlson suggests for you to let go of your expectations - or as I see it, don't let them stop you on your journey, acceptance is freedom.

This leads me to the title of this chapter ***Wabi-Sabi***. It's a Japanese term that helps us understand nothing is perfect and that it's okay to accept the imperfections. I think the original concept was referring to pottery & gardening. *Wabi* - feels that less is more, refined beauty, being understated is a true compliment and more difficult to achieve than in-your-face attractiveness - minimalist is how I interpret it. Pleasing to the soul may be my stretch of understanding. *Sabi* - is attentive melancholy that has been called aged, mellow beauty. Maybe not striking but appealing in a way that your mind is drawn back to it. When you put these two words together it's a magic potion that shows you how to strive to be excellent even if that doesn't mean perfect.

My wife thinks I have a bit of a screw loose at times because if I cannot find something or struggle to accomplish a task, I will not give up. I guess, according to her, I take this zeal to a place that borderlines mental dysfunction. Obsession. I hate giving up. Failure is not an option until there is just no way to get the outcome I desire. I bring this up because I think it is natural to have a *Yin & Yang* personality. Yin is defined as negative, dark and feminine. The yang is seen as positive, bright and masculine. Their interaction is thought to maintain the harmony of the universe and to influence everything within it. The Chinese philosophers who came up with the concept had to be male. I like how it describes how opposites can be unified, mutually prolonged together creating forces that compliments each other. Genius! But the "female" being negative and the "male" positive shows it's age of creation. Dualism makes sense to me because I know I have that little devil *(yin)* on one shoulder and the angel *(yang)* on the other.

To succeed in business I believe you need to be a perfectionist to a large degree and know when to accept the liberty of wabi-sabi. They literally are the yin-yang opposites, but both play an important role in success. Let me explain how I see it and maybe you'll agree. This "scripture" can go for business or personal. I'm being facetious of course, but I do think it's important to allow yourself to feel both, it's a religious experience. You open yourself up to letting go, but along the path you want things to be the way you know they need to be. You forgive the sins of imperfection as you push for spiritual immaculateness. Freedom to me is being your own person. Creating a company, writing a book, making something from nothing, is an "aha" moment that gives you a high. A moment of sudden realization, inspiration, insight, recognition, or comprehension that you are really living. Nothing feels better than an accomplishment. The first step, as I've said, is deciding you are going to ***Try***. But try at what is the question of your life?

After deciding your "Freedom to What?" you have to approach that goal full tilt-boogie. Don't get hung-up on little details to the point that you stop moving forward. The wabi-sabi tells you to accept and appreciate the imperfections in yourself and your project. Don't let small things stop you. Move forward and things will work themselves out. The important thing is to TRY and not stop. Does that mean not to strive for perfection? No, but embrace the calmness. There is value in authenticity. Don't over complicate things is my best advice. You need to hold your ground on what's important and what truly matters. Wabi-sabi also asks you to value the unique skills of yourself and those who you are working with. Keep an open mind to something that's not fitting into a mold you had envisioned, could it add to your concept? With all this said you still need to drive the bus. Importantly, you need to *focus*. Warren Buffet and Bill Gates were asked to name possibly the most important trait behind their success. They both answered with the word "FOCUS!" When you're making cookies, as wonderful as the cookies at Levain Bakery in New York City, there are multiple ingredients that have to be just right. Every measurement has to be exact. It's the same for success. Your zeal, resilience, perseverance, drive, wabi-sabi and perfectionism - I will say that the word "focus" encompasses many of these powerful adjectives. Maybe Buffet & Gates are onto something - Yes, I had a shit grin on my face as I typed that last sentence.

Frank Sinatra sings the Paul Anka lyrics "My Way" and for most entrepreneurs this is exactly what they do. Perfectionists, many of the world's most successful people, have this element of being demanding, not comprising, as a strong reason for their ability to stand out and succeed. We are demanding control freaks. I get obsessed with the lighting in my bars. If I pop-in unexpectedly to one of our places at 10pm and it's too bright in the room it drives me bonkers. I need every little detail to be right. This is not a "want" this is a "need" to have the atmosphere perfect. There is a lot of competition out there and the slightest variation can knock you off the podium. The mind's eye is a powerful tool that guides our thoughts and tells us if we like something or if it doesn't feel right. We have a snap-judgement built into our minds that has gathered millions of unconscious experiences & images. These brain caches tell us organically if something is off. Stranger-Danger, this person puts off red-flags, if a situation feels sketchy and wrong in some way. These highly efficient mental warnings are our safety blanket. Benjamin Spock said, *"Trust yourself. You know more than you think you do."* Our wonderful defense systems help keep us safe and also tell us if a room feels cozy. Do we like this place? Is it upscale? Is this a cool place to chill? Is this product trustworthy? Is there anything about, whatever you're seeing and faced with, that makes you feel uncomfortable? We evaluate everything in a snap with our 2.5 petabytes of capacity for memory. A petabyte is 1,024 terabytes or a million gigabytes. That means us humans have 2.5 million gigabytes to store our instincts, our hunches and intuitions. We need to trust this gut feeling in all aspects of life. In building and creating your freedom you must follow your heart and what you feel will be the most successful way to do something. If you do this you can't blame anyone but yourself if things don't go as hoped. Have no regrets. Swing for the fences! Or as the great Carl "Moose" Payne told little Ricky, "Run to the woods!" meaning to see the finish line past the end zone. Have a greater vision than just a touchdown. Go for greatness is what I think Ric Payne's dad was instilling in his children..

I am reminded of the famous Steve Jobs' story, he delayed the release of the first Macintosh until he felt the circuit boards were esthetically pleasing to the eye although nobody would actually see them. Maybe unconsciously, in a part of unknown telepathy, we do know that the circuit board is beautiful? The thorough confidence you emote when you feel good, to your very core, that you did your very best is sensed. It's an assured cockiness that makes people believe in your dream. A swagger, a conviction in what you're doing, is something you should feel when you release the hounds.

With all this "Perfectionist" talk I want to make sure we understand that *Wabi-sabi's* imperfections can make perfection at work. The important thing is to move forward and embrace the possibilities. You want to achieve more than is assumed. You are reaching for greatness and striving for perfection. I know, I've been there, but don't let perfection be your goal. I titled this chapter Wabi-Sabi because I want you to leave knowing perfection should not be a goal. It can lead to failure or even stop you from trying. It's a form of OCD. We value perfectionism in society but even Steve Jobs let go of the reins and hired creative people he gave trust to. Perfectionist vs Control Freak, both are similar but treated differently. Obviously, a control freak always has a negative connotation. Going after excellence does not mean you can't have flaws. We can apply this to our personal life and business ventures. Some of the sexiest, most creative, successful people I know are far from perfect. The same can be for a business.

You can create a culture of high standards by letting go of perfectionism. It's healthy in all aspects of our life to take a deep breath and accept the little bit of belly fat that seemed to suddenly appear. Obsession can lead to work stop, love stop, friend stop. The unhealthy stress will take you down. I'm NOT saying to not make sure things you want to accomplish are not done well, or that they shouldn't be the way you want them to be, but let being perfect only be a few drops in your magic potion.

A few more points are merited. To want to be perfect is a self-esteem issue too. This is our social world now. It's not in a vacuum for an individual person. It's around all of us now and it's debilitating. Social media bleeds over into our human psyche. This refers to "all parts of the human mind that affects personality," according to Sigmund Freud. "The psyche consists of the id, the ego, and the superego and it functions at different levels: the conscious, preconscious, and subconscious." - I'm not pretty, I'm not skinny enough or rich enough or seen as successful enough. We begin to fear other people will notice our shortcomings. Our centerfolds are our

Facebook, Instagram and TikTok accounts. We seek validation. It's a black hole, a sucking vortex that is very hard to not fall into. We create our "real self" as we want others to see us. Our perfection becomes woven into our future because of what we've created for others to see. Do we create a business or go on a vacation for our own satisfaction or to impress others? This is your own personal Ponzi Scheme that will collapse like a house of cards. Perfectionists are hard workers but it leads to burning out and self-sabotage.

I can be a stickler for details. As stated - Ric, Kerry and I also own the bar *Burnside Inn* in Indianapolis. It's possibly considered the best bar for the local hipster crowd. The day after Thanksgiving my wife and I go in to really deck the place out with an old school Christmas vibe. The more we dug in the more things I found wrong. The tables and chairs were set up wrong, the stage was in disarray, things were not where they are supposed to be, the "Live Music" neon sign was not in the window but shoved above a cooler - the little details I strive to make perfect were esthetically wrong in so many areas of the bar. It wasn't that the Burnside Inn was in gloom or doom. Quite the contrary, 2023 was one of my best years. I told my wife we need to take a chill pill and realize it won't be exactly like we want it to be unless we decide to do what we did the first 2 years it was open, which was to basically live in it 4 nights a week, forgo vacations and become bar rats again. Obviously, neither of us had any plan to do that. I realize there are tradeoffs that need to be balanced. Yes, the ship needs to be righted from time to time. Maybe a few people need to walk the plank, but letting go of the little things will allow us to enjoy life now. I've seen self-sabotagers forget to enjoy their spoils. Know what & when something needs to be closer to your idea of perfection. A little *wabi-sabi* opens up the key to balancing success perfectly.

Myself and Mr.DiVona Factor Himself
(Venice 2012)

David DiVona, Remember this Face!

The DiVona Factor

CHAPTER NINETEEN

•

"And on my deathbed I will pray to the gods and the angels, like a pagan, to anyone who will take me to heaven!."
—Audioslave (Like a Stone)

POSSIBLY ONE of the best voices in music history is how most people describe Chris Cornell. He was the lead singer for Soundgarden & Audioslave. I heard him sing Prince's song *Nothing Compares 2 U* and it blew me away. Cornell was/is David DiVona's favorite singer. I think they were even guests on the The Howard Stern Show together. I can promise you that "nothing compares to" David, or as I often call him: Rocker Dave. I also refer to him as "Teflon Dave" when I'm talking about the resilience of this man. I grew up in an era when guys often called their friends by their last name, so I'll refer to David as DiVona from here on out. Sounds cool too. It could be the lead character's name in any mafioso movie, but in fact the origin of the name is from "The Divine" along the Pyrenees Mountains in France. I only bring this up out of humor, because it also means something like "angry people" that specialize in manufacturing linen. To be fair, the surname DiVona has some link to Italy too but we'd need a 23 & Me to confirm anything. I like the angry people version because outwardly DiVona has an "angry" sense of humor. It's his shtick. "I'm sick over it" as he often says. It adds to his allure and is probably one of the reasons he's able to accomplish the remarkable.

DiVona grew up on Long Island and has that New Yorker attitude oozing from his soul. Before I met him he had some success as the lead guitarist for the rock band called *Lint* and later the *Good Rats* revival. Since then he's had nine lives and always seems to land on his feet. He goes from broke to a millionaire, then back to broke and millionaire again like most people put their shoes on in the morning. His financial swings would put most of us in the looney bin, but he consistently shakes it off and claws himself back from the brink of disaster. I call this chapter **The DiVona Factor** because we all need a whack-a-doodle friend like DiVona. He can get you into the best unbelievable situations in life. Some may think he's full of it, but I can tell you that mostly he's the real deal and more. During one of his upswings, he and I, along with Conrad Ricketts, started a company called Proven Entertainment Development. Conrad had won a few Emmy's with Extreme Home Makeover and was looking to create new shows. Us three bonded together. Conrad had the connections and know-how, DiVona had the tenacity & brains and I would be the money guy. Next thing we know, DiVona is booking himself as the guest speaker at film festivals across the US. We were helping small filmmakers get distribution through several streaming platforms. Later he hooked up with George Schlatter, the creator of Laugh-In, and became the catalyst that got it back on the air again. It's beloved fans were thrilled for a chance to relive the laughs.

DiVona set up other deals with Rowan & Martin, Liza Minelli, Carol Burnett, Nikki Haskell and countless content distributor and development deals. I remember being out in LA with him and we were hanging with Robert Wagner. He knows Hollywood dynasty. DiVona can always get us a table at Craig's in Beverly Hills where we might be sitting next to Sylvester Stallone & family. Larry King may come by our table to say "Hi". Who knows? It's part of the allure.

He is bi-coastal, hell — let's be honest, he's connected all over the world. If you are in NYC he'll pull strings for Mr Chow's or whatever is the hottest spot in town. It's usually a restaurant you're never getting into, but voilá (wa-la), "Right this way Mr. DiVona" and you're at the best table in the house. You could tell him you were going to Paris, London, any big city, and he'd tell you where to eat (Michelin Star) and somehow get you a table. David DiVona and I have been to 40+

states together and quite a few countries as well. It's never dull around him. We drove my 1977 Ford Bronco out to Venice Beach from Indiana. He had contacts in nearly every city we passed through along the way. How he does this is a mystery I will never understand.

Here's a good one, my wife and I are in New York City and decided to go to the fancy-dancy bar at the top of the Peninsula Hotel called the Pen Top. I opened the menu and there's a drink named The DiVona. WTF! You can't make this stuff up.

With all this praise of David DiVona it can't go without being said that he can be difficult too. He used to drink too much and that brought on a whole set of issues that were hard to deal with. The funny thing about DiVona is he doesn't seem to curb his appetite for the best things in life no matter what his current income is. I'm all for being a free spirit but this level of extremes is a sight to be seen, not lived. We all know a person or two who makes you ask, "How do they live like this?" - "Where do they make their money?" He usually lives in the best homes, drives luxury cars, collects oddity art, dines in the finest restaurants and typically travels all over the world First Class.

When DiVona is living high on the hog so are you. He will get you in situations that no-one else can. We are thick as thieves and his loyalty towards his friends is legendary.

I decided to add this chapter because we all need the DiVona Factor. It's friends like these that make life grand. They make you scratch your head with wonder. How did I get into this amazing situation? Friends who are different can make you want to run away, avoid, but I recommend taking a deep breath and appreciate their oddities. Buckle-up and be thankful life is not boring. Embrace the people in your life that shake things up. Say "Yes!" a whole lot more.

DiVona invited me to Pamplona, Spain to run with the bulls. Although, to this day my right thumb has lost all strength from a bull pushing me over a barrier in the bullring, it was an experience of a lifetime. This is a typical DiVona spur of the moment adventure. It's usually expensive and dangerous. This ticked both boxes. I met Dr. William Graves on this boy's trip for the first time. He goes by Billy with his friends. Billy is a Maxillofacial surgeon in Amarillo, TX. He is actually a big deal. I've been told he's one of the finest dental surgeons in the world by doctors who didn't even realize how good a friend he is to me. Billy owns 30+ Full Smile clinics in the Southwest and keeps expanding. This is a typical case where wild man David DiVona introduced me to another unique outlier who is also living life to the fullest. Billy does dental foundation clinics for free all over the world. My wife, Jill and I, have volunteered in the Dominican Republic and Ecuador to assist dentists who are there to help improve people's lives. That lead us to exploring the Galapagos Islands and seeing a part of the world I never thought I would. Divona and Billy are unique life sherpas. They both offer a nontraditional way of chasing life. We can all get caught up in our normal circle of friends, people who are like us. People who earn around the same amount of money and believe in the same religion or politics. Don't push that occasional different person away from you too quickly. They might just be the dose of adventure you need. Let them push you down an uncomfortable path. After you wade out into their fiery, unknown waters, you can always swim back to your normalcy. It keeps you sane. Let a DiVona Factor effect your destination in life. Kiss of life!

After starting Proven Entertainment, Ric & Kerry Payne and myself opened a new concept bar in downtown Indianapolis called Burnside Inn. I tried to invoke all the incredible experiences I've had with my DiVona Factor friends and give our new drinking establishment a great vibe. People and experiences create a new way of looking at life. As aggressive as I've been in living, I still felt the pangs of TRY from people who are exciting me with crazy adventures. I use the word "pang" because it is not always easy to take on a new challenge. Your natural reaction may be to say "No" to an invite to Bali, Indonesia when one of your outlier friends asks you to go. Let people shake you out of your comfort zone. Be thankful for the non-vanilla box when it's placed under your tree of life. Rip it open like it's that Cabbage Patch Doll you thought you'd never get for Christmas. It's the official Red Ryder, carbine action, 200-shot, range model air rifle, with a compass in the stock and that thing that tells time.

Over the years the DiVona Factor opened my eyes to adventurous people like Brad & Stephanie Stout. They are our landlords for the *Burnside Inn* in Indianapolis and own the oldest continual running shoe store in the United States aptly called *Stout's Shoes*. They've invited us hiking at some of the best National Parks in the world. We've gone to Iceland, Key West, traveled to Paris to see Jimmy Buffet and they continue to open our eyes to experiences we would not have thought of.

Another DF person in my life is Kevin Carter. A financial wizard and legitimate wild man. He was living on a boat in Marina del Rey that cut the cost of housing in SoCal by 75%. That planted the seed in my mind to do the same thing. GENUIS! I met Kevin at the Indianapolis 500 Mile Race on Carb Day. Carb stands for "carburetor" from long ago when IndyCars had such a thing. It's the last day before the race for the cars to get their final tuneups. For the fans there are pit stop competitions and big name concerts, but the main draw is to PARTY! Remember, I went to Speedway High School and know all things Indy 500. I have been going to the track as long as I can remember.

Carb Day is an homage to the throwback days when the infield was a mini-Woodstock, but far more wild. Partiers hung-out in the Snake Pit, a name it's been called since 1961. As kids, we were warned to never go there. It was a living & breathing urban legend that was actually true. The bikers, hippies, rednecks, and any other part of humanity that wanted to let loose, settled in the center of the track, oblivious to the cars racing around them. Back in the day, you were guaranteed to see a streaker or two and a whole lot of breasts. The "Show Us Your Tits" signs in the 70s & 80s were the drunk rallying cry. There were buttons, bumper stickers, t-shirts and homemade signs all begging for exposure. Most ladies smiled and ignored the hoopla, but every once in a while there would be a taker who would climb on top of the hood of some jalopy to flash the cheering crowd. It was a rowdy bunch for sure.

Back to meeting Kevin. I see a guy dressed in country bumpkin overalls with the pants cut short like Daisy Dukes. American flag bandana, no shirt, wearing cowboy boots and mirror sunglasses. He looked hilarious and somewhat dangerous so I had to talk to him. He had heard the legends of the Snake Pit / Carb Day and someone told him it was equivalent to a hillbilly Halloween Party. Now, the wild side of the track has calmed down over the years. Since 1992 it's been more of a musical festival, but Kevin didn't get the memo and he was a total hoot to hang out with. Whoever played that practical joke on him helped me meet a truly unique person who has, like David DiVona, Billy Graves, Brad Stout, Richard Deer, Jim Irsay - brought or continue to bring, a unique aspect or experiences into my life.

The moral of the story is - keep an open mind when you meet people who are not like you. Variety is the spice of life. Making different types of friends will bring different kinds of experiences. I call this *The DiVona Factor*.

If you embrace "T*he DiVona Factor*" people, when they cross your path, you might actually graduate to being one yourself. I've seen it happen to me. I've now become the friend that might just add an unusual twist to their lives. 'Pay it Forward' could be re-coined The *DiVona Factor*! *Giving someone experiences is a true gift.*

Epilogue

•

"Be yourself, everyone else is taken."
—Oscar Wilde

TRY, TRY; TRY - nothing is beyond your imagination, nothing is impossible. In Shakespeare's play 'The Merry Wives of Windsor', 1602, a line is often quoted, "The world's mine oyster" which emotes the strength that you can do anything if you set your mind to it. That quote often has an important part left off. The next words completing Pistol's thoughts are, "Which I with sword will open." Yes, the world can be yours for the taking, your 'oyster' but you will have to fight for it. Put forth a great effort to get to your dreams. No one is going to knock on your door and deliver it. Most likely you're going to have to kick a few doors down along your path. From time to time I've gotten bad advice over the years. I might not have known, as well as I do now, how bad it was but my snap judgement smelled horse-doo-doo. My brain's instinctual *snap judgment* kicked in. I was told "Don't put the horse before the cart" more than once. I say, "PLEASE put the horse before the cart." Let the damn horse catch up. You need to run out of the starting gate like your life depends on it.

To be successful you need a certain amount of drama. Fly by the seat of your pants is my advice. When will you ever really be ready? If you wait to know everything, that horse will be long gone out of the barn of opportunity. I always take the position that everything will work itself out. I had no cheerleading experience - but I tried. I had never been a maître d', but that fib got my Hollywood days rolling. I invented a product that was basically a dog toy that did $50M in sales. I'm a successful bar & nightclub owner but I'm not a bartender. The list of me putting the cart before the horse should be my mantra. Hell, it could have been the title of this book. I jump in headfirst even if I'm not sure I can swim.

I became a part of corporate America, a "salaryman" in Japan, international model, Hollywood actor, Playboy host on TV worldwide, bar & nightclub owner and a successful inventor of a couple well known household products. I keep dreaming and keep my mind open to new experiences I feel compelled to follow. I got that "pluck" from my grandmother. She was a mean old goat that I learned a lot from. My mother always had the "drive" for freedom. Growing up without much planted a seed in her to create a better life. Possibly through mom, or knowing that if I wanted to succeed, I'd need to buckle down and "focus", which Gates & Buffet credit as their means to success. Who am I to argue with advice from two billionaires, right? First you TRY, then you FOCUS on what you are trying at. I've always worked hard in spurts. I've learned over the years to delegate responsibilities and trust good people. A man cannot be an island. Don't measure your pleasure in nickel and dimes. Find your "What to" and go after it 100%. Listen to your "Pooh" whenever you come to a fork in the road. Follow your instincts!

Robert M. Sapolsky released a book in 2023 titled Determined with a tagline: "A Science of Life Without Free Will" and this stopped me in my tracks. I have been tossing a theory around in my head for 20 years. There is some inner-self, nature-vs-nurture partnership, that we all must listen to. Human behavior, the good, the bad and the ugly, can be unnerving if we start to acknowledge that we may not be a total free willed spirit. If you look at worker bees they all have a role to make the hive succeed. Humans may very well have a hidden blueprint within the synapses of our brains too. The neurons connect and communicate information. Besides the memories, the gunk stored in our hippocampus, could also be a "rough draft" of which "worker bee" you're best suited to be? My best advice for us all is to listen to our heart. It can help us be true to ourselves which encourages the pathway to peace, happiness and fulfillment. Wow, I'm not meaning to be so zen-like but I'm laying it on the line. We all have just one chance on this wild ride. Recognize your own specialness. You have one! Believe in yourself. Find it.

The "*The Power of Good*" is a concept a friend of mine named Adham Badwan introduced to me in Baños, Ecuador. We were both there helping people with free dental needs. It is like 'Doctors Without Borders' but for teeth. It's organized by Dr. William "Billy" Graves through his program *Full Smile*. Adham is a talented dentist/surgeon and motivating philosopher. *The Power of Good* philosophy believes *"Tapping into the power of good is committing to touch every life that crosses your path in a positive way or at least vowing to dish out no harm. When presented with a negative worldly issue transcend it by rising above and seeing the bigger picture and then transmit the energy it gives you to fuel the positive moving forward," says APGB.* As I wind down my story I want us all to remember who we really are. Stay good.

I don't like to think that success or fame changes who you are. The ultimate gift in my life is my freedom and having someone to love. My wife has added a quality to my life I did not have before meeting her. You've read my crazy life story now. I didn't settle down and get married until I was 50 years old. In life you never know what will happen next so we do need to "Live Like We're Dying" like the Tim McGraw song says. When you reflect back on your life I hope you don't think "I needed to ***Try*** more" because stepping up to the plate and swinging for the fences is one of the best experiences in life. Like I've mentioned several times before, my mom used to say, "Can't never did anything." ***Try! Try! Try!***

Venice Beach Morning of 2012

Thank You Mister Steamy the Dryer Ball

Made in the USA
Las Vegas, NV
10 October 2024

721d300e-4afd-4f48-81db-aed045a26283R01